Property Tax Planning

Seventh Edition

Philip Spencer BSc (Econ), FCA
Tax Partner, BDO Stoy Hayward

Tottel
publishing

Tottel Publishing
Maxwelton House,
41–43 Boltro Road,
Haywards Heath,
West Sussex,
RH16 1BJ

A CIP Catalogue record for this book is available from the British Library.

ISBN 978 1 84766 060 2

Typeset by Phoenix Photosetting, Chatham, Kent

Printed and bound by Athenæum Press Ltd, Gateshead, Tyne and Wear

Preface

In the first edition of this book I included the following statement in my preface.

> I have not sought to produce a comprehensive reference work on property tax. Whilst such texts are invaluable reference material for the specialist, they inevitably fail to highlight the 'do's', and 'don'ts' that arise in most tax planning situations. It is this gap in property tax books that I wanted this manual to fill.

The fact that this book is now in its seventh edition would suggest that this objective has been fulfilled.

The sixth edition was published in Autumn 2004. Since then, there have been Finance Acts in 2005 (two), 2006 and 2007, introducing yet further complications, pitfalls and reliefs into our already complex tax legislation. In addition, we have had a consultative document on capital allowances and a Pre-Budget Report in 2007 with significant changes to capital gains tax. There has also been a flow of judicial decisions and pronouncements from HM Revenue and Customs (formerly the Inland Revenue and HM Customs & Excise).

The changes that have taken place as a consequence of all this activity are distributed around the chapters of this book. Furthermore, many statutory references have had to be updated to reflect the consolidation of income tax aspects into two new Acts ie the Income Tax (Trading and Other Income) Act 2005 and the Income Tax Act 2007.

Just a few of the changes worthy of mention are:

- the proposed withdrawal of taper relief announced in the 2007 Pre-Budget report;

- the tightening up of the stamp duty land tax relief rules, with the consequent restrictions on avoidance techniques and use of reliefs;

- the introduction of the UK Real Estate Investment Trust and the exit opportunity this can provide to owners of a property investment company;

- the changes in the tax regime to accommodate alternative finance structures, particularly to remove tax disadvantages for Islamic-compliant finance arrangements;

- the anticipated impact of the Government's consultative document issued in July 2007 with an indication of likely changes to the capital allowance regime for machinery and plant;

- a revamping of the Construction Industry Scheme from April 2007.

We do not yet know at the time of writing how the proposals announced in the 2007 Pre Budget report will look. A 'Stop Press' note after this preface summarises the principal changes that we are currently aware of. There are appropriate references to these changes in the relevant chapters.

This book continues to adopt the popular format of previous editions. Each chapter has been set out as a series of important tax planning opportunities and pitfalls which, for ease of reference, are summarised at the beginning of each chapter by a chart. This arrangement is designed to help the busy reader to use it as a checklist of the points he or she might want to consider. In addition to a practical explanation of the position, relevant cases, statutes and other authorities are quoted to facilitate further reference by the interested reader.

I am certain that many of the fundamental points highlighted in this book are not widely appreciated because tax reference material generally does not successfully separate the main planning points from the detailed rules.

Those familiar with past editions will know that it is divided into four parts. These reflect the four categories of property ownership, viz:

Part A – Property Investors

Part B – Property Dealers and Developers

Part C – Trading Premises

Part D – Private Residences

Each category has its own particular topics which are dealt with in the chapters in that part – although there are some cases where the same topic is relevant to more than one category. To avoid too much duplication, certain points cross refer to other parts of the book where the same topic is covered in detail.

Judging from the feedback from past editions, I can predict that this book will appeal to the following:

- Individuals and companies owning property.

  Investors, dealers/developers, trading organisations and owners of private residences are always on the lookout for ways to reduce tax. These companies and individuals would welcome a book which provides them with ideas which they could in turn 'bounce' off their professional advisors.

- Practising accountants.

  The book can assist the busy accountant in keeping abreast of the latest in property tax planning opportunities.

- Tax practitioners.

  The book provides a useful compendium of tax planning points in property situations for the tax practitioner's reference.

- Other professionals.

  Solicitors, surveyors, estate agents and bankers involved in property situations often need to be aware of the tax aspects of situations they encounter, without necessarily having to sift through technical detail.

In managing to complete this edition of this book, I am indebted to a number of my colleagues at BDO Stoy Hayward LLP, notably Adrian Benosiglio for his technical review. In addition, Stephen Keogh from our VAT department, Mike Sutherland on the Construction Industry Scheme, Malcolm Pengelly on stamp duty land tax and Maggie Gonzales regarding overseas trusts and private residences all gave me crucial input in these areas. Special thanks also to my secretary Nicola Heath and my wife Juliet, for all their help.

I should mention that, whilst every effort has been made to ensure the accuracy of the contents of this book, neither the author not the publisher can accept any responsibility for a loss arising to anyone relying on the information contained herein. Indeed, specific professional advice on possible tax implications should always be sought in relation to any proposed transaction or situation.

The law is stated as at 31 October 2007.

Philip Spencer
BDO Stoy Hayward LLP
31 October 2007

Stop Press

Pre-budget Report – October 2007

On 9 October 2007, the Chancellor of the Exchequer delivered the Government's Pre-Budget Report, outlining proposals for tax changes for the forthcoming financial and fiscal years.

Included in these proposals are measures which, if implemented, would have an impact on certain tax planning points in this book. During the final editing of the book, during October 2007, amendments have been made in the relevant chapters to reflect these possible tax changes. At the time of writing, there are indications of possible modifications to the original proposals, but no details are yet available.

Summarised below are two particular areas of change which could impact on planning points in this book:

Capital gains tax

Significant changes were announced to capital gains tax for disposals after 5 April 2008 for individuals, trustees and personal representatives.

Most notable is the withdrawal of taper relief and indexation allowance. Instead, there will be a flat rate of capital gains tax of 18%.

There has been much debate in the media about the losers in this situation. These will include individuals who sell property or property-owning companies after 5 April 2008 that would previously have qualified for full business asset taper relief. Their capital gains tax liability effectively rises from 10% to 18%.

Also losing out will be those individuals and trustees with property assets acquired before April 1998 where they might have benefited from the indexation allowance. This allowance was frozen at 5 April 1998. Under tax proposals that accumulated indexation figure will now be lost.

Among the possible winners are property investors whose rate of capital gains tax on disposals pre 6 April 2008 will be somewhere in between 40% and 24%, depending on how long the asset has been held. Many of these can now benefit from this lower rate of 18%.

There may well be further changes in this area. The Government have responded to criticism of the measures, notably the withdrawal of business asset taper relief, by indicating that there may be a restricted relief retained in certain situations. This may take the form of a specific limit of, say, £100,000 on which the relief may still be available. However, no details have been made available at this stage.

A further area of change, though less significant, relates to the tax-base cost of assets that were owned at 31 March 1982. Before 6 April 2008, capital gains can be computed by reference to either original cost or 31 March 1982 value, whichever produced the lower chargeable gain (or larger loss). For disposals after 5 April 2008, only the value at 31 March 1982 can be used.

Non-UK domicilaries

The proposals intend to bring in a flat tax charge of £30,000 on any individuals who are not domiciled in the UK for tax purposes and wish to claim the benefit of the remittance basis. This will only apply to individuals who have been tax resident here for at least seven years.

Up to 5 April 2008, individuals who are not UK tax domiciled can avoid tax on any income arising abroad which is not brought into the UK. Those individuals who did want to enjoy these funds in the UK at some future stage were also able to plan their affairs by closing down the source of income in a previous fiscal year or routing the related funds back to the UK indirectly and thus breaking the remittance link. The Pre-Budget proposals intend to remove these benefits.

As mentioned above, these proposals are still subject to revision at the time of writing.

31 October 2007

Contents

4   Repairs, renewals and improvements   51

5   Stamp duty land tax   59

6   Capital allowances on plant and machinery   69

Table of statutes

Table of statutory instruments

Table of cases

Abbreviations

CAA	Capital Allowances Act
CNR	Centre for Non-Residents (within HM Revenue and Customs)
FA	Finance Act
FRS	Financial Reporting Standard
HMRC	Her Majesty's Revenue and Customs
IHTA	Inheritance Tax Act
IM	Inspectors' Manual
IR	Inland Revenue (now known as HM Revenue and Customs – which also incorporates the former HM Customs & Excise)
ITTOIA	Income Tax (Trading and Other Income) Act
ITA	Income Tax Act
Para	Paragraph
RI	Revenue Interpretation
S	Section
Sch	Schedule
SI	Statutory Instrument
SP	HM Revenue and Customs' Statement of Practice
SSCD	Simon's Special Commissioners' Decisions
STC	Simon's Tax Cases
TA	Income and Corporation Taxes Act
TC	Tax Cases
TCGA	Taxation of Chargeable Gains Act
TMA	Taxes Management Act
VATA	Value Added Tax Act
VATTR	Value Added Tax Tribunals Reports

Part A Property Investors

CHAPTER 1 – ACQUISITION OF A PROPERTY THROUGH A NON-UK RESIDENT COMPANY

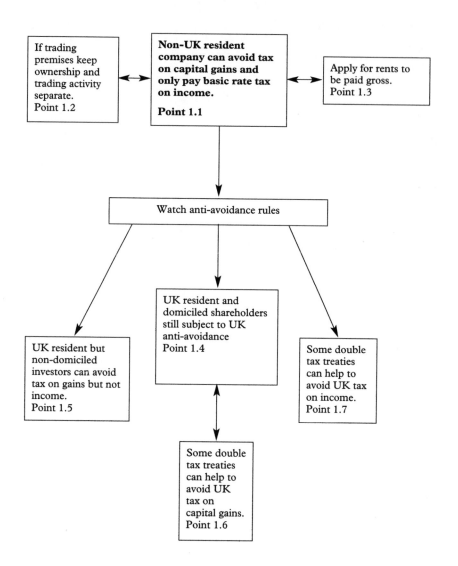

If trading premises keep ownership and trading activity separate.
Point 1.2

Non-UK resident company can avoid tax on capital gains and only pay basic rate tax on income.

Point 1.1

Apply for rents to be paid gross.
Point 1.3

Watch anti-avoidance rules

UK resident and domiciled shareholders still subject to UK anti-avoidance
Point 1.4

UK resident but non-domiciled investors can avoid tax on gains but not income.
Point 1.5

Some double tax treaties can help to avoid UK tax on income.
Point 1.7

Some double tax treaties can help to avoid UK tax on capital gains.
Point 1.6

1 Acquisition of a property through a non-UK resident company

Point 1.1: *A company resident outside the UK is a useful vehicle for the ownership of investment property in the UK, since capital gains on sale can be realised free of UK tax. However, the tax benefit can only be fully exploited by individuals who are or become non-UK resident or domiciled.*

The principal advantages enjoyed by a non-UK resident investment company are:

- Exemption from tax on capital gains realised on the disposal of investment assets (*TCGA 1992, s 2*). The exemption does not extend to assets used in connection with a trade conducted in the UK (*TCGA 1992, s 10*).
- Income arising in the UK will only be subject to basic rate income tax. Non-resident companies are not subject to corporation tax unless they carry on a trade in the UK through a permanent establishment (*TA 1988, s 11*).
- Income arising outside the UK cannot be subject to UK tax.

As explained in Points 1.4 and 1.5 below, these benefits may not be fully available where the non-resident company's individual shareholders (or ultimate shareholders) are resident or ordinarily resident and domiciled in the UK when the capital gain is realised.

The capital gains exemption provides an important tax planning opportunity. A company not resident in the UK for tax purposes can realise tax-free gains on the sale of an investment property which has not been used for trading purposes in the UK. The exemption from tax on capital gains should also apply where there is letting of commercial furnished holiday accommodation which, although regarded as a trade for some purposes of the Taxes Acts, will not be so regarded in this context (*TA 1988, s 503(1)*).

Point 1.2: *A non-UK resident company can still benefit from the favourable UK tax position even if trading premises are to be acquired.*

Where trading premises are to be purchased, the ownership of the property and the trading activity should be separated.

For example, where it is proposed to buy premises for a retail business in the UK, a non-UK resident company should acquire and own the property. A separate company, which may be a UK resident company, could carry on the retail trade. The trader would occupy the premises under a lease from the non-resident owner.

The lease to the trader would be a short lease at a market rental and subject to regular review. In this way, none of the capital appreciation in the property over time would accrue to the UK trading entity.

Rent payments by the trader should attract full corporation tax relief as long as they do not exceed a reasonable arm's length figure. The foreign property investment company, on the other hand, will only pay basic-rate UK tax on the income after finance costs and expenses.

Where a non-UK landlord is receiving rents on property in the UK, there is potentially a withholding tax issue. This is discussed in Point 1.3 below.

Point 1.3:   *Where a UK tenant or agent pays rent to a non-UK based landlord, basic rate tax may have to be withheld. This can be avoided by entering into a special arrangement with HMRC.*

Any tenant paying rent to a landlord who is not resident in the UK is under an obligation to pay to HMRC each quarter an amount equivalent to the basic rate of income tax (22% pre 5 April 2008, 20% thereafter) on the rent paid (*TA 1988, s 42A & SI 1995/2902*).

If there is a letting agent acting, then the obligation shifts from the tenant to the letting agent. If the agent is responsible for paying any expenses on the property, those expenses can be deducted from the income in computing the tax due – providing that the expenses are allowable for tax purposes (*SI 1995/2902 (9)*).

The landlord can deduct any tax paid by the tenant or agent from any tax due when filing the annual self-assessment tax return in the UK. Excess tax paid can be recovered.

There are two situations where the tenant or agent need not account for tax to HMRC. These are where:

- a tenant's gross rent is £5,200 or less per year, or
- the non-resident obtains HMRC approval to receive the rents with no tax withholding.

Obtaining this approval is a relatively straightforward procedure. It involves the submission of a form (form NRL1) by the non-resident to the HMRC's Centre for Non-Residents (CNR). If the non-resident landlord is a company, the appropriate application form is NRL2; if it is a trust, NRL3. CNR will grant approval where the following applies to the non-resident landlord:

(a)   the tax affairs are up to date; or
(b)   the landlord does not expect to be liable to UK tax; or
(c)   the landlord has never previously had any UK tax obligations.

The landlord must undertake to comply with all his UK tax obligations in the future.

Where properties are jointly owned, a separate application needs to be submitted for each non-resident owner.

Any agent acting for a non-resident landlord must register with CNR. Registration should be within 30 days of the date the agent became liable to operate the Non-Resident Landlord Scheme. Tax must be paid within 30 days of the quarter dates which for these purposes are 30 June, 30 September, 31 December and 31 March. The agents must also prepare an annual return (form NRLY) detailing all income, expenses and tax deducted. This must be sent to HMRC by 5 July following the end of the tax year. Agents must by the same date provide the landlord with a certificate of tax deducted. They may use the form NRL6 for this purpose.

The entitlement for a landlord to receive rents gross and account for any tax annually on a normal self-assessment return can be withdrawn. This will happen if the landlord suffers any late payment surcharges or delays sending information to HMRC. If this happens, the non-resident will have to wait at least two years before being approved to go back to the annual self-assessment basis.

Point 1.4:   *Anti-avoidance rules and the need to establish non-resident status create hurdles in the use of non-resident companies.*

For UK tax purposes, a foreign company is not resident here if its central management and control is abroad (*De Beers Consolidated Mines Ltd v Howe* (1906) 5 TC 198). A UK incorporated company will always be resident in the UK regardless of where it is managed and controlled, subject to the provisions of certain double tax treaties.

An HMRC Statement of Practice (SP 1/90) raises a number of issues in determining 'central management and control' which can be summarised as follows:

*   Do the directors of the company in fact exercise management and control?
*   If so, where do they exercise it (which is not necessarily where they meet)?
*   If not the directors, by whom and where is central management and control exercised?

(SP 1/90).

In practice, there are many non-UK incorporated companies involved in UK activities where their residence is accepted without question as being outside the UK. However, that does not mean that investors in UK property can simply avoid tax here by using an offshore vehicle.

In the first place, HMRC have stated that they will look at such companies 'to see whether there has been an attempt to create the appearance of central management and control in a particular place without the reality'. That could well defeat a situation where local directors in a tax haven location are merely rubber stamping instructions issued by a UK based individual or company.

For the company to be resident outside the UK, all or most of the directors should be based outside the UK. The non-UK directors should be active in making business decisions. All major policy decisions must be decided at board meetings outside the UK. These include purchasing and selling the property, issuing instructions to any managing agents in the UK and negotiating any financial arrangements. Although not necessarily critical to the issue of corporate residence, ideally agreements should be concluded outside the UK.

In the recent cases of *Wood & Another v Holden* [2006] STC 443 and *News Datacom Limited & Another v Revenue & Customs* (SpC561), the High Court and Special Commissioners respectively found in favour of the taxpayer companies whose overseas tax had been challenged by HMRC. The cases served to emphasise the importance of the need for active involvement by the non-resident directors in the business of the company and the evidencing of that by company minutes.

UK residents can establish non-resident companies but, to benefit from optimal UK tax treatment, they must sit back as shareholders and appoint non-resident directors to decide matters and run the company. HMRC may look closely at the company's affairs to ensure that the individuals do not involve themselves in any executive decisions.

Even where the non-residence of a company can be established, the benefit of the capital gains exemption to the company can be denied to UK-based shareholders. There is an exception where the company is established in a country with a suitable double tax agreement (see Point 1.6 below). Subject to that exception, HMRC will follow through any gain arising in such a company (providing it would have been a close company if resident in the UK). Individual shareholders (or ultimate shareholders) who are resident or ordinarily resident and domiciled in the UK when the gain is made will be taxed on the gain in proportion to their interest in the company (TCGA 1992, s 13). Following *FA 2001*, this only applies where the interest exceeds 10%.

Further anti-avoidance provisions may tax shareholders who are ordinarily resident in the UK (whether or not they are domiciled here) on any income arising in the company (*ITA, s 714* – formerly *TA 1988, ss 739 & 740*) if the income arises directly or indirectly from a transfer of assets.

It is overseas-based investors who reap the full benefits of using non-UK tax resident companies. This still leaves opportunities for their exploitation by UK individuals who are not domiciled in the UK (Point 1.5 below) and for UK residents investing via a company resident in a suitable tax treaty country (Point 1.6). There is also an opportunity for individuals who are normally based in the UK, but can plan for several years of non-residence when the company realises its gain on the property or they sell the shares in the company.

Point 1.5:   *A UK resident who is not domiciled in the UK can benefit from investing in UK property via a non-resident company.*

Point 1.4 above referred to the fact that capital gains arising in a foreign, non-resident company can be taxed directly on individual shareholders who are resident or ordinarily resident and domiciled in the UK (*TCGA 1992, s 13*).

On the other hand, an individual who is not domiciled in the UK can avoid any UK tax on that gain. That can be the case even if that person is a full-time resident in the UK (*TCGA 1992, s 13(2)*).

Note that the Government's Pre-Budget proposals announced in October 2007 are likely to affect the UK tax position of non-domiciliaries from 5 April 2008. Reference should be made to the 'Stop Press' note at the beginning of the book for the possible changes in this area. The points below should be read in the context of these. Not only can tax be avoided when the gain is realised, but it can also be avoided if the company is liquidated following the sale of the property which generates a capital gain directly for the shareholders.

This is because capital gains arising abroad (and in some cases, foreign income) realised by non-domiciliaries will only be taxed in the UK if and when the related proceeds are brought into the UK. This is subject to the proviso that the individual chooses to be subject to tax under the 'remittance basis'. In that case, as long as the funds are retained outside the UK, the non-domiciled shareholder can retain the gains tax-free.

Unlike the capital gains rules, the anti-avoidance provisions referred to in 1.4 above relating to income do apply to non-domiciled individuals. The remittance basis does, however, apply to foreign income. Such income received by non-domiciled individuals will not be taxable in the UK unless remitted here. If the income is rent from a UK property, on the other hand, it is potentially taxable under these anti-avoidance rules. So there is considerably less scope for protecting UK income arising in the non-resident company from UK tax.

Domicile is a legal concept that extends beyond tax law. Generally, anyone who intends the UK to be his or her permanent home will be UK-domiciled. Someone born in the UK will be presumed to have a UK domicile, unless one or both parents were born and bred abroad. Displacing that UK domicile will involve that person establishing a permanent home in another country and severing all links with the UK.

On the other hand, someone born abroad but living in the UK will be non-UK domiciled if that individual's intention is to return to his or her country of origin. It does not matter whether this is a short-term or long-term intention. However, in agreeing an individual's non-UK domicile status HMRC might wish to see a specific intention (eg returning after retirement or spouse's retirement) combined with family/social links with that country.

Generally, an individual who is not domiciled in the UK might find that a non-resident trust is a more flexible vehicle for acquiring UK property tax efficiently (see Point 2.2).

Point 1.6:   *Some countries have tax treaties with the UK which prevent HMRC from using anti-avoidance rules to tax UK shareholders on non-trading property gains in overseas companies. UK-based shareholders can invest via companies in these jurisdictions to shelter property gains from UK tax.*

As mentioned in Point 1.4 above, anti-avoidance provisions can subject any individual shareholders to tax on their share of capital gains realised by a closely controlled non-resident company in which they have a sufficiently large interest. This would be the case for individuals who are resident or ordinarily resident and domiciled in the UK.

Certain tax treaties that the UK has with other countries prevent those provisions from applying to companies resident in those jurisdictions. Prominent examples are the Netherlands, Belgium and Luxembourg. Notwithstanding this, the anti-avoidance rules can still apply where the gain arises from the sale of property.

This still leaves scope for sheltering property gains.

For instance, a UK shareholder could set up a Netherlands resident company (Nethco). This, in turn, holds shares in a property investment company managed and controlled in Jersey (Jco). Jco buys a UK investment property.

If Jco realises a gain on selling the property, there is no protection from the anti-avoidance provisions of *TCGA 1992, s 13*. These will apply to UK shareholders on the property gain unless the shareholders are not UK domiciled.

On the other hand, if Nethco sells the shares in Jco, then the gain realised is protected from UK tax by the treaty. The gain arises from shares rather than property. This, therefore, offers the opportunity for indefinite deferral of tax on gains. When the funds are paid to shareholders, tax will arise if at that time they are resident in the UK.

If, however, any of the ultimate shareholders of Nethco are trustees, then the treaty will not protect them. Any gains realised in Nethco or Jco will be apportioned to trustee shareholders (*TCGA 1992, s 79B*) and the relevant tax consequences will follow. The taxation of trusts and beneficiaries is outside the scope of this book.

For the purchaser, buying a company represents a different proposition from buying the property itself. At worst, some buyers may seek a discount for the inherent tax in the company that would be paid when the property is sold. At best, the status of other buyers may enable them to enjoy any future gain tax-free within Jco.

The purchaser can also avoid up to 4% stamp duty land tax by buying the company.

Point 1.7:   *UK anti-avoidance rules can tax income and gains accruing to an offshore company although the use of a non-UK resident company in certain jurisdictions may provide shelter.*

If there is evidence that a property is purchased for reasons other than long-term investment, a gain on sale could be chargeable as trading income or under special provisions relating to certain transactions in land (*ITA, s 755* and subsequent sections – formerly *TA 1988, s 776*).

If either of these treatments applies, a company's non-resident status will not afford any exemption from tax. In view of this, it must be expected that HMRC will look at the possibility of taxing gains as trading income or under the provisions of, s 755. However, depending on where the company is resident, some double tax treaties may protect gains from this charge.

Certain countries have tax treaties with the UK that can give rise to a lower UK tax bill on trading gains realised by companies resident in those countries. These include Cyprus, Isle of Man and Guernsey.

Where UK companies own UK or overseas property assets through overseas incorporated companies there is a further tax hurdle to surmount apart from the residence and anti-avoidance issues already mentioned. This hurdle is the UK's Controlled Foreign Company ('CFC') legislation. Broadly, any undistributed income arising in a low-tax jurisdiction can be treated as the UK taxable income of the UK parent company unless there is a commercial reason for the siting of the company in that jurisdiction or some other exceptions apply (*TA 1988, ss 747–756*). A low-tax jurisdiction would be where the local tax is less than three-quarters of the UK liability. The CFC provisions do not tax capital gains. However, if the company is close for tax purposes, then the provisions of, s 13 (see Point 1.4 above) may apply to apportion the gain to the UK company.

A detailed discussion of the complex CFC rules is outside the scope of this book. It should be said that as European Community law develops, there seems greater scope successfully to resist a CFC challenge on an EC subsidiary by HMRC. Furthermore, at the time of writing, the Government have issued a recent Consultation Document seeking to explore a new regime for taxing overseas gains.

CHAPTER 2 – PROPERTY OWNERSHIP THROUGH A NON-UK RESIDENT TRUST

Non-domiciled individuals can shelter property gains in offshore trusts. Other individuals can also enjoy tax-free gains if they cease UK residence for at least 5 years.

Point 2.1

Trusts of UK domiciled persons defer tax on gains if the beneficiaries are parents, brothers and sisters, nieces and nephews, great-grandchildren or non-relatives.
Point 2.2

Trust gains are not taxed after the settlor's death. This is useful for longer-term trusts and will trusts but may only be a deferral mechanism.
Point 2.3

2 Property ownership through a non-UK resident trust

Point 2.1: *Individuals based in the UK can benefit from using a non-resident trust for UK property investment, but only if they are not domiciled in the UK or plan to live outside the UK in the future.*

Capital gains on the disposal of investments realised by non-UK resident trustees are not prima facie subject to tax. However, the UK has anti-avoidance provisions which, in many cases, tax settlors on gains realised within trusts they have created (*TCGA 1992, s 86 & Sch 5*).

The legislation applies where any of the following individuals ('defined persons') can benefit under a trust:

(a) the settlor;
(b) the settlor's spouse or civil partner;
(c) any child or step-child of the settlor or of the settlor's spouse or civil partner;
(d) any grandchild or step-grandchild of the settlor or of the settlor's spouse;
(e) any spouse of such a child or grandchild;
(f) any company controlled by persons within (a)–(e) above; and
(g) any company associated with a company within (f) above.

If a gain arises in a year in which any one of them receives a benefit or can benefit, that gain is treated as accruing to the settlor (*TCGA 1992, s 86(4)*). This is so even if no benefit is actually received by the beneficiaries.

The gain is calculated as if the trustees were UK resident except that there is no annual exemption. Unused trust capital losses can be deducted (*TCGA 1992, Sch 5, para 1(1), (2)*). Taper relief for disposals before 6 April 2008 is allowed where appropriate. *Note that the Government's Pre-Budget report in October 2007 included provisions for the removal of taper relief after 5 April 2008. Reference should be made to the 'Stop Press' note at the beginning of the book for the possible changes in this area. The points below should be read in the context of these.*

For 2003/04 onwards, the gains treated as accruing to the settlor can be offset by personal losses and still attract the personal annual exemption.

This tax charge cannot apply where the settlor is domiciled outside the UK. As explained in Point 1.5, an individual who does not intend to make the UK his or her life-long home may not be domiciled here even if he or she has been living here for some years. Typically, such an individual would have been born outside the UK or have parents of non-UK origin. *Note that the Government's Pre-Budget proposals announced in*

October 2007 are likely to affect the UK tax position of non-domiciliaries from 6 April 2008. Reference should be made to the 'Stop Press' note at the beginning of the book for the possible changes in this area. The points below should be read in the context of these.

Anyone who is able to establish non-domicile status can potentially avoid tax on UK investment property gains where that person creates and owns the property through an overseas trust *(TCGA 1992, s 86(1)(c))*.

It is also possible for UK domiciled settlors to escape this tax charge if the trust realises the gain at a time when they are no longer UK-resident or ordinarily resident, provided that at least five complete tax years elapse between the year in which they cease to be resident and ordinarily resident and the year in which they resume residence and ordinary residence. In that situation, the gain cannot be taxed on them *(TCGA 1992, ss 86(1)(c) & 10A)*.

The avoidance of tax on capital gains does not extend to income tax on income from UK property. Anti-avoidance rules on UK source income do not distinguish between domiciled and non-domiciled settlors.

Point 2.2:   *Apart from the avoidance of capital gains tax by non-UK domiciled settlors, there are also a few situations where UK domiciliaries can avoid tax through non-resident trusts.*

If a non-resident trust is created which expressly excludes any of the beneficiaries listed in Point 2.1 above, then it is not caught by the anti-avoidance rules mentioned therein.

There is, therefore, the scope to create trusts to benefit other relatives, eg parents, brothers, nieces, great-grandchildren. The beneficiary can also be a friend.

In these cases, gains can accrue in the trust free of UK tax. Any UK-domiciled and resident beneficiaries will be taxed on the gains when the beneficiary receives any capital payment from the trust. The tax liability is increased by 10% of the tax for each year the gain is retained in the trust, up to a maximum of 60% *(TCGA 1992, ss 87 & 91)*. This can give rise to a maximum effective tax rate of 64%.

To take advantage of these arrangements, the settlor must set up the trust out of his or her own funds and without any element of reciprocity. If, for example, Adam gives money to his sister Linda to set up a trust for himself, Adam (and not Linda) will be treated as the settlor. Alternatively, arrangements whereby Adam settles a trust for Linda in reciprocation for her settling a similar sized trust for him would also not work. Adam and Linda would be treated as settlors of their own trusts *(ITTOIA 2005, s 620))*.

Point 2.3: *Non-resident trusts holding longer-term growth assets for the next generation can avoid UK capital gains tax.*

A settlor cannot be taxed on gains arising after his or her death. Nor can gains be taxed in the UK in the tax year of death (*TCGA 1992, Sch 5, para 3*).

Therefore, the individual keen to settle property for the benefit of future generations could create a non-resident trust in the knowledge that, after death, gains accruing to the trust fund will not be subject to UK tax. Capital gains tax will, however, be due when capital payments are made to UK domiciled and resident beneficiaries as discussed above.

Alternatively, the trust might be created by will. Inheritance tax would normally arise where UK investment property is transferred on death into a will trust.

CHAPTER 3A – RELIEF FOR FINANCE COSTS INCURRED BY INDIVIDUALS, TRUSTEES AND NON-UK RESIDENT INVESTMENT COMPANIES

Accrued interest on finance to buy, improve or repair property or repay loans for that purpose is deductible against letting income for tax purposes.

Point 3.1

↓

Surplus interest costs can be carried forward to offset against future letting income.
Point 3.2

↓

To avoid carrying forward unusable losses, it may be better to grant a lease at a premium instead of a sale or assignment.
Point 3.3

↓

Funds can be borrowed from UK and overseas associates but these must be on commercial arm's length terms.
Points 3.4 & 3.5

↓

20% withholding tax deduction but reduced or eliminated where interest is short or there is a double tax agreement or discounted loan stock.
Points 3.6 & 3.7

↓

The introduction of rules for 'alternative finance' has improved tax relief for financing structures which are compliant with Islamic law.
Point 3.8

3A Relief for finance costs incurred by individuals, trustees and non-UK resident investment companies

Point 3.1: *Accrued interest and other finance costs can be deducted from total rental income. Excess interest must be carried forward.*

Although HMRC do not regard letting as a trading activity, taxable profits from property letting are computed as if it were a trade (*ITTOIA 2005, s 272(1)*). That means that any finance costs incurred are deductible from total rents received. The deduction is for the accrued costs, regardless of whether they are actually paid.

The finance must relate to the purchase or improvement (including repairs) of the let property or the repayment of another loan that had been taken out for these purposes. Personal borrowings or loans for other activities would not qualify even if secured on the let property.

All properties let by a landlord are treated as a single business. If finance costs and other costs exceed that year's total rental income, only the loss attributable to any capital allowances can be offset against the landlord's other income or gains (*ITA 2007, s 120*). The surplus costs can, however, be carried forward against future income from the letting activity (*ITA 2007, s 118*).

Point 3.2: *If there are surplus finance costs following a property sale these can be used against the rental income from a property owned and let subsequently.*

As mentioned in Point 3.1 above, surplus finance costs cannot be offset against other income or gains but they can be offset against future profits from the letting of property. Therefore, following a sale of a property, unused past finance costs can be used to shelter tax on income from another property whether owned at the time or bought subsequently.

HMRC will allow the losses to be carried forward indefinitely whilst the letting business is being carried on. However, if the letting actually ceases, the unused expenses will be forfeited.

This does not mean that losses cannot be carried forward if there is any gap in the letting activity. Where a property is sold but there is the clear intention to carry on a letting business, the costs can be carried forward. Therefore, if there is a gap in time following a sale of a property and in that period the investor is actively looking for a replacement property, the loss carry forward should not be affected.

Point 3.3:   *Where finance costs exceed rental profit throughout ownership, tax on a capital gain on sale can be reduced if a short lease can be granted at a premium prior to a sale of the main interest in the property.*

If a property is sold for more than its cost, after deducting indexation allowance up to 5 April 1998 (see Chapter 12) and taper relief for disposals pre 6 April 2008 (see Chapter 35), a capital gain will arise unless the vendor is a company is not UK tax resident (see Chapter 1). Unrelieved finance costs cannot be offset against this gain for tax purposes. If there is to be no further rental income from this or any other properties, future relief for these costs will be forfeited.

Where there is the prospect of a capital gain that will be chargeable to UK tax, the tax liability can be reduced if the capital gain were partially converted to income for tax purposes.

This can be achieved by granting a short lease at a premium with an option for the buyer to buy the main interest at the end of the lease period. For the reasons set out in Point 9.1, such a premium is partly treated as income depending on the length of the lease involved. The shorter the lease, the higher the proportion of premium treated as income.

EXAMPLE

Mrs A owns a freehold property that she lets. The rent is £30,000 per year. Over the past few years, repairs and finance costs have given rise to an accumulated loss of £100,000.

The property is now to be sold after 5 April 2008 for £400,000, which will give Mrs A a capital gain of £100,000 on which she will pay 18% tax, ie £18,000, assuming the proposals announced in the Government's Pre Budget report are implemented (see the 'Stop Press' note at the beginning of the book) .

Alternatively, Mrs A offers the prospective buyer a 4-year lease for no rent and a premium of £107,000 together with the freehold reversion for £293,000.

As a consequence of this transaction, 94% of the premium of £107,000 – or £100,580 – on grant of the 4-year lease will be treated as letting income (see Point 9.1). Against this the £100,000 losses can be offset leaving just £580 in charge to income tax.

The capital gain, following the reduction in the capital element of the receipt by £100,580, has now disappeared. No capital gains tax therefore arises.

Mrs A has, therefore, saved just under £18,000 tax.

There could also be a short-term benefit for a buyer who is using the property for trading premises. The premium rules allow the buyer a trading deduction against taxable profits over each of the four years of the lease of £25,145 (ie £100,580/4, see Point 27.1).

There is exposure in arrangements such as this that HMRC might seek to attack the grant of a lease as an artificial step inserted in the transaction under the principle in *Furniss v Dawson* [1984] STC 153. Ultimately, the dividing line between arrangements that work and those that do not is a matter for the courts rather than HMRC to determine. It is essential in such arrangements for there to be commercial or structural features that make the pure tax avoidance aspects less significant. For instance, the lease could be granted to an entity occupying the premises for trading purposes whilst a separate (but possibly associated) entity bought the reversion for investment purposes.

In some situations there may be no taxable capital gain. This could be, for instance, where the gain is less than the available annual exemption for the individual or trust. In other cases there may be unused capital losses. Where the owners are non-UK resident individuals and non-UK companies, they may not be subject to UK tax on capital gains (see Chapters 1 and 2). In cases such as this, the conversion of capital into income would not give rise to any benefit. Indeed, it may be preferable to preserve losses in case there is a resumption of letting.

Point 3.4: *Finance costs are allowable on funds borrowed from associated and connected persons. This includes lenders based abroad.*

Interest is allowable even on a loan from a connected party. Therefore, finance can be obtained from associated individuals (including spouses and relatives) and trust funds.

For the most part there is no stipulation as to the amount of interest that is allowed other than where it is paid to a non-resident. In that case, the interest must not be at more than a 'reasonable commercial rate' (*TA 1988, Sch 28AA*). The implication is that interest paid at more than a commercial rate to a UK lender would be allowable – probably on the basis that HMRC can tax the recipient. However, excessive finance costs will be disallowed as not 'wholly and exclusively' for the purposes of the business (*ITTOIA 2005, s 34(1)(a)*).

There is also the possibility, since April 2004, that transfer-pricing rules may apply to adjust excessive interest to arm's length rates where one company borrows from another with which it has a 'special relationship', meaning that one company has a controlling or major interest in the other, or the same third person has such an interest in both companies.

Transfer pricing (see also Chapter 3B and Point 3.5 below) now applies also to transactions wholly within the UK. In most cases, however, the transfer-pricing rules now no longer apply unless the person receiving the tax advantage ('the advantaged party'– here the borrowing company) is a 'large enterprise' (which means that it has a turnover or gross assets of many millions of pounds). Even where they do apply, the 'disadvantaged party' (the lending company, which is receiving the excess interest) can claim exemption from UK taxation on the amount of interest that is disallowed for the borrower.

See also Point 3.5 below and Chapter 3B, Points 3.20 and 3.21.

Point 3.5:   *Where the borrower is a non-UK resident company, the terms of any borrowing must be wholly arm's length to obtain a deduction for related finance costs. Where borrowings are from a foreign associate, the terms should be based on those offered by a reputable third-party lender.*

The UK's transfer-pricing rules (*TA 1988, Sch 28AA*) may apply to limit the allowability of finance costs payable by non-UK resident companies. Transfer pricing applies to non-arm's length transactions between two persons, one of whom has a controlling or major interest in the other. It does not therefore apply to transactions between individuals or to non-business transactions but can apply to business transactions between an individual and a company or partnership. Before April 2004 the transfer-pricing rules applied only where one of the parties to the transaction was outside the scope of UK tax. Now, however, the rules apply even where both parties are taxable in the UK, but there is an exemption where the advantaged party – the party whose liability to UK tax has been reduced as a result of the transaction – is an SME (a small or medium-sized enterprise), unless the other party is located in a tax haven or certain other jurisdictions with which the UK does not have an appropriate double tax treaty. For transactions involving UK companies, see Point 3.4 above, and Chapter 3B, Points 3.20 and 3.21.

Under the rules, 'excessive' interest paid to an associated lender abroad will be disallowed. This does not just apply to situations where the rate of interest is too high. It also applies where the amount of the loan is greater than would have been supplied by a third party.

In a situation where a third party might lend up to 85% of the value of a property on purchase, finance higher than this will be considered excessive. The loan does not have to be between two associates for the rule to apply. Interest will also be disallowed where a third party lends a higher than normal amount on the strength of the security of a guarantee or deposit provided by the borrower's associate. So-called 'back to back' arrangements are, therefore, caught.

If the interest paid under the arrangements is greater than would have applied in an arm's length transaction, a deduction for the excess will not be allowed. If the entire loan is not on an arm's length basis – for instance where a top-up loan is required in addition to a normal secured loan, the whole of the top-up interest can be disallowed.

Companies which borrow with the direct or indirect assistance of a foreign associate must now be prepared to justify the loan arrangements as arm's length. It is advisable to approach a bank or other lender for a loan quote which ignores any security from associates. If a reputable third party lender can be found which is prepared to take a greater than usual risk, any loan arrangement with an associate which replicates those terms should be acceptable as arm's length.

As has already been noted, however, if the advantaged party (here the borrower paying an excessive interest rate or in receipt of an advantageous loan) is an SME, the transfer-pricing rules are of no application after 31 March 2004, with two exceptions:

(i)   the lender is located in a tax haven etc; or
(ii) the borrower is a medium-sized enterprise and HMRC directs that the transfer-pricing rules shall apply after an inquiry into the borrower's tax return

(*TA 1988, Sch 28AA, paras 5B, 5C*).

Point 3.6: *If interest is paid to a non-UK resident lender, there is a requirement to deduct income tax at the time of payment unless the loan is non-UK source.*

Any person paying interest to a foreign lender on a long-term loan is required to deduct tax at a current rate of 20% unless the loan does not have a UK source (*ITA 2007, s 874*).

There is no statutory definition of UK source, this being an area where HMRC have formulated their own guidelines. In connection with the introduction of the EC Interest and Royalties Directive (see below), HMRC raised the possibility of a statutory definition and issued a consultation document in December 2003. However, it was decided not to proceed with such a definition, which would simply have provided that interest had a UK source if the payer was resident in the UK. Notwithstanding, HMRC will still regard any loan as UK source where the borrower is UK resident. In other cases, they will be looking to designate loans as UK source and will take into account:

(a)   whether the interest is paid out of the UK source rents;
(b)   if the interest is paid in the UK;
(c)   whether the loan is secured on UK property;
(d)   if the loan agreement is governed by UK law

(Revenue Tax Bulletin November 1993 page 100).

If any of the above features apply, there is a potential withholding problem, although in each case whether the loan has a UK source will be determined by looking at each of the factors to see on which side of the fence the indicators fall. The borrower is best advised to try and clear the position with HMRC's Centre for Non-Residents (CNR) before it makes payments without withholding tax.

Note that where the withholding of tax is required of the borrower, it is only on payment of the interest. It is quite separate from the tax deductibility of the interest from profit which is on an accrued – rather than paid – basis.

Tax withholding will still apply even if the interest is not allowable for tax purposes (for instance, where it is disallowable under Point 3.5 above). However, if excess interest is disallowed under the transfer-pricing rules (see Point 3.5 above), it is now possible for the recipient of the interest to claim exemption from withholding tax (*TA 1988, Sch 28AA, para 6C*).

Point 3.7:   *Where a deduction of tax might otherwise apply, it can be avoided in a number of situations. These are where the lender is in a country with a suitable tax treaty with the UK, where the EC Interest and Royalties Directive applies, where the interest is short interest or if the interest is in the form of a redemption premium on a discounted security.*

There will be no tax withholding requirement where the lender is resident in one of a number of foreign countries with which the UK has a suitable double tax agreement – for instance, Germany or the USA. In that case, however, it is still necessary for the lender to obtain advance clearance from CNR that the interest can be paid without tax deduction.

It is possible to pay or receive interest without deducting or suffering a tax withholding where the payment is made between a lender and borrower within the European Union Specific advice would be necessary depending on the countries involved and the nature of the borrowing.

Where the loan is not capable of exceeding 12 months, any interest paid is referred to as 'short' as opposed to 'yearly' interest. Deduction of tax only applies to 'yearly' interest (*ITA 2007, s 874*). Therefore, no tax deduction is necessary on interest on short-term facilities from a foreign lender.

A 'discount' payable on the redemption on a discounted security (ie one that is issued at a discount to redemption price) is similarly not yearly interest for the purposes of the withholding rules. Accordingly, another way around the withholding rules is to borrow funds on a discounted security. This typically has a low or zero interest rate but where the borrower must repay a specific sum over and above the original sum borrowed (see Point 3.28 for further details regarding discounted securities).

Point 3.8:   *The introduction of rules for 'alternative finance' has enabled tax relief to be obtained for costs incurred in relation to financing structures which are compliant with Islamic law.*

See Point 3.29 in Chapter 3B for an outline of the typical structures that have been accommodated by changes in the UK tax rules as introduced by *Finance Acts* in 2005, 2006 and 2007.

CHAPTER 3B – FINANCE COSTS FOR UK PROPERTY INVESTMENT COMPANIES

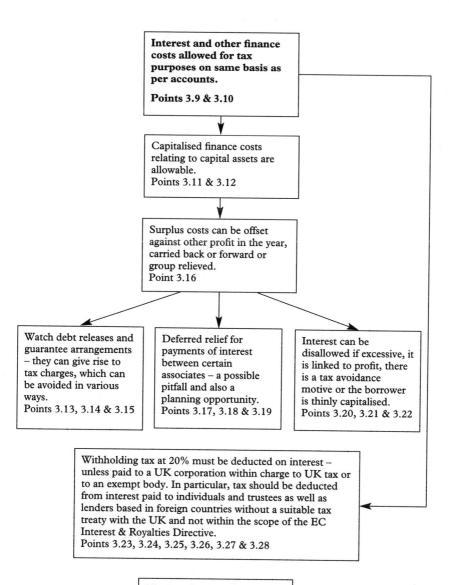

Interest and other finance costs allowed for tax purposes on same basis as per accounts.

Points 3.9 & 3.10

Capitalised finance costs relating to capital assets are allowable.
Points 3.11 & 3.12

Surplus costs can be offset against other profit in the year, carried back or forward or group relieved.
Point 3.16

Watch debt releases and guarantee arrangements – they can give rise to tax charges, which can be avoided in various ways.
Points 3.13, 3.14 & 3.15

Deferred relief for payments of interest between certain associates – a possible pitfall and also a planning opportunity.
Points 3.17, 3.18 & 3.19

Interest can be disallowed if excessive, it is linked to profit, there is a tax avoidance motive or the borrower is thinly capitalised.
Points 3.20, 3.21 & 3.22

Withholding tax at 20% must be deducted on interest – unless paid to a UK corporation within charge to UK tax or to an exempt body. In particular, tax should be deducted from interest paid to individuals and trustees as well as lenders based in foreign countries without a suitable tax treaty with the UK and not within the scope of the EC Interest & Royalties Directive.
Points 3.23, 3.24, 3.25, 3.26, 3.27 & 3.28

The introduction of rules for 'alternative finance' has improved tax relief for financing structures which are compliant with Islamic law.
Point 3.29

3B Finance costs for UK property investment companies

Point 3.9: *A company that obtains conventional finance from an unconnected lender for property investment is entitled to a tax deduction for the related finance costs. The deduction for the interest and other costs is normally given on the same basis as they are treated in the accounts.*

Finance costs are, generally speaking, deductible for tax purposes on the same basis as they are reflected in the accounts. This applies to:

- interest;
- incidental costs of obtaining finance or repaying a loan;
- a premium/discount payable on redemption of a loan.

More specifically, a deduction is available for the following:

- discounts (including a variable discount influenced by market conditions);
- premiums;
- losses arising from the repurchase of debt;
- costs of obtaining loan finance including the issue expenses incurred in connection with quoted debt;
- abortive expenditure and expenses incurred in connection with a loan facility which is never drawn;
- termination costs (including any penalty on loan redemption);
- any other payments made under the terms of a loan including payments to reimburse a lender's costs.

(FA 1996, s 84(1), (3)–(6)).

The general rule on deductibility is subject to the condition that the indebtedness in question is a 'loan relationship'. Loan relationships arise in the following situations:

(a) a money debt resulting from a transaction involving the lending of money;
(b) an instrument issued to represent security for a money debt; or
(c) an instrument issued to represent rights of a creditor in a money debt.

(FA 1996, s 81).

Unpaid trade debts or outstanding consideration on the purchase of an asset do not satisfy the above criteria and are not loan relationships. Shares carrying normal distribution rights are also excluded from the definition.

There are specific rules allowing tax relief on interest on debts which are not loan relationships (*FA 1996, s 100*). The interest is treated in the same way as costs incurred under loan relationships.

In many situations for borrowers, there should be no practical difference between the treatment of a debt that is a loan relationship and the treatment of one that is not.

As a general rule the tax treatment of finance costs follows the accounting treatment. In most cases the costs accrued in the profit and loss account will be deductible for tax purposes (see Point 3.10 below). There are, however, special rules where the borrower and lender are associated, which can result in the deferment of tax relief for accrued but unpaid interest (see Points 3.17 to 3.19 below).

Borrowers will receive relief for any discount paid on 'relevant discounted securities'. There are rules that defer tax relief until the discount is paid where the holder and issuer of the security are associated and the holder is not assessable on an accruals basis (eg when the holder is an individual, trustee or non-resident company).

There is still the potential for mismatch where the holder of the security is not connected with the borrower/issuer and not associated with a participator in the borrower/issuer. If the recipient of the income from the security is not taxable under the loan relationship rules, then that person may only be taxed when the income is received. That would be the case with unconnected individuals or unconnected foreign holders of the security. The borrower can still enjoy a tax deduction as the expense accrues.

A company that issues convertible debt can claim a deduction for interest on an accrued basis providing it is issued on normal terms. This is subject to the disallowance of that interest if the convertible debt is a security which is neither listed on a stock exchange nor issued on 'comparable terms' to those securities. Any debt falling foul of that proviso could give rise to disallowance of the interest, which is, instead, treated as a distribution (*TA 1988, s 209(2)(e)(ii)*).

On conversion, the face value of the indebtedness may exceed the nominal value of shares to be issued. Any such difference credited to share premium account in the borrower's books is not taxable under the corporate debt rules because it is not recognised in computing the company's taxable profits (*FA 1996, ss 85A(1), 85B*). In accounting periods beginning before 1 January 2005, there was a specific exemption for amounts transferred to the share premium account (*FA 1996, s 84(2)(a)*, repealed by *FA 2004, Sch 10, para 1(3)*). Hence there is no clawback of accrued discount for which tax relief has been obtained.

Unpaid but accrued interest will be treated as paid on conversion, which could trigger a requirement to deduct tax and pay this over to HMRC (see Points 3.23 to 3.28 below). Where a tax withholding applies, it is as well to remember that the lender should be entitled to a net sum rather than gross interest. This may be relevant to the terms of the conversion.

Point 3.10:   *The deduction is for all the costs reflected in the accounts in accordance with generally accepted accounting practice.*

Most companies will be claiming a deduction for the costs reflected in the profit and loss account on an accruals basis.

There are a number of ways to accrue expenses. To minimise the scope for creativity here, the rules require the basis adopted to be in accordance with generally accepted accounting practice (GAAP) or International Accounting Standards, as appropriate.

For interest or other expenses of a loan relationship to be recognised under GAAP in determining the borrower's taxable profits, they must be brought into account in its:

(i)   profit and loss account/income and expenditure statement; or
(ii) its statement of recognised gains and losses; or
(iii) its statement of changes in equity; or
(iv) in any other statement of items brought into account in computing its profits and losses,

except for those items recognised in order to correct a fundamental error (*FA 1996, s 85B(1)*).

The actual payment dates or due and payable dates do not themselves influence the timing of the deduction – other than for certain connected-party loans (see Point 3.17 below).

Methods in accordance with GAAP, such as the amortised cost basis would similarly apply where there are either stepped or 'balloon' pay-ments of interest. This may mean smaller payments in earlier years and larger amounts later. For the payer and the recipient, the effect of accru-ing these costs in the accounts over the period of the loan under the amortised cost basis would be to 'flatten' out the payments. This has the effect of recognising a larger tax-allowable expense for the borrower in the early years compared to the actual amount paid. The lender, on the other hand, would be taxed on accelerated income.

This treatment is also relevant for discounted borrowing (see Point 3.28 below).

Accrued costs may not be allowable if the parties to the loan are con-nected and the payments are deferred (see Point 3.17).

The rules just described are those applying to accounting periods begin-ning after 31 December 2004. They have been revised to take account of the obligatory adoption of IAS (International Accounting Standards) by publicly quoted companies in the European Union for those accounting periods. In the UK, companies not required to adopt IAS may do so on a voluntary basis.

For earlier accounting periods, although the terminology was different, the rules were essentially the same. Companies were required to account for loan relationships using 'authorised accounting methods', of which there were two – the authorised accruals basis and the mark-to-market basis. These have now been effectively replaced by the amortised cost basis and the fair value basis, respectively.

Point 3.11:   *If finance costs are capitalised in the balance sheet, tax relief can still be claimed in that year where the finance is in respect of capital assets.*

The normal rule provides for a deduction for any finance costs that are properly charged to the profit and loss account or the equivalent statement.

Where finance costs are included in the value of a fixed asset in the balance sheet a deduction can be claimed for tax purposes (*FA 1996, Sch 9, para 14*). This would include interest on finance for purchases and development of investment property or the purchase of shares in a property company.

However, in accounting periods beginning after 31 December 2004, no deduction will be allowed in respect of any amounts representing a writing-down of the asset which is attributable to the finance costs or in respect of amortisation or depreciation representing a writing-off of the interest component (*FA 1996, Sch 9, para 14(4)*). This is to prevent a 'double dip' for any impairment or depreciation provided in respect of the interest element in the cost of the fixed asset.

The costs appear to be allowed on an accruals basis although the wording of the relevant provision is unclear. It refers to a bringing into account of the relief in the accounting period for which the related debit is 'given' (*FA 1996, Sch 9, para 14(2)*). The best interpretation of this is that the relief is available on an accruals basis.

HMRC regard the relief as only relevant to costs in relation to capital assets. In the absence of such a provision, capital-related costs in respect of, say, finance for a property or company purchase might not be tax deductible if they are never charged to the profit and loss account. On the other hand, where a company treats costs as deferred revenue expenditure which is released to the profit and loss account over a period of time, the company will get its tax deduction spread over the period as the cost is expensed.

3.12:   *For UK corporate borrowers funding purchases of investment property or related capital projects, fees should be allocated as far as reasonable to the funding.*

The purchase of investment property – or indeed any capital asset – gives rise to costs that may not be deductible from taxable profit. Such costs are of a capital nature and normally cannot be expensed for tax purposes against the profits of this or any other year.

The exception to this rule is funding costs. As indicated above, any legal or professional fees that are part of the finance exercise can be deducted from taxable income.

It is, therefore, worthwhile liaising with professionals supplying their services in relation to a property acquisition, reconstruction or refurbishment to ensure they allocate an appropriate portion of their fees to the related funding exercise.

Point 3.13: *Watch debt releases as these can generate taxable income.*

In the same way that costs and expenses reflected in the profit and loss account are allowed for tax purposes, so will be any credits.

For the borrower, it will be a rare event to have a credit in the profit and loss account in respect of finance it has received. However, as we have seen in past years, many distressed property situations have been resolved by arrangement between the lender and borrower resulting in forgiveness of some or all of the debt.

Any credit to a company's profit and loss account as a result of such a release gives rise to taxable income if the parties are not connected. This is also the case if the credit is posted directly to reserves (*FA 1996, s 85B(1)*; and for accounting periods beginning before 1 January 2005, *FA 1996, s 84(2)*).

The rule does not apply to a voluntary arrangement under the *Insolvency Act 1986* or an arrangement with creditors under, *s 425* of the *Companies Act 1985* (*FA 1996, Sch 9, para 5(3)*). Such releases are tax-free. Where the release of the debt takes place after 9 December 2003, the number of occasions on which a release of the debt is tax-free is extended to include situations in which the creditor company is in:

(a)   insolvent liquidation;
(b)   insolvent administration;
(c)   insolvent administrative receivership;
(d)   insolvent provisional liquidation; or
(e)   foreign proceedings equivalent to any of these

(*FA 1996, Sch 9, para 6A*).

The legislation does refer to releases (*FA 1996, Sch 9, para 5(3)*). This would seem to apply whether or not the borrower recognises the release in the accounts. A lender, on the other hand, does not need to release a debt to get tax relief. It is sufficient for this purpose to provide against a specific recoverable debt or write it off.

When a debt release is contemplated that is not an arrangement under the Insolvency or Companies Acts, the alternative actions suggested in Points 3.14 and 3.15 below should be adopted where possible. This may also apply to payments under a guarantee by another party (see Point 3.15).

Debt releases between connected parties are generally tax neutral under the corporate debt rules (*FA 1996, Sch 9, para 6*). There are exceptions to this rule where:

- the creditor has become insolvent (*FA 1996, Sch 9, para 6A*); or
- the debt precedes the connection (*FA 1996, Sch 9, para 6B*); or
- the connection has ceased (*FA 1996, Sch 9, para 6C*).

See Point 3.17 below for an explanation of 'connected'.

The tax charge on release will similarly not arise where a debt is novated from one group company to another with the consequence that the first borrowing company is thereby released from the debt (*FA 1996, Sch 9, para 12(2)*). The effective release in that situation is ignored. Different rules apply where the transferor company (the original creditor) uses fair-value accounting (or, for accounting periods beginning before 1 January 2005, the mark-to-market basis) to account for the loan relationship.

Point 3.14: *A loan that is on the point of being released could be converted into shares which the original lender sells for a nominal sum.*

If Smith Limited owes Browns Bank £100,000, any release of that debt by the Bank will trigger taxable income of £100,000 in the company.

It might be possible for the loan to be transferred from the Bank to Mr Smith at its nil market value. Smith Limited is now indebted to Mr Smith. Mr Smith could then release the debt.

Mr Smith, as an individual, is not subject to the loan relationship rules. The waiver of the debt would not crystallise any tax adjustment in his hands. When he releases Smith Limited from the consequent debt, the transaction is neutral for tax purposes as it is between connected parties (see Point 3.17 below).

One technical problem with this is that the transfer of the debt from the bank to Mr Smith might be treated as an effective release on novation.

The legislation provides for another way of getting around the problem. This can be achieved by capitalising the debt through the issue of shares with a low nominal value.

In the above example, Smith Limited could issue, say, 10 £1 ordinary shares to the bank in satisfaction of the debt. This would entail crediting the balance of £99,990 to Smith Limited's share premium account. Although a credit to profit and loss account or reserves would be taxable, an amount which is credited to share premium should not be (see Point 3.9 above).

Browns Bank could sell the shares to Mr Smith for £10. The Bank should still be in a position to claim a deduction for the loss in value of the debt.

Point 3.15: *Guarantee fees are deductible. However,*
watch for adverse tax consequences for the debtor if the
guarantee is about to be called upon.

HMRC has accepted that guarantee fees are deductible under the loan relationship rules (see HMRC Bulletin December 1996). However, there can be a problem if and when a guarantee is called upon. The problem arises because a guarantee is normally called upon when the borrower is unable to meet its obligations. Part and parcel of the guarantee process is that, on payment of the guarantee, the debtor would be released from its indebtedness.

Such releases from third party lenders give rise to a taxable credit (Point 3.14 above). The fact that the borrower and the guarantor are connected does not avoid this problem.

In view of this, the following alternatives might be considered where the guarantor and borrower are connected:

(a)   The guarantor simply lends the debtor money to pay off the other company's debt. That loan is then released without consequence under the connected party rules (see Point 3.17 below).

(b)   In conjunction with payment under the guarantee, the bank assigns the right to receive the debt to a connected individual. That person can release debt without tax consequence to him/herself (since individuals are outside the corporate debt rules) or to the company (by virtue of the connected company rules).

Point 3.16: *The borrower who has incurred finance costs*
under a non-trading loan relationship has some flexibility
about the manner in which charges are offset. In any case,
careful planning will be required to ensure optimal use of
the tax deduction.

It is important to recognise how non-trade loan relationship debits and credits arise and the extent to which they give rise to non-trading loan deficits or profits.

A company can incur non-trading debits in the following ways:

- interest payable on finance for non-trade purposes;
- bad debts on loans not made in the course of trade;
- losses on non-trade related foreign exchange transactions;
- payments in respect of financial instruments (eg caps, collars and swaps) entered into for non-trade reasons;
- finance and other incidental costs of a non-trade related loan relationship;
- abortive costs of trying to obtain non-trade related finance.

Similarly, a company can make profits from non-trading loan relationships in the following ways:

- releases from indebtedness;
- reimbursement of finance costs;
- non-trade related foreign exchange profits;
- non-trade related financial instrument receipts and profits.

These particular items are relevant when analysing the relief available for net deficits or the manner in which profit may be taxed.

Where a borrower incurs finance costs under a borrowing for non-trading purposes, the finance costs are deductible in several ways. All costs and profits must first be aggregated.

It is possible for a borrower to have surplus profits from non-trading loan relationships. These would be taxed as investment income (under *Schedule D Case III*).

Where a net loss ('a non-trading deficit') arises, which should typically be the case for a borrower, this could be relieved in one of the following ways:

- Offset against the company's total profits in the same year (*FA 1996, s 83(2)(a)*).
- Offset against capital gains of the company arising in the same year (*FA 1996, Sch 8, para 1*).
- Offset against any specified category or categories of income arising in the same year (*FA 1996, Sch 8, para 1*). Specifying categories of income to offset deficits against this option can help preserve, for example, trading profits where there may be past trading losses carried forward which can be set against them. Alternatively, it keeps foreign income in charge to tax thus enabling the company to use any foreign tax credit.
- Surrender as group relief against the total profit of other group companies (*FA 1996, s 83(3A)(a)*).
- Carry-back against the company's previous year's profits arising from non-trading loan relationships (*FA 1996, s 83(2)(c)*). This also includes foreign exchange and financial instrument profits. The carry-back cannot go back before 1 April 1996, when the corporate debt rules started to apply.
- Carry-forward against all non-trading profits and foreign trading income of the following year (*FA 1996, s 83(3A), Sch 8, para 4*). It is possible to 'skip a year' when carrying the deficit forward, providing a claim is made under *FA 1996, Sch 8, para 4(3)*. This allows any foreign income against which double tax relief is available, to remain in charge, thus not wasting the foreign tax credits.

The above claims, with the exception of a claim to use the deficit in the following year, must be made within two years of the end of the accounting period in which the deficit is incurred. A claim to use the deficit in a following year has to be made not later than two years after the end of the period in question.

Where these other options are not used, deficits are carried forward automatically against future profits from non-trading relationships.

Point 3.17: *Where the lender is connected to the borrower and is not subject to UK corporation tax on the full amount of accrued interest, no deduction for accrued interest in a period is available unless the interest is paid within 12 months of the year end.*

The fact that the borrower is connected to a lender does not prevent a deduction for accrued interest. Generally, where the lending is between UK companies, the treatment is no different for the borrower than if the loan were with an unconnected lender, except that fair-value accounting (or, for accounting periods beginning before 1 January 2005, a 'mark-to-market' basis) cannot be used to account for the loan relationship.

However, where the lender and borrower are connected and the lender is not subject to UK corporation tax on the full amount of accrued interest, the borrower will not receive a deduction for interest accrued unless it is paid within 12 months of the year end (*FA 1996, Sch 9, para 2*). In that case, the deduction for tax purposes will be deferred to the accounting period when the interest is paid.

There are four specific situations in which relief is deferred until the interest is actually paid. These are where at any time in the accounting period:

(a)   The borrower company and the lender are connected.

(b)   The borrower is a 'close company' and the lender is a 'participator' in the borrower, an 'associate' of such a participator or a company that the participator controls or in which the participator has a 'major interest'.

A close company is, broadly, any UK or foreign company that is under the control of fewer than six 'participators' or any number of directors. A 'participator' is generally a shareholder, although the term extends to a person with a right to acquire such a share or interest.

In certain circumstances even a company fully listed on the Stock Exchange can be close (*TA 1988, s 415*).

A company has a 'major interest' in another company if, essentially, it and another person together control the other company and both it and the other person have no less than 40% of the total rights, powers and holdings in that other company (*FA 1996, Sch 9, para 20*).

(c)   The lender is a company and the borrower has a major interest in the creditor company or the creditor company has a major interest in the borrower company.

(d)   The loan is made by pension trustees; and

(i)   the borrower company is the employer of scheme members; or

(ii)   the borrower company and the employer are connected; or

(iii)   the employer is a company and the borrower company has a major interest in that employer or the employer has a major interest in the borrower company.

This point clearly has to be watched since a borrower might find its tax liability retrospectively increased having failed to pay its accrued interest by this deadline. Alternatively, a fellow group company that has relied on group relief could find that the losses it has claimed from the borrower have disappeared.

Anyone buying a company from a group where such relief is being relied upon would need to ensure that there is an appropriate warranty in place in the purchase agreement. By the same token, anyone buying a company with past relief for unpaid interest might be required to ensure that the company it buys pays the interest by the requisite date.

Since UK resident companies and non-resident companies trading in the UK are taxable on accrued interest and related income under the corporate debt rules, this situation would typically only arise where the lender is an individual, partnership, trust or an investment company tax resident outside the UK.

A revised definition of control has applied from accounting periods beginning after 30 September 2002.

A company is connected with another person in any accounting period if at any time in that period:

(a)   the other person is a company and one controls the other; or
(b)   the other person is a company and both companies are under the control of the same person.

Control can be exercised by holding shares or otherwise possessing voting power. A person may also exercise control by means of any powers conferred on him by articles of association or any other documents. In all cases, control means the power to secure that the affairs of the company are conducted in accordance with that person's wishes. In the case of a partnership involving one or more companies, the assumption is that any powers, rights or property vesting in the partnership can be exercised by the partners separately according to their profit-sharing ratio. Banks or financial traders are generally excluded, since control by shares or voting power is not taken into account if a sale of the shares would give rise to a trading receipt.

(*FA 1996, ss 87, 87A*).

As noted in Point 3.20 below, tax relief for interest on loans from connected parties might be restricted under the transfer-pricing rules.

Point 3.18:   *The fact that a company might not get a tax deduction for interest until it is paid under the connected party rules could help in planning to ensure that it falls in a period when the tax relief can be fully exploited.*

As noted in Point 3.17 above, where the borrower is connected with certain lenders there will be no relief for accrued interest under the corporate debt rules until payment if the interest is paid more than 12 months after the accounting year end. Where the interest is paid late, the borrower is in a similar position to that prevailing before the corporate debt rules when interest in many cases was allowed only on a paid basis.

There are circumstances where that sort of flexibility could be useful. For instance, a deduction may occur in a year when neither the borrower nor any group company has any profit to offset it against nor are there carry-back opportunities. This leaves the unrelieved costs to be carried forward.

The problem with carrying forward costs is that the company may not generate surpluses to offset them against for some years. In the meantime, other future group profits are taxable. In this situation, deferring payment of interest can crystallise relief in a year when the group can use it.

EXAMPLE 1

Wills Ltd borrows £1 million from its controlling shareholder, Charles. Wills Ltd is loss making. Wills Ltd has a subsidiary, Harry Ltd, that also makes losses.

In its years to 31 December 2005 and 31 December 2006, Wills Ltd accrued £90,000 interest to Charles but did not pay this.

In the year ended 31 December 2007, Wills Ltd continued to lose money but the subsidiary company, Harry Ltd, had surplus income in excess of £90,000.

If Wills Ltd pays the year 2005 accrued interest in either the year to 31 December 2005 or the year to 31 December 2006 (ie within 12 months of the year end), Wills Ltd will get a deduction on the accrued basis in the year to 31 December 2005. The unrelieved interest will simply be carried forward. An expense in the year ended 31 December 2005 cannot be group relieved in the year to 31 December 2007 against Harry Ltd's income.

On the other hand, if Wills Ltd delays paying until the year to 31 December 2007, the deduction is allowed on a paid basis in that year. In that year, it can offset these costs by way of group relief against Harry Ltd's income.

The above example illustrates that the paid basis can be used to get greater flexibility in relieving finance costs.

Point 3.19: *The mismatch between the accruals basis of relief under the corporate debt regime and the received basis of taxation for certain lenders offers a cash flow tax planning opportunity.*

Point 3.17 above referred to the situation where the borrower will not be entitled to a tax deduction for interest accrued in a year if the interest is not actually paid within 12 months of the year end (*FA 1996, Sch 9, para 2*). Instead, the deduction will be allowed in the accounting period when the interest is subsequently paid.

Individuals, trusts and non-resident investment companies are outside the corporate debt regime. Where individuals, trusts and non-resident companies are liable to UK tax on interest, it is normally on a received basis.

In many cases, that gives rise to an opportunity to exploit a potential cash flow tax advantage.

EXAMPLE 2

Wayne borrows £1 million on 1 April 2007, which he lends to his property company, Rooney Limited, on 30 April 2007 (its year end) at 7% interest. Wayne earns £120,000 plus from other sources.

Rooney Limited uses this money together with accumulated funds to buy a £2 million property yielding £120,000 rent. It does not pay Wayne any interest until 29 April 2009, ie just within the deadline of 12 months after the year end 30 April 2008 to which the first year's interest will accrue. On 29 April 2010 it pays the accrued interest to 30 April 2009 and so on.

Rooney Limited will get a tax deduction in its year to 30 April 2008 and subsequent years for the interest it accrues as payable to Wayne. This will reduce the corporation tax payable on 31 January 2009 by, say, £14,000 (20% of £70,000) and slightly higher amounts on subsequent 31 Januarys (reflecting the increase in the small companies rate to 22%)

Wayne can claim tax relief in the two years to 5 April 2008 and 5 April 2009 for the £70,000 a year paid on the bank loan for the property company (worth £28,000 each year at 40%). He will enjoy the benefit of this on 31 January 2009 and 31 January 2010 (and possibly earlier depending on his payment on account position).

Wayne does not receive any taxable interest until 29 April 2009 (in the tax year 2009/10) at which stage Rooney Limited must deduct 20% tax ie £14,000. Wayne will pay higher rate tax on this (£14,000 if rates stay at 40%) until 31 January 2011.

Therefore, on 31 January 2009 and on 31 January 2010, the cash impacts are:

	£
Corporate tax saved	14,000
Personal tax relief	28,000
Income tax deducted by company	(14,000)
Interest free loan from HMRC in each of two years	£28,000

Point 3.20:   *Foreign investors need to be aware of potential restrictions on tax relief when they are using associated funds to finance UK property acquisitions.*

Tax relief on interest paid to associated lenders may be restricted or disallowed if the interest is excessive or the finance involves a 'top-up' to normal commercial lending. This is particularly relevant where foreign investors are behind purchases of UK investment property.

There are provisions (known as the transfer-pricing rules) in the tax legislation which aim to prevent reductions in UK tax liability as a result of arrangements between associated persons on uncommercial terms (*TA 1988, s 770A & Sch 28AA*). For periods beginning after 31 March 2004, the transfer-pricing rules apply to transactions wholly between UK persons. In previous periods, they applied only to transactions between UK persons and non-UK persons. However, together with the extension of the rules to all-UK transactions, has come their exclusion where the person attempting to derive the UK tax advantage is a small or medium-sized enterprise (SME) (*TA 1988, Sch 28AA, para 5C*).

A small enterprise is one with no more than 50 employees and with either an annual turnover of less than €10 million (approx. £6.67 million) or a balance-sheet total of less than €10 million. A medium-sized enterprise is one with no more than 250 employees and with either an annual turnover of less than €50 million (approx. £33.33 million) or a balance-sheet total of less than €43 million (approx. £28.67 million). If a company is a member of a group, these criteria are applied to the group as a whole. It will be seen that the UK to UK transfer-pricing rules should only apply to relatively few enterprises.

There are two exceptions to this exclusion of SMEs. The first is where one party to the transaction is resident in a territory with which the UK has no double tax treaty or has a treaty that does not have an appropriate non-discrimination article. Such territories will normally be tax havens. The second exception applies to medium-sized enterprises only. In certain circumstances, when an inquiry is opened into the tax return of a medium-sized enterprise, HMRC can direct that the transfer-pricing rules apply.

These rules apply to finance transactions where the lender or borrower participates directly or indirectly in the control, management or capital of the other (*TA 1988, Sch 28AA, para 4*). They bite in the following situations:

1. where interest payable to the lender exceeds an arm's length amount or other terms are agreed that would not have been agreed in the absence of the special relationship between the parties;
2. where the loan is in addition to or greater than a normal loan that a third party lender would be prepared to make in the circumstances;
3. where the loan would not have been made at all in the absence of the special relationship.

The provisions aim to correct the loss of UK tax arising from these situations. They do this by treating the transactions as having taken place at arm's length. Whilst they do not prescribe the exact mechanics, the inference is that excessive interest will be disallowed for tax purposes as will interest on excessive loans. These rules supplement HMRC's ability to treat certain interest payments as distributions (*TA 1988, s 209(d)*) – including situations where the interest is payable to a UK lender (see Point 3.21 below). For accounting periods beginning after 31 March 2004, they replace the former 'thin capitalisation' rules.

In these instances, there is the element of subjectivity as to what is excessive.

With regard to situations 1 and 2, any indications from established third party lenders as to how much they would be prepared to lend and on what terms would provide a basis for acceptable associated party lending. If a third party can state that it would lend, say, 80% of a property's value at 9% interest, then those terms should be regarded as commercial if taken up with an associated lender.

Additional security or guarantees available from the prospective borrower's overseas associates cannot influence the third party's terms. For example, if a third party is prepared to increase its lending from 80% to 100% of the property value because of guarantees from overseas shareholders of the borrower, that extra lending is uncommercial. Related interest would, therefore, be disallowed. This is the case even if it is actually the third party that lends the funds. Similarly, HMRC will look at loans routed through third parties (*TA 1988, Sch 28AA, para 3(3)*).

The transfer-pricing rules now explicitly cover situations where a loan is received on favourable terms from a third party because of a guarantee given by a party connected to the borrower, as well as loans from a connected party.

Where any of the following circumstances would have applied in the absence of the special relationship (between the borrower and the guarantor or the borrower and the lender):

(a)   the guarantee would not have been provided at all; or
(b)   a smaller amount would have been guaranteed; or
(c)   the consideration for the guarantee would have been greater and other terms would have been less favourable,

any excess interest arising as a result (which could amount to the whole of the interest, if the loan would not have been made at all between independent third parties in the absence of the guarantee, for example) is disallowed (*TA 1988, Sch 28AA, para 1B*).

These rules apply to accounting periods beginning after 31 March 2004, but are intended to replace the previous thin capitalisation rules rather than introduce new restrictions.

A possible way around such a problem might be for the foreign associate to provide funds by way of subscription for ordinary or preference shares. That would improve the borrower's balance sheet and increase the security for the lender. This, in turn, may secure a larger commercial loan than would otherwise be available.

With regard to the issue of thin capitalisation, HRMC has commented as follows:

> ... we have in recent years tended to accept that, where a loan otherwise meets the arm's length test, if the United Kingdom grouping remains geared at something less than 1:1 and its income cover is at least 3:1, its financing should be regarded as satisfying the test as a whole. If not, further consideration would be appropriate. It must be stressed, however, that there are no hard and fast rules in this area and each case has to be considered on its own facts.

(*Tax Bulletin* Issue 17, June 1995).

These comments remain valid now that thin capitalisation has been subsumed into the transfer pricing legislation. However, banks in recent years have been prepared to lend on much larger loan to value multiples particularly on good quality let commercial property. HMRC have, accordingly, had to recognise that this needs to be taken into account when considering whether a loan is on arm's-length commercial terms.

The restriction on the tax deduction for interest in these situations is not restricted to non-UK lenders. This is covered further in Point 3.21 below.

Connected parties to a loan relationship cannot get around the rules by routing the debt through a bank or other third party lender. HMRC can look through such arrangements (*FA 1996, s 87(5)*).

Genuine commercial transactions that, say, a bank has with parties that happen to be connected with each other should not be caught by the provisions. For instance, associated entities may use the same organisation for deposit and lending transactions. It may be important to be able to demonstrate that the transactions are not related.

Interest disallowed under the transfer pricing rules is not treated as a distribution (dividend), in contrast to the situations described in Point 3.21 below. Since April 2004, it has also been possible not to deduct tax at source from payments of disallowed interest if the lender is able to, and makes, a compensating adjustment (so that in effect the lender is taxed as if the disallowed interest had not been paid to it).

3.21:   *Where the lender is UK based, the deductibility of loan interest can be restricted in certain other situations.*

There are situations where interest will be treated as a distribution by the company rather than a deduction from taxable profit. The disallowance principally arises in the following situations:

(a)   Interest paid on a security to the extent that the interest exceeds a reasonable return for the use of the principal (*TA 1988, s 209(2)(d)*). This has applied even where the lender is based in the UK and taxable on that interest. 'Reasonable' for that purpose can take into account the lender's commercial rationale, notably risk.

(b)   Where the interest arises on a security on which the return is linked to the profits of the business or part of it. As with situation 1, there is no disallowance if the return is reasonable and the interest is payable to a UK company (*TA 1988, ss 209(2)(e)(iii) & 212(1)*).

The above situations, therefore, will be relevant where the lender is an individual, trustee or exempt fund such as a pension fund. If the recipient is an individual or trust, the reclassification of the payment as a distribution would mean that the receipt would be taxed as if it were a dividend rather than interest.

Point 3.22:   *There is a general anti-avoidance provision which can prevent a deduction for finance costs where the objective of the loan is tax avoidance.*

There is a rather notorious provision in the corporate debt rules. This appears to empower HMRC to resist any deduction for finance costs where finance has been advanced for an 'unallowable' purpose (*FA 1996, Sch 9, para 13*).

Unallowable purposes include those where the sole or main purpose of the loan is tax avoidance. This could be tax avoidance by the borrower, the lender or some other person.

Tax avoidance is sufficiently wide to include any arrangement designed to reduce a company's tax liability and has led to widespread concern. In response to concerns, the Economic Secretary to the Treasury at that time, Mrs Angela Knight, announced that the measure was primarily aimed at artificial avoidance. However, there remains some uncertainty about the scope of the provision. This is, no doubt, deliberate to discourage exploitation.

It is quite possible that the provision will have little more scope in practice than the established restriction on the allowability of loan interest where tax avoidance is the main motive for the transaction (*TA 1988, s 787*). As with that section, it may well be sufficient to show a business motive for the borrowing.

The fact that there was also a tax advantage or that the finance could have been structured less tax-efficiently should be irrelevant. On the other hand, routing loans through companies which themselves have no commercial justification for being involved in the loan relationship could be challenged under this provision.

This 'unallowable purpose' test has to be satisfied each accounting period. It is not enough to show that the loan was taken out originally for an allowable purpose, if its ongoing existence is for an unallowable purpose.

Point 3.23:   *There is no requirement to withhold tax at the lower rate from interest payments made to UK companies that are within charge to corporation tax.*

There is no requirement to withhold income tax from any interest payments made by a company within the UK to any other companies that are within charge to UK corporation tax (*TA 1988, s 349A*). As a consequence, UK companies can enter into loan arrangements without the need to deduct tax from any interest payments or comply with the requirement to complete the related quarterly returns to HMRC. Payments may also be made gross to the UK branches of non-resident companies, provided that the branch carries on a trade in the UK and the interest will form part of its profits chargeable to UK tax.

Point 3.24: *Since 1 October 2002, interest may also be paid to exempt funds without deduction of tax.*

The abolition of the withholding requirement on interest paid to UK companies has been extended to payments made to UK bodies that are exempt from tax. Thus, payments since 1 October 2002 to pension funds and charities, among others, may be made without deduction of tax, if the payer is a company or local authority.

Point 3.25: *The borrowing company should ensure that the lender is a UK company subject to corporation tax or an exempt body before paying interest without tax deduction.*

The abolition of the tax deduction requirement still leaves categories of lenders that will be subject to withholding tax. This would apply to lenders such as individuals and trustees as well as companies not resident in the UK without a trading branch here.

An exception applies where the loan is not capable of exceeding 12 months. Any interest paid on such loans is known as 'short interest'. There is no tax deduction requirement on short interest.

Borrowers need to have a reasonable belief that the lender is subject to UK corporation tax or is an exempt body before making interest payments gross. It may be prudent to obtain a confirmation from the lender's professional advisers to this effect before paying interest.

Point 3.26: *Where an individual borrows to lend to a company, he or she needs to take into account the cash flow shortfall.*

Non-corporate lenders should be mindful of the cash flow effect of the tax deduction requirement. Where an individual borrows from a bank personally and on-lends to a company, his or her interest payments will have to be made gross to the bank. Unless extra interest is charged on the loan on to the company, there will be a shortfall as between the interest net of 20% tax received from the company and the gross interest payable to the bank.

As far as the paying company is concerned, the timing of interest payments subject to deduction of tax at source can secure a cash flow advantage. In that connection, the tax must be accounted for to HMRC no later than 14 days after the end of a return quarter. Return quarters end on 31 December, 31 March, 30 June and 30 September. Where a company's year-end does not coincide with one of these dates, then its accounting date will form the end of a fifth return period.

It is easy to see that paying the interest at the beginning of the following return quarter is better than paying at the end of the previous quarter.

EXAMPLE 3

Andy Limited pays interest on its loan from Andy on 30 June 2007. 20% tax must be withheld from the payment and sent to HMRC by 14 July 2007.

If Andy Limited pays the interest one day later – ie 1 July 2007, the tax does not need to be paid over until 14 October 2007 – ie 3 months later.

Point 3.27: *Tax must be withheld from annual interest payments made abroad. There are exceptions, however, for treaty countries and for payments to associated companies within the EU.*

The general rule is that interest payments made to a foreign lender must be subject to a deduction of income tax, currently at a rate of 20%. This tax must be accounted for to HMRC in the same way as other withholding situations already referred to.

The required withholding may be reduced, in some cases to nil, if the lender is resident in a foreign jurisdiction that has a double tax treaty with the UK that provides for this. For example, the US/UK and Germany/UK treaties provide for a nil withholding.

The reduced or nil withholding cannot apply unless and until the borrower has received express authorisation from HMRC. To receive this authorisation the UK borrower must complete a form obtainable from the HMRC's Centre for Non-Residents. This is sent to the lender who, in turn, submits it to the relevant local tax office in that country. Once approved in that jurisdiction, the form is forwarded to the UK authorities who issue the formal authorisation to the borrower.

The procedure can take several months but will be necessary if a withholding is to be avoided. Often overseas lenders will not be prepared to suffer a tax deduction from the interest payments, so the borrower will need to act quickly once a loan is entered into.

Since January 2004, tax has not needed to be withheld from payments by UK companies or UK permanent establishments of foreign companies to 'associated' companies elsewhere in the EU, as provided by the EC Interest and Royalties Directive. Companies are associated if one has an interest of at least 25% in the other or the same third company has an interest of at least 25% in both of them. This interest reduces to 10% from 2009.

However, before paying interest gross, the UK paying company will need to have an exemption certificate from HMRC. HMRC issue the certificate on application from the foreign lender, if they are satisfied that the lender meets the necessary criteria. Applications must be made to the Charities, Assets and Residency office.

When setting up loan arrangements between companies in EU member states, it is worth checking from which date the EU state in question will be complying with the Directive. Some of the newer member states are not required to comply immediately.

Short interest is not subject to withholding (Point 3.24 above).

Point 3.28:   *Other ways to avoid tax withholding are to structure the loans as non-UK source or to structure the return on the loans as a discount on a discounted security or to list the debt on a recognised stock exchange.*

Where a favourable double tax treaty does not apply, a borrower may find that a lender still expects to receive the gross interest and thus the borrower will have to bear the cost of any tax withheld. In that situation, the borrower should explore the possibility of siting the loan outside the UK. Interest on a non-UK sourced loan is not subject to UK withholding.

The following factors should ensure that a loan is sited outside the UK and the withholding requirements:

(a)   the borrower is resident abroad;
(b)   the interest is paid abroad;
(c)   the nature and location of the security is abroad;
(d)   the interest is paid from foreign funds;
(e)   the debt is subject to foreign law.

It is arguable whether the fact that the majority of the above conditions apply will be sufficient to site a debt abroad. HMRC do not necessarily take that view. See also Point 3.6. It may well be advisable to obtain express agreement that a loan is outside UK jurisdiction from HMRC's Centre for Non-Residents.

There was a proposal to simplify the law in this respect, so that a loan would have a UK source if and only if the borrower was resident in the UK. Following consultation, the decision was taken to leave the law as it is. This proposal could be revived in future, however.

Where the borrower is UK-resident it may help if the loan is established as a 'specialty debt'. This involves having the loan agreement drawn up and executed under seal outside the UK. The debt is then treated as situated where the document is physically kept. As long as the document is abroad, so is the debt.

Another way to avoid withholding tax is by structuring a debt as a discounted security or series of discounted securities. Discounts are not interest and HMRC accept that discounts are not subject to withholding.

One exemption from the withholding requirements applies where interest is paid in relation to a debt which qualifies as a quoted Eurobond

(*TA, s 349(3)(c)*). This would cover a debt listed on a recognised stock exchange (*TA, s 349(4)*). Accordingly, where a UK company borrows from, say, an overseas entity, it may be possible for that debt to be issued in the form of loan notes which could become listed on, a stock exchange in, for instance, a Channel Island.

Point 3.29:   *The introduction of rules for 'alternative finance' has enabled tax relief to be obtained for costs incurred in relation to financing structures which are compliant with Islamic law.*

The Government introduced measures in the *Finance Act 2005* which were largely aimed at the growing volume of transactions which are structured to comply with Islamic Sharia law.

There are a number of areas where commercial transactions undertaken by Muslims are expected to comply with religious and ethical precepts. These cover, amongst things the lending of money. In particular, the charging of interest by lenders is prohibited and arrangements for the provision of finance need to involve a return other than the payment of interest.

- As a consequence, finance structures have evolved and continue to evolve which are compliant with Islamic law. Typically, these have taken a number of forms, for instance:
- Diminishing Musharaka – Musharaka more generally involves the financing party entering into a form of partnership arrangement with the commercial owner of the property. A profit share is secured by the financing partner which would be comparable to a finance return in a more conventional lending arrangement. Typically, the return paid by the commercial owner to the financing party is in the form of rent. Property financing structures generally involve a diminishing musharaka arrangement. Under this, the initial ownership of the asset is held between the two parties according to the contribution to the finance. The finance party's share then diminishes over the specified period as payments are made by the commercial owner, who as a consequence, progressively acquires a greater share of the property until it is fully owned at the end of the finance period.
- Mudaraba/Wakala – As a form of investment limited partnership, these are variations on the above arrangement which involve the finance party advancing funds for the acquisition of the property in return for a share of profits (or losses) arising.
- Murabaha – This has some similarities to a finance lease. The financing party actually buys the asset in question and on-sells it to the commercial venturing party at a mark-up and on deferred terms which again give rise to a similar level of return that a conventional lender might expect.
- Sukuk – This is a form of securitisation. A security, or sukuk, is issued by a special purpose vehicle which would typically buy the

property and let it to the commercial owner. Often, the sukuk vehicle will acquire the property in a sale and leaseback arrangement. As with Musharaka, the owner pays a return in the form of rent. This in turn is distributed by the SPV to its Sukuk holders as a profit distribution.

As the global Islamic community has become more influential in commercial transactions here in the UK in recent years, there has been an increasing interest in these alternative finance structures. With that, there has been the growing recognition that our tax rules would not necessarily accommodate a tax deduction even though a similar level of costs in a conventional finance arrangement would be tax deductible.

One particular problem has been the nature of the payments. As they are expressly not interest payments, it has been difficult to find a basis in the UK tax code for their deductibility. In the absence of relieving legislation, where a company makes Mudaraba or Wakala payments as profit shares, these would be generally treated as distributions and disallowed (*ICTA 1988, s 209 (2) (e) (iii)*). Other problems can arise with Murabaha payments given that what otherwise would be annual costs of finance are presented as a series of payments for the asset, probably totalling more than that asset's market price.

Even with Musharaka and Sukuk transactions, where the payments are in the form of rent, there might ordinarily be a tax deductibility problem if the annual payments are greater than the normal commercial rent.

A further issue arises with non-UK based financing parties as involvement in a Mudaraba or Wakala arrangement could result in that party having a taxable activity in the UK.

With these concerns in mind, the Government introduced a series of provisions, initially in the *Finance Act 2005*, to enable tax relief to be available in circumstances where that previously may not have been the case.

To come within the new rules, the arrangements in question must involve a financial institution, which should include one of the following:

- a bank (within *ICTA 1988, s 840(a)*);
- a building society;
- a wholly-owned subsidiary of a bank or building society;
- a person licensed under the *Consumer Credit Act 1974* to carry on credit or hire business; or
- a person authorised in a jurisdiction other than the UK to receive deposits or repayable funds from the public and grants credit for its own account

(*FA 2005, s 46(2)*).

The ensuing sections in the *Finance Act 2005* together with subsequent amendments in 2006 and 2007, again set out various forms of arrangement which are typical of Sharia financing structures.

The provisions specify that providing the return, profit share or mark-up as the case may be reflects a reasonable arm's-length finance return, the payment can be allowed for tax relief purposes.

In the case of a situation where a 'turn' is made in the form of a mark-up on goods purchased from the financing party, the part payments for the goods each year are treated as principle with interest and the allowable element computed accordingly (*FA 2005 s 47*).

With regard to the profit-sharing, Mudaraba style arrangements, the provisions introduced in the *Finance Act 2005* have stopped the distribution rules in *ICTA, s 209* from preventing a tax deduction (*FA 2005, s 54*).

In the *Finance Act 2006*, the rules were extended to include Wakala and diminishing Musharaka type structures. Furthermore, the SDLT rules were amended to ensure there was not a double charge to SDLT as ownership of a property changed progressively under the Diminishing Musharaka or Murabaha style arrangements.

The *Finance Act 2007* has further introduced into the UK tax regime the concept of the Sukuk type security to the extent that the return enjoyed by the investors is on a par with a commercial return for the provision of funds. The return is then assessed on the bond holders in the same way as would interest and allowed to the payer on a similar basis.

The modification of pre-existing rules has gone a long way to assisting with the tax effectiveness of these various arrangements. There remain areas, however, where the strict tax position is still unhelpful. For instance, the structure can fall outside the alternative financing reliefs where the financing party has an interest in the future income or capital growth of the property. This has been a feature of the partnership style arrangements.

Also, no special rules exist for VAT. Accordingly, the financing party in a Sharia compliant structure may be treated as principal or part principal in a property transaction for VAT purposes and thus have to consider different VAT consequences to a conventional lender.

Although the primary focus of these new rules is to legislate for the tax deductibility of costs in these financing transactions, there is no reference to Islamic law in the legislation or to the terms referred to above. The Government have deliberately sought to ensure that such rules should not be specific to any particular religious group or community. As a consequence, it is open for any commercial arrangements that want to use structures such as these in preference to a conventional financing scenario.

CHAPTER 4 – REPAIRS, RENEWALS AND IMPROVEMENTS

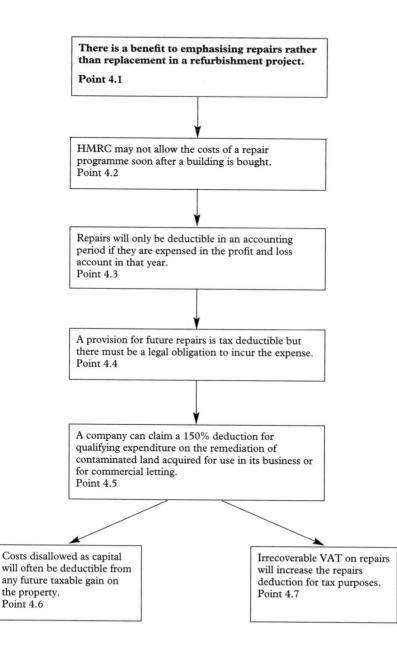

There is a benefit to emphasising repairs rather than replacement in a refurbishment project.

Point 4.1

HMRC may not allow the costs of a repair programme soon after a building is bought.
Point 4.2

Repairs will only be deductible in an accounting period if they are expensed in the profit and loss account in that year.
Point 4.3

A provision for future repairs is tax deductible but there must be a legal obligation to incur the expense.
Point 4.4

A company can claim a 150% deduction for qualifying expenditure on the remediation of contaminated land acquired for use in its business or for commercial letting.
Point 4.5

Costs disallowed as capital will often be deductible from any future taxable gain on the property.
Point 4.6

Irrecoverable VAT on repairs will increase the repairs deduction for tax purposes.
Point 4.7

4 Repairs, renewals and improvements

Point 4.1: *A landlord contemplating an expenditure programme can influence the deductibility of amounts spent by putting the emphasis more on repairs than improvements.*

Where substantial refurbishment or redecoration is carried out, the related expenditure may not be fully deductible against rental income for tax purposes. To be allowable, such expenditure must be in respect of repairs or maintenance rather than improvements.

The distinction between repairs and improvements can give rise to problems. The courts have distinguished between repairs, which are allowable, and renewals, which are not.

Judicial decisions on this suggest that the restoration or replacement of part of an asset is a repair. The replacement of an entire asset is a renewal (see *O'Grady v Bullcroft Main Collieries Ltd* (1932) 17 TC 93 and *Jones (Samuel) & Co (Devondale) Ltd v IRC* (1951) 32 TC 513).

It is not easy to determine whether there has been a replacement of the whole asset or just part of it. Within the building there are a number of assets which make up the whole. A possible approach might be:

(a)   For assets within a building, such as lifts or heating systems, the initial installation and subsequent complete replacement are renewals. If the system is overhauled or parts replaced, then that is a repair (*Lurcott v Wakely & Wheeler* [1911] 1 KB 905).

(b)   If there is no separate asset, the test is whether the work performed enhances the asset as a whole. A new roof, for instance, could improve the building and would then be a capital item. The stripping down and repair of an entire roof on the other hand should still qualify as a revenue expense.

If an old building is repaired using modern materials, that is a repair. In one case, the old wooden oak floors of a 400-year old building were replaced much more cheaply and effectively by a concrete floor covered with terrazzo tiling. In the same case, steel joists encased in oak replaced wood lintels. The High Court upheld the Commissioners' decision that these were repairs and not improvements (*Conn v Robins Bros Ltd* (1966) 43 TC 266).

In one of its Bulletins, HMRC has stated:

> Generally, if the replacement of a part of the 'entirety' is like-for-like or the nearest modern equivalent, we accept the expenditure is allowable revenue expenditure. (IR Tax Bulletin 59, June 2002).

Giving the example of double glazing, the bulletin added:

> In the past we took the view that replacing single-glazed windows with double-glazed windows was an improvement and therefore capital expenditure. But times have changed. Building standards have improved and the types of replacement windows available from retailers have changed. We now accept that replacing single-glazed windows by double-glazed equivalents counts as allowable expenditure on repairs.

A landlord might well review any proposed refurbishment programme to see whether repairs rather than improvements could be carried out. Furthermore, where both repairs and improvements are included in a work specification at the outset, a quantity surveyor could be asked to identify the related costs separately. General costs can then be allocated between them. In the absence of such a split, it is likely that the builders' invoices would not contain sufficient detail to support a revenue deduction for an appropriate part of the costs.

Point 4.2: *If there is a large repairs cost soon after a building is bought, HMRC is likely to treat this cost as capital and not allow a deduction from taxable income.*

Expenditure is not deductible from taxable income if it formed part of the acquisition cost of the property. Furthermore, if a property is purchased in a dilapidated state, restoration expenditure will be treated as part of the capital cost of the property (*Law Shipping Co Ltd v IRC* (1923) 12 TC 621 and *Jackson v Laskers Home Furnishers Ltd* (1956) 37 TC 69).

To obtain a deduction for the repairs, it is necessary to establish that a building was commercially habitable without carrying out the repairs. The best evidence of this would be if the repairs did not take place until some time after occupation commenced (see *Odeon Associated Theatres Ltd v Jones* (1971) 48 TC 257).

Point 4.3: *There may be no deduction for repairs expenditure which has not been reflected in the profit and loss statement of the investment activity. Therefore, repairs which are 'capitalised' in the accounts are likely to be disallowed.*

The rules determining how a profit from a property investment activity is taxed now closely follow the accounting treatment. This, in turn, is determined by normal accounting principles as applied also to trading activities (*TA 1988, s 21A(1)* for companies and *ITTOIA, s 272(2)* for non-corporate landlords). It does not matter whether the investor is a company, individual, partnership or trust.

HMRC will regard the profit and loss account of the entity as showing the proper measure of profit and loss for tax purposes on the premise that it is prepared in accordance with generally accepted accounting principles. There will be no deduction for items that are specifically disallowable such as depreciation, entertaining or capital expenses. Subject to that, HMRC will be reluctant to see an adjustment to profit for expenditure which it was not considered appropriate to include in the profit and loss account in the first instance.

In view of this, there is a clear conflict between maximising profit for accounts purposes and minimising profit for tax purposes. In either case, of course, the objective must be subservient to the proper treatment of the item to ensure that the accounts give a true and fair statement of the position.

Point 4.4: *A deduction is available for a repairs provision providing that there is a contractual obligation to undertake the expenditure and the repairs are specific.*

It had been assumed in the past that provisions for repairs were not tax deductible. HMRC's position on this was successfully challenged when the owner of a department store sought a deduction for a provision for refurbishment costs to be incurred in accordance with a feasibility report (*Jenners Princes Street Edinburgh Ltd v IRC* [1998] STC (SCD) 196). As the store was about to undertake the specific and detailed work set out in the feasibility report, the Special Commissioners felt that was sufficient to say that the funds had been 'expended' in an accounting sense. Thus *TA 1988, s 74(1)(d)* was satisfied.

In another case on the allowability of future costs, a firm of solicitors was held entitled to deduct for tax purposes the future rent commitment on its business premises (*Herbert Smith v Honour* [1999] STC 173).

Since these cases, the Accounting Standards Board has published FRS 12 ('Provisions, Liabilities and Assets'). This sets out the circumstances in which provisions are acceptable if the accounts are going to present a true and fair view. The fundamental change now is that there must be an actual obligation to pay a sum of money before it can be the subject of a provision. HMRC will not allow a provision for tax purposes if it does not satisfy FRS 12.

HMRC's present position is as set out in a Tax Bulletin (Tax Bulletin 40, April 1999). In this, it is stated that an accounts provision will be allowable for tax only if:

- it is in respect of revenue expenditure;
- it is required by UK generally accepted accounting practice;
- it does not conflict with any specific statutory tax rule;
- it is estimated with sufficient accuracy.

The message is that a provision for repairs can attract tax relief in a year, as the law currently appears to stand, even though monies are not paid out until a future period. This should be the case where there is a specific programme of work to be undertaken and a legal commitment to incur the expenditure.

Point 4.5: *Companies can obtain deductions of 150% on qualifying expenditure on cleaning up contaminated land they acquire for their own trading purposes or for commercial letting.*

A company incurring 'qualifying land remediation expenditure' qualifies for a deduction of 150%.

The company must acquire the land for the purposes of its trade or for commercial letting. If all or part of it is contaminated, and the contamination is not due to any action or inaction on the company's own part, or on the part of any connected party, certain types of expenditure on remedying the contamination qualify for the relief.

The expenditure must satisfy five conditions to qualify, as follows:

- the land in question must be in such a condition that harm of a defined environmental nature (injuring the health of living organisms, interference with ecological systems etc.) is being caused or may potentially be caused or that pollution of controlled waters is being or is likely to be caused;
- the expenditure must be undertaken directly by the company or on its behalf and consist of works, steps or operations designed to prevent, minimise, mitigate or remedy the harm or pollution;
- in the case of in-house costs, it must be incurred on employee costs or the cost of materials. There is no relief for the cost of support staff or items eligible for capital allowances;
- it must not be partly or wholly funded by any grants or subsidies nor must the cost of it, in fact, be borne directly or indirectly by a third party. This restriction might be a problem if there is a specific discount negotiated with a seller to reflect the remediation costs;
- the expenditure must be of a kind that would not have been incurred if the land had not been contaminated.

Provided that the above conditions are met, the company can opt to claim a deduction of 150% of the expenditure when computing its taxable profits (either of the trade for the purposes of which the land was acquired or of the commercial letting business in which the land is being used) for the accounting period in which the expenditure is incurred. If, in that period, the company makes a loss that is unrelieved, it may instead claim a tax credit equal to 16% of the smaller of the loss and 150% of the qualifying expenditure. A loss is unrelieved to the extent that it has not been, and could not be, used to offset other profits of the same period or previous periods or as part of a group-relief claim.

The relief is only available to a UK resident company. Individuals, partnerships, trusts and even non-resident companies will not be able to claim the deduction.

It is worth noting that a property investment company that incurs such costs can elect to claim a tax deduction for these even though they may be included in the balance sheet cost of the property. A company which holds the property as trading stock, on the other hand, can only get the deduction when the stock is sold.

The credit is not treated as taxable income of the company and can be applied against any corporation tax liability the company may have, or be claimed as a repayment. It will, however, be more beneficial to claim the deduction rather than the tax credit where the landlord has sufficient other income to shelter.

Point 4.6: *If expenses are disallowed by HMRC on the grounds that they represent improvements, ensure that these costs are included in the capital cost of the property when computing any future chargeable gains.*

If refurbishment or related expenditure (including any irrecoverable VAT thereon) is disallowed as capital, it is important to keep a note of these amounts. They should form part of the capital gains tax base cost of the property as enhancement expenditure, assuming the related improvements are reflected in the state or nature of the property when sold (*TCGA 1992, s 38(1)(b)*).

These expenses will reduce any subsequent capital gain arising.

Point 4.7: *Remember that irrecoverable VAT will attract a tax deduction.*

Where VAT on repairs expenditure is irrecoverable, the non-recoverable VAT will be a deductible expense for income and corporation tax purposes.

CHAPTER 5 – STAMP DUTY LAND TAX

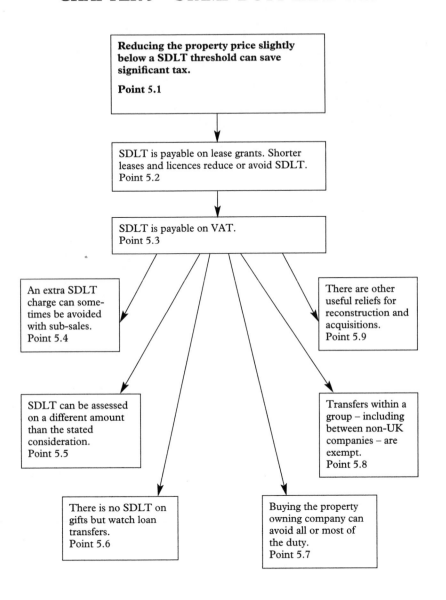

Reducing the property price slightly below a SDLT threshold can save significant tax.

Point 5.1

SDLT is payable on lease grants. Shorter leases and licences reduce or avoid SDLT.
Point 5.2

SDLT is payable on VAT.
Point 5.3

An extra SDLT charge can sometimes be avoided with sub-sales.
Point 5.4

There are other useful reliefs for reconstruction and acquisitions.
Point 5.9

SDLT can be assessed on a different amount than the stated consideration.
Point 5.5

Transfers within a group – including between non-UK companies – are exempt.
Point 5.8

There is no SDLT on gifts but watch loan transfers.
Point 5.6

Buying the property owning company can avoid all or most of the duty.
Point 5.7

5   Stamp duty land tax

Point 5.1:   *Full stamp duty land tax at the appropriate rate is payable on property purchases exceeding certain thresholds. Reducing a price slightly could have an impact on the stamp duty land tax. Also avoid contingent amounts where possible.*

Since 1 December 2003, stamp duty land tax (SDLT) has applied to land transactions instead of stamp duty.

The SDLT thresholds on transfers of non-residential (or mixed non-residential/residential) freeholds and lease assignments are currently as follows:

£150,000 or less – 0%

£150,001–£250,000 – 1%

£250,001–£500,000 – 3%

Over £500,000 – 4%

In the case of residential property, the nil rate band is restricted to £125,000 (*FA 2003, s 55(2)*).

The above rates would apply to transfers of property and most other land transactions, eg options and waiver of rights. The grant of leases is, however, subject to a different regime mentioned in Point 5.2 below.

Paying for example, £100 more than £250,000 increases the SDLT by 2% ie by £5,002. In that case, it would be worth the purchaser's while to negotiate the price down to £250,000. Similarly, where the threshold of £500,000 is exceeded, there is an increase in SDLT by 1% to 4%. The difference between the duty payable on a sale for £499,999 and that for £500,001, ie £2 more, is £5,000. These amounts are inclusive of any VAT due (see Point 5.3).

A possible pitfall for buyers is to have consideration contingent on a future event. Under SDLT, that contingency will be assumed to occur and thus the SDLT is calculated on the higher amount (*FA 2003, s 51(1)*). It is, however, possible to make an application to defer the tax payable in certain circumstances (*FA 2003, s 90*). In the event that the contingency does not eventually happen, any overpaid SDLT can be recovered (*FA 2003, s 80*).

5.2:   *SDLT is payable by tenants on lease grants. Shorter leases and licences can help to minimise the charge as can appropriate allocation to non-rent amounts such as service fees. There is also an exemption for certain sale and leasebacks.*

SDLT must be paid by tenants entering into a new lease.

The rate is 1% and this is applied to the present value of rents reserved under the lease over £150,000 (£125,000 for residential property). The SDLT calculation is based on a present value formula. It is possible to access HMRC's on-line calculator for assistance with computing the liability (which can be found on HMRC website at www.hmrc.org.uk).

The rules surrounding this charge are complex, particularly in determining the SDLT where there are variable and uncertain rents or the potential for future large rent hikes. As such, any detailed discussion of the rules is outside the scope of this book. Some of the key planning pointers in this area can be summarised as follows:

- The consequence of the calculation is that the longer the lease and the higher the rent, the higher the SDLT charge.
- No SDLT is due on licences.
- Service charges and other non-rental amounts do not figure in the calculation. Therefore, it is sensible to separately identify such amounts from the rent in any lease. Note that the amounts in question must be reasonable otherwise the SDLT due is open to challenge by HMRC.
- Lease grants of residential property may be subject to the disadvantaged area relief. An exemption is available for the first £125,000 of value in the case of grants of leases of residential property situated in a disadvantaged area. Lists of current qualifying areas are included in the *Stamp Duty (Disadvantaged Areas) Regulations 2001 (SI 2001/3747)* and are available on the HMRC website.
- A lease grant will not be subject to SDLT where it is part of a sale and leaseback arrangement (*FA 2003, s 57A*).

Point 5.3:   *SDLT is payable on VAT.*

A controversial aspect of SDLT is that it is charged on the VAT inclusive price of a property. There is thus an element of tax on tax.

The position can be summarised as follows:

- Where the VAT exemption on a commercial property has been waived VAT is chargeable on the sale price or, where relevant, the rent. In this case, SDLT is payable on the VAT-inclusive consideration or, with a lease grant, the present value of future VAT inclusive rents.
- Similarly, where VAT must be charged – ie on the sale of new commercial property – SDLT would be computed on the price inclusive of VAT.

- If the sale is of a property where the exemption from VAT has not been waived at the time of completion (ie the sale is exempt), no VAT would be charged on the sale and thus would not affect the SDLT due (*FA 2003, Sch 4, para 2*).
- In the case of grants of leases, SDLT will only be charged on the VAT inclusive rent figure, if VAT is chargeable at the date the lease is granted. If, at that point, there has been no election to waive the exemption, SDLT is calculated on the VAT exclusive rent figure (*FA 2003, Sch 4, para 2*).
- Where a property transfer is outside the scope of VAT as it is a transfer of an asset as a going concern, SDLT is levied on the price exclusive of VAT.

A purchaser needs to consider the SDLT position in relation to the VAT status of the transaction and anticipate the SDLT on the VAT as an extra cost. VAT could also have the effect of pushing the sale price of the properties over the relevant stamp duty threshold (see Point 5.1 above).

For further reference on the VAT position for properties, see Chapters 18 (for investors), 26 (for property dealers and developers) and 39 (for trading premises).

Point 5.4: *SDLT may arise on a property transaction even where a contract of sale has not been completed. An important exception is available to enable certain sub-sales to proceed without double tax provided there has not been 'substantial performance'.*

A common way to avoid stamp duty on commercial property transactions in the past has been to transfer the beneficial ownership under a contract which is never formally completed. The transfer to the purchaser of shares in a nominee company holding the legal title in the property was normally sufficient to effectively 'complete' the transaction. As there was no formal conveyance, no stamp duty arose.

With the introduction of SDLT in December 2003, this technique no longer avoids tax. SDLT can still arise in relation to an uncompleted contract providing there has been 'substantial performance' (*FA 2003, s 44*).

Substantial performance can occur where the buyer becomes entitled to occupy the property, or, where relevant, to receive the rental income arising. Alternatively, there is also substantial performance when the seller receives 90% or more of the sale consideration (*FA 2003, s 44(5)*).

A commercial situation where the substantial performance rule can be particularly helpful is in the area of sub-sales. Sub-sales is the term normally applied to situations where the buyer acquires land with a view to selling-on immediately or very shortly afterwards. Normally, this would mean two occasions of charge to SDLT. However, sub-sale relief avoids the double charge (*FA 2003, s 45*). If, however, the buyer completes, or pays more than 90% of the purchase price, any possibility of sub-sale relief is lost.

There is a specific exemption from SDLT where a house builder buys property from individuals who are selling their current residences to acquire a newly built home (*FA 2003, Sch 6A*). The subsequent purchaser from the house builder becomes liable to SDLT in the normal way.

Point 5.5:   *SDLT would normally be assessed on the consideration payable by the purchaser for the property, subject to certain exceptions where the amount may be more or less than this figure.*

For the most part, property transactions will stipulate the consideration payable and the calculation of the SDLT thereon would be relatively straightforward. There are, however, a number of exceptions.

One such situation is where there is a transfer of a property to a connected company, other than a transfer within a 75% group (*FA 2003, s 53*). In this situation, HMRC will seek to apply market value where the consideration passing is less than this figure.

A further situation arises with respect to loans. Where the consideration for the sale of property is the assumption or release of debt, the face value of the debt is treated as the consideration subject to SDLT (*FA 2003, Sch 4, para 8*). There may be some scope for reducing SDLT in this situation where the debt assumed has a higher market value than face value. This might be the case if the loan carried a particularly high interest rate.

Sometimes, properties are sold where the final consideration is not easily ascertainable at the outset. This may be because there is a contingency provided for or because there is some formula on which the consideration will be based.

The position with contingent consideration has already been referred to in Point 5.1 above. With regard to unascertainable consideration, the SDLT would be charged on a reasonable estimate (*FA 2003, s 51(2)*). It is possible to reclaim any overpaid SDLT, or pay over further amounts, once the actual consideration can be determined.

Point 5.6:   *A gift – other than a gift to an associated company – will not attract SDLT. However, if the donee agrees to take over any loan obligations the amount of that loan will be treated as consideration subject to SDLT.*

Where there is no consideration, no SDLT arises. Typically, that would be the case where there is a gift of a property. The exception to this is where the gift is to an associated company, where market value is substituted (see Point 5.5).

However, if any loan is taken over by the purchaser as part of the transfer, that would be consideration and subject to SDLT.

Point 5.7: *SDLT can be saved by buying the shares of the property owning company, particularly non-UK company, rather than the property itself.*

Whilst SDLT payable on the purchase price of a property can be up to 4%, stamp duty on the purchase of shares in a UK company is only 0.5%. With shares in non-UK companies no stamp duty at all is payable even if that company is resident and active in the UK, provided the shares remain outside the UK.

Buying and selling companies is less straightforward than buying the properties that they own. A problem for the seller has been capital gains tax. Within a corporate group, the issue is highlighted in the example below.

EXAMPLE

London Limited (London) owns all the shares in Manchester Limited (Manchester) which two years ago bought a property for £8 million. Manchester financed the property purchase with £6 million external borrowings and £2 million was lent by London. London only subscribed a nominal amount for the shares.

The property is now worth £10 million. If that property is sold to Birmingham Limited (Birmingham), Manchester would make a capital gain of £2 million (ignoring indexation allowance) on which it would pay £600,000 corporation tax.

After paying off the £8 million debt, the balance of £1.4 million can be distributed to London tax-free by way of dividend. The purchaser will pay £400,000 SDLT or possibly more, if VAT is chargeable on the sale (see Point 5.3 above).

An alternative is for London to sell the shares in Manchester for £2 million. Birmingham would take responsibility for repayment of the £8 million indebtedness which means it is still paying for £10 million.

In this case, London will have a capital gain of £2 million on the sale of the company. This would give rise to the same corporation tax £600,000 liability for London.

The purchaser's stamp duty is limited to 0.5% of £2 million ie £10,000 a saving of £390,000.

The problem is that the purchaser is also inheriting a tax liability within Manchester of £600,000. If the purchaser is going to be a long-term holder of that property, the cash flow benefit of avoiding stamp duty now could exceed the prospect of a distant future tax liability. In that case it could be an attractive proposition. Otherwise, the inherent tax liability could exceed the SDLT saving. The purchaser will, of course, have extra due diligence and contractual issues when buying a company as compared to the relatively more straightforward purchase of the property.

Clearly if the gain was exempt or there was only a modest gain or no gain at all, this structure is potentially beneficial all round. Gains might be exempt where the companies in question are not UK resident (see Chapter 1) or where the substantial shareholdings exemption applies (see Chapter 36).

Transferring a property into a special purpose company when a sale has been contemplated is unlikely to be effective for SDLT purposes (ie the intra-group exemption would not be available – see Point 5.8 below). Furthermore, it will give rise to an immediate corporation tax liability on the gain within the transferee company if the company is sold within six years (*TCGA 1992, s 179*). The seller group can absorb any such liability by electing to transfer the deemed gain into one of the retained group companies (*TCGA 1992, s 179A*) If roll-over would normally have been available in the group, this liability ('the degrouping charge') can now be rolled over into the cost of a qualifying asset (such as land) acquired no earlier than a year previously or no later than three years subsequently (*TCGA 1992, s 179B*). See Chapter 34 for roll-over relief.

Where the property-owning company is owned by a UK-based individual or trust keen to get direct access to the sale proceeds, the prospect of selling the company rather than the property may be relatively more attractive. The individuals or trustee shareholder cannot extract the profit of the company tax-free in the way that London Limited could in the above example. Therefore, if the company sells the property, there is the prospect of two levels of tax charge in extracting the proceeds. This would be corporation tax in the company on the gain and either income tax or capital gains tax on extraction of profit.

Point 5.8: *Many transactions within a group – including sales to overseas group companies – are exempt from SDLT.*

An important exemption relates to transfers of properties between group companies (*FA 2003, Sch 7, para 1*). For companies to be treated as within a group, there must be 75% common ownership (*FA 2003, Sch 7, para 1(2), (3)*).

This relief also extends to the grant of leases between group companies.

It does not matter whether or not the companies in question are UK resident. Accordingly, a UK company can transfer property to a Jersey parent and vice versa without an SDLT consequence.

The ownership rules are more stringent than simply having shares which confer 75% ownership but none of the economic benefits that come with that. The 75% ownership test looks at various aspects such as entitlement to dividends, voting control and assets in a winding up. This test can also take into account the rights of a lender to acquire shares (*FA 2003, Sch 7, para 1(4), (5) & (6), TA 1988, Sch 18*).

The relief for intra-group transactions is subject to a number of restrictions and potential withdrawal situations.

The restriction operates where, at the time the transaction takes place, there are arrangements under which:

(a)   another purchaser can take control of the buying company at some stage; or

(b)   the purchasing company can cease to be a member of the same group as the seller, or

(c)   the consideration for the sale is to be provided directly or indirectly by a third party. It is understood that HMRC do not regard normal commercial bank finance as affecting this

(*FA 2003, Sch 7, para 2*).

In addition, relief is not available if the transaction is not effected for bona fide commercial reasons or forms part of arrangements of which the main purpose or one of the main purposes is the avoidance of a liability to tax (not just SDLT).

Relief previously given will be withdrawn if the purchasing company ceases to be a member of the same group as the buying company within three years whilst still owning the property. It will similarly be withdrawn if there are arrangements within the three years for this to happen (*FA 2003, Sch 7, para 3*). There are exceptions to this rule such as where the company leaves the group because another company is wound up. It is also possible to avoid this withdrawal in some circumstances where the seller and buyer both leave the group (*FA 2003, Sch 7, para 4*).

Point 5.9:   *There are other reliefs for reconstructions and acquisitions.*

Apart from group relief, the SDLT rules also allow certain commercial transactions which do not result in a change in the property ownership to be carried out SDLT-free.

Exemption from SDLT is available for a reconstruction (*FA 2005, Sch 7, para 7*). Typically, this occurs when a company is put into liquidation and the company's undertaking, including the property it owns, is transferred to a new company. The shareholding of the acquiring company must be almost the same as that of the former company.

Acquisition relief, is potentially of wider application. This reduces the rate of duty to 0.5%. This is available where a company acquires the property and related undertaking of the target company in consideration of the issue of non-redeemable shares or the assumption/discharge of indebtedness. Up to 10% of the share nominal value can be in cash (*FA 2003, Sch 7, para 8*).

There are similar restrictions and withdrawal circumstances as for group relief (see Point 5.8 above).

CHAPTER 6 – CAPITAL ALLOWANCES ON PLANT AND MACHINERY

Capital allowances are available on machinery and plant fixed to and let with a building. For new builds, reconstruction and purchase of second-hand property, it pays to identify eligible items.

Points 6.1 & 6.2

There are restricted allowances on certain long-life assets.
Point 6.16

Maximising claims involves proper descriptions and cost allocations particularly of electrical and plumbing work and also in relation to floors, walls, ceilings and professional fees.
Points 6.3, 6.4 & 6.8

Allowances available with furnished holiday lets and restricted allowances on furnished lettings.
Point 6.9

There are lower 10% allowances on certain assets which are integral fixtures in a building from April 2008.
Point 6.5

100% allowances on plant are available in several situations.
Point 6.7

Long-life assets will attract a rate of 10% allowances from April 2008 (formerly 6%).
Point 6.6

Lessees can claim allowances on their expenditure and in respect of capital sums paid on grant/assignment.
Point 6.10

A buyer of second-hand property can claim allowances. There is a need to ascertain what previous claims have been made, if any, and also the opportunity to agree a claim with the seller.
Points 6.11, 6.12, 6.13 & 6.14

No allowances on equipment leased to tax exempt lessees.
Point 6.18

Allowances are claimable in the period when expenditure is incurred.
Point 6.15

A landlord can claim allowances on contributions made to a tenant's fixtures.
Point 6.17

Surplus allowances can often be offset against other income or gains.
Point 6.16

Plant used in estate and company management attracts allowances.
Point 6.19

It is better to claim repairs where possible.
Point 6.20

Allowances on irrecoverable VAT.
Point 6.21

6   Capital allowances on plant and machinery

[*Note* – At the time of writing, there are proposed reforms to the regime for capital allowances on plant and machinery which are outlined in a Government Consultative Document issued in July 2007. The proposals in that document are summarised in this chapter. Final details of the changes will not be available until some time after the consultation period ends in October 2007.]

Point 6.1:   *A property investor can claim capital allowances on expenditure in respect of plant and machinery that is fixed to, and let with, a building.*

The letting of any property on a commercial basis is treated as a qualifying activity for capital allowance purposes (*CAA 2001, s 15(1)(b)*). So where plant and machinery are included in a let building, the property investor can claim allowances on capital expenditure in respect of qualifying items. These allowances are deductible from the letting income.

Up to 1 April 2008 (for companies within the charge to corporation tax) and fiscal year 2007/08 (for other taxpayers who are subject to income tax), annual allowances at a rate of 25% apply to the tax written-down value of the plant in each year unless the items of plant and machinery are long-life assets (see Point 6.6 below).

After these dates, there have been changes to the capital allowance regime and the rates of allowances as announced in the 2007 Budget. As a result of these changes, the main rate of writing-down allowances reduces from 25% to 20%.

In the year of transition straddling April 2008, a hybrid rate applies to the pool of expenditure. Using the example of a company with a 31 December year end, this will mean that one quarter of its year falls in the period when the 25% writing down allowance applies. The remaining three quarters will fall in the period when the 20% rate applies. The result is a hybrid rate of 21.25% (ie 3/12ths of 25% plus 9/12ths of 20%) which is applied to the pool of expenditure at the end of the year. In practice, the hybrid rate is calculated by the number of days in each period.

See Point 6.15 for a summary of the rules for identifying when expenditure is actually incurred for these purposes.

There is also a new separate category of certain 'integral fixtures' within a building. It is proposed that these will attract a reduced annual writing down allowance of 10%. The Government's proposals regarding integral fixtures were set out in a consultative document issued jointly by HMRC and the Treasury on 26 July 2007 (see Point 6.5 below).

No capital allowances can be claimed on plant or machinery installed in a 'dwelling house' (*CAA 2001, s 35(2)*). This restriction is confined to the residential unit. In the case of an apartment block, this should not preclude claims in respect of the common areas, eg lifts and boiler equipment. Items installed in the individual flats would not qualify.

100% allowances are available in several situations (see Point 6.7 below).

Point 6.2:   *Whether the expenditure is on the construction of a new building, reconstruction work at an existing building or the purchase of a second-hand building, it pays to identify the items on which capital allowances could be due.*

Capital allowances are claimable on plant and machinery installed in a new building, purchased as part of the building or installed subsequently.

Where plant has become a fixture in a building and the price paid for the building includes an element in respect of the fixture, capital allowances are potentially claimable on the amount attributable to the plant (*CAA 2001, s 181(1)*). This would be the case where:

(a)   a freehold is purchased; or
(b)   consideration is paid for the assignment of a lease; or
(c)   a premium is paid on the grant of a lease.

Although there is normally little problem in identifying items of machinery, 'plant' has proved more difficult – and further complications arise following the implementation of the 2007 Budget reforms in relation to integrated fixtures (see Point 6.5 below).

Up to 30 November 1993, the determination of which items qualified as plant was solely a matter of interpreting the decisions in a succession of tax cases. Two general principles have emerged from the cases over the years. These are:

(a)   the item should perform a function in the business; and
(b)   it should not be part of the setting in which the business is carried on.

With effect from 30 November 1993, legislation was introduced that specifies certain items in a building on which the related expenditure qualifies for capital allowances. It also sets out expenditure that will not qualify (*CAA 2001, ss 21–24*). These items are summarised in Appendix I. Note that expenditure on some of the items of plant listed there will, from April 2008, be regarded as integral fixtures and be part of a separate pool attracting just 10% writing-down allowances (Point 6.5). Furthermore, some expenditure in certain buildings will be on 'long-life assets' which also attracts a 10% writing-down allowance (Point 6.6).

The above legislation needs to be read in conjunction with case law where the distinction between plant and non-plant has been explored in a number of cases, as noted below.

Whilst the present legislation has resolved some of the issues, areas of expenditure will continue to arise which do not fit neatly within any of the specified categories. There remain areas where it is not easy to apply the legislation in practice and where further analysis is useful to ensure that allowance claims are maximised. Some of the more typical problem areas are examined in Points 6.3 and 6.4 below.

Point 6.3: *The Inspector of Taxes often challenges allowances claimed on electrical and plumbing work. It is useful to be familiar with the extent to which such expenditure is eligible for allowances.*

Electrical installations and cold water systems which become part of a building can qualify as plant (CAA 2001, s 23 List C Item 2). They must be either provided mainly to meet the particular requirements of the qualifying activity or serve specific plant used for the purposes of the qualifying activity, for example a cold water system for industrial machines. Otherwise, they will be regarded as part of the business's setting and hence not qualify as plant – although from April 2008 the expenditure may qualify under the new integral fixtures rules (Point 6.5 below).

Where processes are carried on which will require an electrical and/or cold water system, the concept will be easy to apply. It will be less obvious where there are office, retail or leisure situations.

Two cases are helpful in throwing light on this area.

In *IRC v Scottish and Newcastle Breweries Ltd* [1982] STC 296, light fittings installed in a hotel were held to be plant. In that case, new lighting was installed to create ambience appropriate to the newly designed lounge, restaurant and discotheque areas. The House of Lords accepted that part of the hotel's trade was to provide the right atmosphere for people using its facilities. The lighting was considered to be part of the apparatus of the trade.

In *Cole Bros Ltd v Phillips* [1982] STC 307, a similar argument in respect of electrical works in a John Lewis Department store failed. This was after the Special Commissioners had decided that the installation of electrical wiring and lighting was an integral part of the construction of the building and part of the setting in which the trade was carried on.

In the *Cole Bros* case, the House of Lords did not wish to overturn the Special Commissioner's decision of fact but did have sympathy with the argument that the whole electrical system was one item of plant specially designed for the purposes for which the store was used. HMRC did subsequently accept that entire electrical systems like that in the John Lewis case might well qualify as plant following an unreported Special Commissioner's decision that went against them. Where relevant, claims should certainly be made on that basis.

General wiring for ordinary lighting and power purposes would be disallowed. Electrical work for specific items of plant, including computers and communication equipment, would be allowable.

On a similar principle, ordinary cold water plumbing together with related drainage is normally disallowable. On the other hand expenditure on hot water and heating systems is eligible for allowances.

As mentioned above, there are indications that the proposed new capital allowance category of integral fixtures may include items such as general wiring or cold water systems (see Point 6.5).

Point 6.4:   *HMRC will disallow all expenditure on certain items such as floors, walls and ceilings. Check whether the descriptions of these items are appropriate and also the way expenditure has been allocated to them.*

Expenditure on walls, floors or ceilings would normally be regarded as part of the setting in which the business is carried on. Even if the wall, floor or ceiling in question is part of the 'apparatus' of the trade including creating the right ambience, it is still not plant for capital allowances purposes.

This was established in the cases involving Wimpy and Pizzaland Restaurants. However, decorative items such as fixed murals which provided ambience were accepted as plant (*Wimpy International Ltd v Warland; Associated Restaurants Ltd v Warland* [1989] STC 273).

Similarly, suspended ceilings and raised flooring can perform a function in a business. Often they provide a cover or housing for ventilation ducting, piping and IT cabling. Nevertheless, HMRC will not give capital allowances on these items because the tax legislation excludes them (*CAA 2001, s 21 List A Item 1* – see Appendix I). This is supported by case law (*Hampton v Fortes Autogrill Ltd* [1980] STC 80).

In view of this, consider the extent to which expenditure is properly attributable to these items.

In the first place, the description may not be altogether appropriate. For instance, expenditure on a 'mezzanine floor' has been allowed when, as a matter of fact, it was demonstrated to be a suspended demountable storage area (*Hunt v Henry Quick Ltd; King v Bridisco Ltd* [1992] STC 633).

Another example is walls that are formed by demountable partitioning. If that partitioning is actually to be moved as the requirements of the business changes, it is plant and the related expenditure will be allowable (*Jarrold v John Good & Sons Ltd* (1962) 40 TC 681). Any doors or windows that are integral with that partitioning should be similarly allowable.

In addition to description, the allocation of expenditure may merit further analysis.

It is advisable to ask the builder or project manager whether any proportion of the cost attributed to suspended ceilings or raised floors relates to the heating, air-conditioning, electrical or other plant installation since that element would be allowable. An element of any three-dimensional structure such as raised floors and suspended ceilings designed to allow the passage of ducting or cabling, should be part of that installation. This argument becomes even stronger if the existing flooring or ceiling has had to be modified to facilitate a new installation.

It remains to be seen whether any items disallowed under these heads might alternatively attract allowances under the new rules relating to integral fixtures.

Point 6.5:   *Expenditure from April 2008 on 'integral fixtures' must be separated from other plant and machinery as this attracts a lower, 10%, rate of annual allowance. This may include some items for which allowances were not previously available.*

The Government announced in the 2007 Budget that there would be a new category for certain fixtures which are considered integral to the structure of a building and which it regards should be eligible for a lower, 10%, rate of annual writing down allowance. The announcement was followed by a consultative document which went a little further in outlining the Government's thinking on this. At the time of writing, the consultation period had not expired and the Government was still contemplating the simplest way to define the assets within this category.

Unless the Government finally opt for a general definition of 'integral fixtures', there is likely to be a short but specific list of items that would only be eligible for this lower allowance. In that case, the probability is that this would include items such as lifts, escalators, air conditioning, heating and ventilation equipment. This would cover the more significant areas of plant expenditure within a construction or refurbishment project.

Whilst this new lower rate category, combined with the reduction of rates on other plant from 25% to 20%, will reduce overall capital allowance relief, there may be some new benefits. In that connection, some expenditure which previously was not eligible for writing-down allowances as plant or machinery, might now attract the 10% allowance under this category. The items the consultative document tentatively refers in that regard include:

- general electrical and power systems;
- cold as well as hot water systems;
- certain fixed, non-moveable parts of building structures which are energy efficient (the consultative document gives the examples of brise soleil and active facades).

On the transition to the new regime, the consultative document proposed that the new 10% rate applied to expenditure – including expenditure on fixtures acquired in a second-hand building – from April 2008 (1 April for companies in charge to corporation tax, 6 April for individuals and other entities subject to income tax). Qualifying expenditure and ongoing capital allowance pools before that date are unaffected by the introduction of this new category.

The full 10% allowance will be due in the first transitional period. Therefore, a company with a 31 December year end that incurs the expenditure on the integral fixtures in June 2008 receives a full 10% allowance in the year to 31 December 2008.

Since expenditure relating to integral fixtures incurred prior to the regime continues to attract 20% allowances, this suggests that buying a property company with its ongoing pool of integral fixtures may be more beneficial than buying the property. In the first scenario, the company can carry on claiming writing-down allowances at a rate of 20% a year. If the property were acquired, only 10% allowances might be available on that expenditure.

See point 6.15 for a summary of the rules for identifying when expenditure is actually incurred for these purposes.

Point 6.6:   *In some property situations, it is also necessary separately to identify long-life machinery and plant which from April 2008 also attract a 10% annual writing down allowance.*

Writing-down allowances for certain 'long-life' plant and machinery are available at a reduced rate which is 10% from April 2008 and 6% per year before then (*CAA 2001, ss 90–104*).

The reduced allowance relates to items where there is a reasonable expectation of a useful economic life of at least 25 years when they are first brought into use. These provisions do not apply where the plant and machinery in question is a fixture in a building used as a retail shop, showroom, hotel or office or for a purpose which is ancillary to any of these (*CAA 2001, s 93*).

Typical items of plant installed as fixtures of buildings would not have an expected useful life over 25 years and many of the more common commercial buildings have been excluded in any event. Where buildings are used for purposes that are not excluded – the leisure and nursing home sectors being notable examples – the category of 'long-life' assets could be relevant. However, as mentioned in point 6.5 above, a similar 10% rate is being introduced for certain other fixtures in a building from April 2008.

Point 6.7:   *100% capital allowances are available for energy-saving/environmentally beneficial plant, for renovating disused property for business use and also, from April 2008, for the first £50,000 expenditure under the new Annual Investment Allowance scheme.*

100% allowances – which provide the opportunity for a complete write-off of costs in the year in which they are incurred – can be claimed in the following situations:

(a) Expenditure is incurred on new qualifying energy-saving or environmentally beneficial plant and machinery. The Government publishes details of the products that will qualify for these enhanced capital allowances (or ECAs) in an Energy Technology Product List (ETPL). The ETPL can be accessed on the internet at website www.eca.gov.uk (*CAA 2001, ss 45a–45c; 45h–45j*). Note that under the 2007 budget proposals, companies that cannot fully benefit from these allowances (eg due to losses) should be able to opt instead for a tax refund. Details of this proposal have not been finalised at the time of writing. This opportunity is only to be made available to companies.

(b) A 100% allowance has been available since 11 April 2007 for the cost of converting or renovating property situated in an 'assisted area' to bring it back into business use. Although the relief was introduced in the *Finance Act 2005*, its introduction was delayed pending EU consent and the consequent need to reduce the areas in which the property could be situated. The relevant rules are now contained in he Business Premises Renovation Allowances Regulations SI 2007/945 and the assisted areas are those specified in the Assisted Areas Order 2007 plus Northern Ireland.

To qualify, the property must been vacant for a period of at least 12 months, after having last been used for the purposes of a trade, profession or vocation, or as offices, but not as a dwelling.

A number of business uses are excluded from the relief including fisheries; shipbuilding; coal and steel; synthetic fibres; the production of certain agricultural products; and the manufacture of substitute or imitation milk or milk products.

(c) The first £50,000 of expenditure of plant and machinery incurred by a business from April 2008 under the annual investment allowance scheme.

This proposed relief will include qualifying expenditure on integral fixtures (Point 6.5) and long-life assets (Point 6.6). As envisaged at the time of writing it is aimed at all sizes of businesses and replaces the previous system of special first year allowances to small and medium-sized enterprises from April 2008 (Point 29.1).

The intention is that only one £50,000 allowance is available for a group of companies each year. The provisions will also seek to prevent associations of companies from gaining a multiple entitlement to the allowance by fragmenting their expenditure between a number of companies.

100% allowances are also technically available where plant and machinery is installed in a qualifying enterprise zone building although, following the expiry of the zones, the situations where this can now be relevant will be rare (see Chapter 33 for enterprise zones).

There is also a 100% allowance on the renovation or conversion of vacant or underused space above certain premises to residential use. This is primarily aimed at unused space above shops and similar commercial property which was formerly used as a dwelling.

Proposals were also announced in the 2007 Budget to extend relief to the clearance of derelict or long-term unused land. This remains subject to a consultation process.

Point 6.8:   *Do not ignore professional fees. HMRC accept that some of these are attributable to plant and machinery installation.*

A significant element of expenditure on any building project will be professional costs. These will include fees charged by lawyers, surveyors, architects, structural and mechanical/electrical engineers.

Professional costs relating to the acquisition of the site – particularly lawyers' and surveyors' costs – would normally be disallowed. If any of this expenditure is in respect of related finance, it might be appropriate to have this charged separately since this could well qualify as an incidental cost of raising finance for income tax purposes or under the corporate debt rules for companies within charge to corporation tax.

The fees of mechanical and electrical engineers are often linked to the installation of plant and these fees are part of that qualifying expenditure.

Expenses like design fees and project management costs are more problematic. An initial approach might be to allocate this pro rata between plant and non-plant although further negotiation with the tax inspector is likely.

Point 6.9:   *Although no allowances are available on residential property, capital allowance claims can be made for furnished holiday lettings and, on a more restricted basis, for ordinary furnished lettings.*

As a general rule, no capital allowances are available on machinery or plant installed for use in a dwelling house (*CAA 2001, s 35*).

Landlords of furnished accommodation generally may be entitled to some deduction for their expenditure on plant and machinery.

There is an HMRC Extra Statutory Concession under which landlords are entitled to opt for tax relief in one of the following ways:

- on a renewals basis, ie there would be no relief for the initial cost of plant and machinery but the future replacement cost of the items could be deducted in full;
- an annual deduction equivalent to 10% of the net rents in a year.

(ESC B47).

The letting of furnished holiday accommodation is treated as a separate qualifying activity for capital allowances purposes (*CAA 2001, s 15(1)(c)*). Allowances are, therefore, available under the normal rules

(*CAA 2001, s 55*) treating it as a separate qualifying activity from any other letting business carried on.

Point 6.10:   *Lessees can claim allowances in respect of fixed plant in a building even though as a matter of law these items belong to the freeholder.*

Lessees are entitled to allowances on fixed plant in the following circumstances:

(a)   Where a lessee incurs expenditure on fixed plant for use in a qualifying activity, capital allowances can be claimed on that expenditure (*CAA 2001, s 176*).

(b)   Where a lessee takes an assignment of a lease and pays a capital sum that wholly or partly represents expenditure on fixed plant, the lessee can claim allowances on that element of the payment in respect of the plant (*CAA 2001, s 181*). A claim cannot be made if anyone else has an interest in the property and has claimed allowances as a result. Thus if a remaining sub-tenant has claimed allowances the new landlord cannot claim for any capital sum paid in respect of the tenant's fixtures. Similarly, the lessee cannot become entitled to allowances on assets on which the freeholder is entitled to claim (*CAA 2001, s 181(2), (3)*).

The amount on which a lessee can claim allowances is restricted to the original cost of the plant, where that original cost was claimed as a capital allowance by a previous owner of the fixture (*CAA 2001, ss 185–187* – see Point 6.12 below).

(c)   A lessee can claim allowances where a capital sum is paid on the grant of a lease and the sum wholly or partly includes expenditure in respect of fixed plant. However, if the lessor would otherwise have been entitled to the allowances, both the lessee and the lessor must make an election within two years of the commencement of the lease if the lessee is to claim the allowances (*CAA 2001, s 183*). If no election is made, the lessor might be entitled to the allowances.

No election is necessary if the lessor would not have been entitled to allowances (*CAA 2001, s 184*). An election cannot be made where the lessor and the lessee are connected.

Point 6.11:   *A buyer of second-hand property with fixtures that qualify as plant and machinery can potentially claim significant allowances. Steps should be taken to establish eligibility and the likely quantum of allowances.*

Tax relief arising from capital allowances on the purchase of a property enables the buyer to recoup a part of the cash outflow.

In some cases, 40%–50% of the purchase price of modern buildings has been attributable to fixtures and equipment eligible for allowances. From April 2008, some of these items will be 'integral fixtures' (see Point 6.5).

The actual entitlement to allowances will be influenced by the following factors:

(a)   Whether the plant allowances attach to the interest being purchased – the freeholder is normally the person owning the plant and entitled to allowances. However, in the past an election may have been made in favour of a lessee (see (c) in Point 6.10 above). Alternatively, the allowances may arise from expenditure by the lessee, for example, the retail tenant that fits out empty premises. Clearly, whether the freehold or a leasehold interest is bought, it is important to establish the capital allowances background to that interest.

(b)   Whether the property is commercial or residential (see Point 6.1 above).

(c)   For properties bought after 23 July 1996, what was the claims history of the previous owner or owners and is the seller looking to do some deal on the allowances (see Point 6.12 below)?

(d)   For properties not affected by (c), what 'reasonable value' can be attributed to the plant (see Point 6.14 below)?

(e)   Whether the plant or machinery is an integral fixture or long-life asset (Points 6.5 and 6.6) and therefore subject to a reduced 10% annual allowance (formerly 6% in the case of long-life assets)

(f)   Whether there could be any eligibility for 100% allowances (Point 6.7 above).

Point 6.12:   *A buyer of property must ascertain what eligible expenditure the seller or any previous seller owning the property claimed after 23 July 1996.*

A property investor or owner-occupier buying a property should find out whether the seller made any claims to capital allowances in respect of plant in the building. If the seller did make such a claim, the allowable expenditure claimable by the purchaser in respect of that plant cannot exceed that amount (*CAA 2001, ss 185–187*).

EXAMPLE 1

Robson Ltd purchased an investment property in 1990 for £8,000,000. £2,000,000 was accepted as being in respect of plant and machinery. Venables Ltd bought that building for £12,000,000 in August 2007.

The amount eligible for allowances to Venables Ltd will be restricted to a maximum of £2,000,000.

It is not relevant whether there have been owners of the property who claimed allowances before Robson Ltd. We are only concerned with owners of the property after 23 July 1996.

EXAMPLE 2

If Keegan Ltd buys the property as an investment from Venables Ltd, Keegan Ltd will be restricted to the same maximum figure of £2,000,000.

As and when the investor incurs capital expenditure on new plant and machinery in the building, the maximum qualifying figure would increase accordingly, although there will also be an adjustment for any plant which is removed or disposed of.

Point 6.13: *The buyer and seller can elect to adopt a specific value for the plant and machinery for capital allowances purposes on the transfer of a property. Such an election can accelerate the use of allowances.*

HMRC will accept a value adopted by both the buyer and seller if it is the subject of a joint election submitted to the Inspector of Taxes within two years of the date of the transaction (*CAA 2001, s 198*). In so doing, both the buyer and the seller have a measure of certainty as to tax implications of the sale and purchase as far as the capital allowances position is concerned. This election is only available for fixtures in a building and not other plant.

The value in the election cannot exceed the seller's eligible expenditure. Thus, in example 2 above, Keegan Ltd and Venables Ltd will be bound by the maximum of £2,000,000. They can go lower than this figure. However, if the value is below the seller's tax written-down value, the seller could face a restriction of the balancing allowance otherwise due – but only if HMRC felt this was an arrangement to generate a balancing allowance (*CAA 2001, s 197*).

A value specified in the election becomes the new maximum for that plant for future buyers of the property.

The election must detail the items that are the subject of the election and attribute values to them. There could be a problem for the buyer if the seller has overclaimed allowances. If HMRC have reason to reduce a seller's original capital allowances claim, they will also seek to reduce proportionately any amount that the buyer may have agreed to.

If the seller has not fully exploited the entitlement to claim allowances by omitting or overlooking a claim on some items of plant in the building, the buyer can initiate claims on those items.

Where a buyer and seller elect for a transfer value lower than the tax written down value of the plant and machinery, this can generate a balancing allowance. This balancing allowance can be offset against other profits or group relieved as with any surplus allowances.

In view of this, there is the potential to reduce that transfer value to a nominal figure and thus get the benefit of the extra allowances arising. This is effectively accelerating the balance of allowances due on the original cost of the assets.

This planning is available whether the sale is to an unconnected party or to a fellow group company. In all cases, however, the sale must be for commercial reasons and not merely part of an arrangement to secure this tax benefit (*CAA 2001, s 197*).

Point 6.14:   *Where Points 6.12 and 6.13 do not apply there is no statutory restriction on the amount eligible for allowances by reference to the vendor's cost. The amount eligible is then determined by estimating a just apportionment of the purchase price.*

There is no statutory restriction on the available allowances if everyone who has owned that property at or since 24 July 1996 has done so without making any claim to allowance in respect of the plant.

This could apply where a builder or property dealer has owned the property throughout the period. Alternatively, an owner for one reason or another may not have claimed allowances.

EXAMPLE 3

In example 1 above, if Robson Ltd had not claimed allowances, Venables Ltd would not be restricted on the allowances it could claim. Similarly, in example 2, if neither Robson Ltd nor Venables Ltd had claimed allowances, Keegan Ltd would not have that statutory restriction.

The significance of there being no restriction is that it would then be open to the purchaser to value the plant and machinery bought within a building. This is an exercise that generally requires quantity surveying techniques to arrive at a hypothetical cost of that plant installed in the building on the assumption that the building was being reconstructed at the time of purchase. The cost of the installed plant could then be expressed as a percentage of the total reconstruction cost and that percentage applied to the purchase price (less land value) to give a total plant value.

EXAMPLE 4

In September 2007, Land Investments Ltd bought the freehold of an office building for £10,000,000. No allowances have been claimed in the past in respect of the plant therein.

A surveyor estimates that the building would now cost £6,000,000 to construct. The cost of the plant installation, which the surveyor has identified in the building, would be £2,400,000. Accordingly, 40% of the building cost would represent plant.

The land element of the purchase price is estimated at £3,000,000 to give a net building price of £7,000,000 (ie £10,000,000 less £3,000,000). The aggregate capital allowance claim would, therefore, be £2,800,000 (ie 40% × £7,000,000).

In practice, the plant would be itemised and the £2,800,000 apportioned accordingly.

For large claims, HMRC have been increasingly involving their own District Valuer and Regional Building Surveyors to agree the estimates used.

Point 6.15: *The allowances are claimable in the chargeable period when expenditure is incurred.*

Capital allowances are claimable in the accounting period or the period of account when expenditure is incurred. This is the date the amount becomes unconditionally payable (*CAA 2001, s 5(1)*).

Once a trade is commenced, future expenditure is treated as incurred when there is an unconditional obligation to pay. This might be when an invoice is issued or a binding agreement signed.

On long-term construction contracts, stage payments are normally made periodically on production of an architect's certificate. When the obligation to pay becomes unconditional on the production of a certificate, expenditure is treated as incurred in a particular accounting period if the certificate is issued not more than one month after the end of the period.

Where payment is due more than four months after the obligation to pay becomes unconditional, the expenditure is treated as incurred on the date(s) it is due to be paid (*CAA 2001, s 5(5)*). The issue of an invoice or signing of a contract designed to bring forward the capital allowances claim to an earlier accounting period than would have been the case in a normal commercial transaction is countered by an anti-avoidance provision (*CAA 2001, s 5(6)*).

Point 6.16: *Investors can use surplus allowances in a number of ways but the rules differ depending on whether or not the claimant is a company.*

An investment company can offset capital allowances as a normal business deduction against its total profits – including capital gains (*CAA 2001, s 253; TA 1988, s 392A*). Unrelieved surplus allowances can then be used as follows:

(a)   by surrender as group relief against total profits of a fellow member of the same tax group (*TA 1988, s 403(3)*);
(b)   by carry-forward to be set off against profits from the letting business (*TA 1988, s 392A(2)*).

Individuals, partnerships and non-resident investment companies can include capital allowances in arriving at the profits or losses from their property rental business. Losses are carried forward against future rental profits.

Where a loss arises following a claim to capital allowances, it is possible to offset that loss against general income in the same year of assessment or the following year. The amount of loss relief will be restricted to the lowest of the following:

(a)   the loss;
(b)   the other income for the year;

(c)   the net amount of capital allowances (ie after deducting any claw-backs of allowances treated as receipts of the rental business)

(*ITA 2007, ss 120 & 121*).

The ability of a limited partner to claim allowances on expenditure incurred is restricted according to the limit of that individual's contribution (*ITA 2007, s 104*).

Point 6.17:   *A landlord can claim allowances on contributions made to a tenant's expenditure. This might be a tax-efficient way for the landlord to offer an inducement to attract an incoming tenant.*

Capital allowances can be claimed in certain circumstances in respect of amounts contributed towards a tenant's expenditure (*CAA 2001, s 537*).

For instance, a landlord might attract a prospective commercial tenant by offering to pay for certain fixtures. The landlord should be entitled to claim allowances on the contribution to the extent it related to items of plant.

The conditions for eligibility are:

(a)   The parties cannot be connected (within the meaning of *TA 1988, s 839*).
(b)   The contribution must be either for the contributor's trade or other qualifying activity (eg commercial letting) or (in the case of industrial buildings allowances or agricultural buildings allowances) for the purposes of the trade or other qualifying activity of a tenant of land in which the contributor has an interest.
(c)   The tenant would normally have been treated as having incurred the expenditure eligible for allowances

(*CAA 2001, ss 537–540*).

If the contributor transfers the trade or land, the transferee will inherit the contributor's entitlement to annual allowances. There are no balancing adjustments (*CAA 2001, ss 538(5), 539(5), 540(5)*).

6.18:   *No allowances will be available to lessors on fixtures which they purchase and let to a tax-exempt lessee.*

Under anti-avoidance rules, lessors cannot claim allowances on equipment which is leased to a tax-exempt lessee such as a local authority or charity (*CAA 2001, s 178*).

Although these rules are not aimed at conventional property lettings, they do apply when a third party leases equipment to a tax-exempt occupier of a building where that equipment becomes a fixture in the building. The lessor cannot claim capital allowances on the capital expenditure it has incurred on that equipment. These provisions apply to leasing arrangements entered into after 24 July 1996.

Point 6.19: *Apart from plant let with a building, a property investor can claim allowances on plant and machinery used in estate management. An investment company can, in addition, claim allowances for plant used in the management of the company.*

Estate management may require the use of plant and machinery. This may, for instance, be installed as fixed plant in premises used as administrative offices. Other items might include an information technology installation, filing cabinets and office furniture. Capital allowances can be claimed on these items and set off against the profits of the letting business.

An investment company can also claim allowances on plant used in the management of the company as distinct from the properties (*CAA 2001, s 253*). Such allowances can be treated as additional expenses of the business.

Point 6.20: *It is worthwhile scrutinising expenditure to see whether it may strictly qualify as repairs and maintenance since this can be fully deductible in the year it is incurred.*

When an item of plant is installed or completely replaced, the related expenditure will be treated as capital and eligible for capital allowances. However, if the expenditure is in respect of the overhaul of plant or the replacement of parts, then this should qualify for a 100% deduction as repairs or maintenance.

A related point is that when reviewing a refurbishment programme, it may well be sensible to consider repairing assets where this is a possibility rather than replacing them. (See Point 4.1 above for repairs v capital expenditure.)

It may be advisable to consider the exact nature of work carried out or to be carried out to determine whether expenditure that might appear to be capital is, in fact, revenue. For instance, if air-conditioning work involves the removal of defective ducting rather than the replacement or renewal of a whole system, that might be shown as repairs. Similarly, if heating expenditure related to the replacement of worn radiators, then it would be repairs as opposed to capital expenditure. However, if the work changes the nature of the original asset then that would not be a repair – such as in the recent case of plastic inner piping inserted within an old cast-iron main (*Auckland Gas Co Ltd v IRC* [2000] STC 527).

Note that to obtain a deduction in a year, the relevant expenditure will need to be reflected in the profit and loss account rather than capitalised in the balance sheet. If the expenditure is capitalised, the tax treatment will follow the accounting treatment with a deduction delayed unless and until amounts are written off as expenses through the profit and loss account.

Point 6.21:   *If irrecoverable VAT is incurred on a building purchase – or building/installation work – the expenditure eligible for capital allowances in relation to plant and machinery is increased accordingly.*

If a property owner cannot fully reclaim VAT on property expenditure, the irrecoverable VAT increases the related cost for direct tax purposes.

Where VAT incurred on plant expenditure is wholly or partly irrecoverable, the amount eligible for capital allowances will include the irrecoverable amount. Furthermore, if adjustments are required under the Capital Goods Scheme, resulting in changes to VAT recovery over a 10-year period, the qualifying capital allowance expenditure will vary accordingly (*CAA 2001, s 235*). See Point 39.7 in Chapter 39 for an explanation of the Capital Goods Scheme.

CHAPTER 7 – CAPITAL ALLOWANCES ON SPECIALISED BUILDINGS

Allowances on capital expenditure on buildings qualifying as industrial buildings, qualifying hotels, and agricultural buildings are being phased out by April 2011. There are still opportunities to claim allowances on these types of buildings and possibly properties situated in an Enterprise Zone. There are also allowances on certain residential conversions and the cost of renovating properties.

Point 7.1

7 Capital allowances on specialised buildings

Point 7.1: *Capital allowances on specialised buildings are being phased out in the period to April 2011. In the meantime, a property investor may still be able to claim allowances on capital expenditure on certain categories of building. These are industrial buildings, qualifying hotels, agricultural buildings and buildings situated in enterprise zones. There is also a 100% allowance available where certain unused commercial space is converted to residential use.*

In Chapters 30 to 33 in Part C of this book, there are points on the capital allowances that are still available over the next few years where expenditure is incurred on certain types of trading premises. These allowances are also available to an investor owning an interest in the property where a tenant occupies and uses the building in the qualifying manner.

The allowances can be claimed in respect of capital expenditure on the construction, reconstruction or refurbishment of a building or the purchase of a new or second-hand building which is used for a trading purpose under one of the following headings:

(a)   Industrial building – see Chapter 30.
(b)   Hotel – see Chapter 31.
(c)   Agricultural building – see Chapter 32.
(d)   Property in enterprise zones and renovations in assisted areas – see Chapter 33.

In the case of categories (a), (b) and (c), the allowances are reducing from 4% in 2007/08 to 3% in 2008/09, 2% in 2009/10 and finally 1% in the last year 2010/11. These are the amounts available on the construction or purchase of new unused buildings. The position, together with the allowances that can be claimed on the 'residue' of the vendor's expenditure when a second-hand building is purchased, is explained in the relevant chapter in Part C.

Note that the above is based on proposed rules announced at the time of the 2007 Budget and may be subject to revision.

Expenditure on a building in an Enterprise Zone attracts a 100% capital allowance. However, the last Enterprise Zones were created in 1996, so the only ongoing claims will be on a very few situations where expenditure is still being incurred under an old building contract (see Chapter 33).

A relief for renovated property in assisted areas, however, has been introduced with effect from 11 April 2007 to confer 100% allowances on bringing business property into use in these areas (see Chapter 33).

There is also a 100% allowance on the renovation or conversion of vacant or underused space above certain premises to residential use. This is primarily aimed at unused space above shops and similar commercial property previously used as residential property.

CHAPTER 8 – HOLDING INVESTMENT PROPERTY THROUGH A COMPANY

Putting an investment property in a company can save tax on income and gains as long as the funds can be retained in the company.

Point 8.1

Shareholders borrowing personally to on-lend to the company can exploit a cash flow advantage.
Point 8.2

Although there is tax on extracting funds from a company, there should be an overall benefit for non-domiciliaries, non-residents and shareholders paying less than 40% tax at exit.
Point 8.3

Companies, unlike individuals, are entitled to indexation relief that can reduce or eliminate taxable gains. However, the 2007 Pre Budget proposals can result in a capital gains disadvantage in holding properties through a company unless there is eventually an exit through a sale to a UK REIT.
Point 8.4

Where a property has attracted business asset taper relief, there has been a disadvantage to owning this through a company.
Point 8.5

8 Holding investment property through a company

Point 8.1: *Individuals paying higher rate tax can shelter investment income in a company where the rate of corporation tax on income and capital gains will be lower.*

There are currently two tax rate bands for corporation tax.

The 'small companies' rate of corporation tax applies to profits of £300,000 or less. For several years up to Financial Year 2006 (ie year to 31 March 2007), the rate was 19%. This has increased following the 2007 Budget with the result that in financial year 2007 the rate is 20% and in each year, 2008 and 2009, the rate rises by 1%. Accordingly, in financial year 2009 (ie the year to 31 March 2010) and subsequently, the small companies rate will be 22%.

For profits of £1,500,000 and above, the full rate of corporation tax applies. This reduced from 30% in financial year 2007 to 28% for 2008 and subsequent years. Between £300,000 and £1,500,000 there is a tapering relief, which results in a gradual increase in the effective rate of tax from the small companies rate to the full corporation tax rate.

Where there are associated companies, these monetary limits are divided by the number of associated companies (including the company in question). For example, if company A has one associated company, the limits applying to company A are £150,000 (for the upper limit of the small companies' rate) and £750,000 (the threshold for the full rate).

'Associated' for this purpose includes any companies under common control, whether or not they are resident in the UK, but dormant companies may be disregarded.

Since an individual's highest rate of tax is currently 40%, there is a potential tax saving by holding an investment property through a company. If the rental, less expenses, amounted to, say, £200,000 there will be a £36,000 saving by channelling this income into a company post-April 2009 (ie 40%–22% of £200,000). The following example illustrates the effect over a five-year period:

EXAMPLE

The following example compares the retained income of an individual paying 40% tax with a company paying 22%. The rental income after expenses is £200,000 per year. Interest at a rate of 5% is assumed and calculated on the previous year-end's balance of accumulated retained profits.

Year 1 (commencing Apr 2009)	Individual £	£	Company £	£
Rental	200,000		200,000	
Tax	80,000		44,000	
	120,000	120,000	156,000	156,000
Year 2				
Rent	200,000		200,000	
Interest on retained profit	6,000		7,800	
	206,000		207,800	
Tax	82,400		45,716	
	123,600		162,084	
		243,600		318,084
Year 3				
Rent	200,000		200,000	
Interest on retained profit	12,180		15,904.2	
	212,180		215,904.2	
Tax	84,872		47,498.92	
	127,308		168,405.3	
		370,908		86,489.3
Year 4				
Rent	200,000		200,000	
Interest on retained profit	18,545.4		24,324.46	
	218,545.4		224,324.5	
Tax	87,418.16		49,351.38	
	131,127.25		174,973.1	
		502,035.21		61,462.4
Year 5:				
Rent	200,000		200,000	
Interest on retained profit	25,101.76		33,073.12	
	225,101.8		233,073.1	
Tax	90,040.7		51,276.09	
	135,061.1		181,797	
		637,096.3		**43,259.4**

As will be seen from the above example, the retained profits at the end of year 5 are over £200,000 greater where a company is used.

There can also be a cash flow benefit in the timing of the tax payments, since individuals will often suffer tax at source on deposits and be required to make tax payments on account during the tax year. For many smaller and medium-sized companies on the other hand, tax is not due until nine months after the company's accounting year end.

The tax benefit arises where the funds are retained in the company for further investment or used to repay the principal of the property finance. As indicated in Point 8.3 below, if funds are eventually paid out to shareholders there is still a benefit, although greatly reduced if an individual is liable to higher rate income tax on the distributed income. As also mentioned in Point 8.3, individuals who are either non-domiciled or non-resident in the UK at that time can avoid any further tax.

Point 8.2:   *A close property investment company and its shareholder who borrows personally to lend funds to the company can take advantage of a cash flow advantage inherent in the corporate debt rules.*

See Point 3.19 for an explanation of this planning possibility.

Point 8.3:   *The realisation of income and investments locked into a company can give rise to further tax liabilities at that time. The extraction of retained earnings can be made by way of dividend. Shareholders who are not fully subject to higher rate tax or who are not resident in the UK at that stage could benefit.*

As illustrated in the example in Point 8.1, there is greater scope for the retention of profits within a company than there is by an individual personally. However, the extraction of these profits will generate a further tax liability where the company is controlled by UK resident taxpayers.

Where a company distributes its profits by way of dividend, the shareholder is treated as receiving a net amount on which 10% tax has been suffered. For the higher rate taxpayer, tax at 32.5% will then be charged on the grossed-up amount to give an effective rate of 25%. For other taxpayers no further income tax should be due whilst they remain below the higher rate tax threshold.

EXAMPLE

Taking the situation illustrated in the example in Point 8.1 above, the company's retained profits of £838.259 are distributed in full at the end of year 5.

Dividend recd	843,259
add: Tax credit	93,695
Taxable income	936,954
Tax at 32.5%	304,510
less: Tax credit	93,695
Tax payable	210,815
Net receipt	632,444

This is less than the net return of some £637,000 if the property had been owned directly by the shareholder. However, the position is improved if, at the time of the payment of the dividend, the shareholder(s) is/are not fully subject to higher rate tax.

The ultimate realisation of the company-owned investment by the shareholder might be achieved by distributing the sale proceeds, by liquidating the company or by selling the shares (see Chapter 14 for the illustration of the tax position in relation to the gains realised).

A shareholder may become tax resident outside the UK in the year of payment and, would therefore, not be subject to UK tax on any dividend payment made in the year of non-residence.

There are anti-avoidance provisions that HMRC could invoke in certain situations where tax avoidance arises from 'transactions in securities' (*TA 1988, s 703*) or certain transactions in land (*TA 1988, s 776*). Advice may be necessary at the time of any realisation of proceeds on the above basis as to what grounds, if any, HMRC might have for invoking these provisions.

Selling a company can also benefit a buyer. There is currently up to 4% stamp duty land tax payable on a direct purchase of a property. This is cut to 0.5% where the purchase is of shares (see 5.7 above).

Point 8.4:   *A company, unlike individuals or trustees, continues to benefit from indexation allowance. This can be advantageous for property assets that have relatively high base costs. Individuals and trustees, on the other hand, could pay tax at a lower effective rate than a company where large gains arise as a result of the Pre Budget proposals in 2007. If implemented, this could mean there is a disadvantage in owning property through a company, unless the shares can in future be sold to a UK REIT.*

Indexation allowance is frozen at its April 1998 value for individuals and trustees – and will be lost altogether on disposals after 5 April 2008 if the 2007 Pre Budget proposals are implemented (see 'Stop Press' at the beginning of the book). On the other hand, a company can continue to uplift the base cost of a property for CGT purposes each month by the cost of living index. This also applies to any enhancement expenditure after acquisition.

At an inflation rate of 3% per year, the base cost of a property would have increased by some 34% after ten years. A £1,000,000 property bought in 2000 would have a base cost of £1,343,916 in 2010. If the value of the property less selling expenses does not exceed this at that point, no taxable gain arises.

For an individual, a taxable gain of £343,916 would have arisen. Pre 6 April 2008, the individual would benefit from taper relief. On an investment asset which does not attract business asset taper relief, the maximum CGT would have been 24%. The tax charge on a gain of £343,916 would thus have been £82,540. However, post 5 April 2008, taper relief is due to be removed following the Pre Budget proposals referred to above and in the 'Stop Press' note referred to. In its place, there will be a flat rate of 18%, giving rise to a lower tax liability of £61,904.

On the other hand, if the value of the property after ten years is £3,000,000, the gain to the company would be £1,656,084 and tax at 28% would be £463,704. The individual would only pay £360,000 on the £2,000,000 gain (ie CGT at 18%) under the 2007 Pre Budget proposals. Of course, there is the added benefit in the latter case that the proceeds are in the individual's hands. Where a company realises the gain, there is usually a further tax cost to extracting funds from the company.

The disadvantage may be avoided if in future the shares can be sold to a UK REIT. See Chapter 14 for an explanation of this possibility.

See Chapter 35 for further details of capital gains tax taper relief.

Point 8.5: *An individual has been entitled to business asset taper relief when selling commercial property which meets certain conditions. There may, therefore, have been a disadvantage in owning such property through a company. Whether this has any on-going significance after 5 April 2008 depends on how the 2007 Pre-Budget proposals are implemented.*

[The comments below will be affected by the 2007 Pre-Budget Report. See the 'Stop Press' note at the beginning of the book for a summary of the relevant proposals.]

An investment property held directly by an individual and let to an unlisted trader could qualify as a business asset for the purposes of capital gains taper relief. This meant that after just two complete years of ownership, the gain on the disposal of such a property was reduced by 75%, which results in an effective rate of tax on the gain of only 10% (or less if the individual is paying tax at less than 40%). An individual has also been able to enjoy the benefit of taper relief where the property is owned through a partnership or LLP.

Before 6 April 2004, such a property was a business asset only if it was let to an unlisted trading company, and not if let to a trading partnership or sole trader. Where the tenant is a trading partnership and the property was owned before 6 April 2004, any gain arising on its sale must be computed in two parts – only the gain relating to the period of ownership from that date is treated as the gain on a business asset.

Neither before 6 April 2004 nor subsequently is a property let to a non-trader of any description a business asset for this purpose.

Whether there is any on-going planning on this basis from a taper relief perspective depends on whether the Government relent from their original Pre-Budget proposals and retain some measure of taper relief going forward.

CHAPTER 9 – PREMIUMS RECEIVED

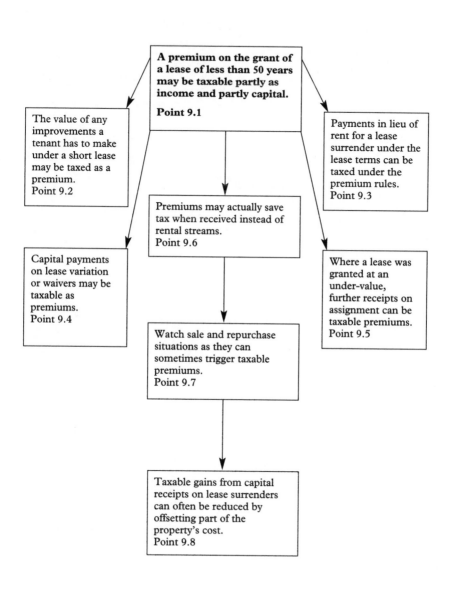

A premium on the grant of a lease of less than 50 years may be taxable partly as income and partly capital.

Point 9.1

The value of any improvements a tenant has to make under a short lease may be taxed as a premium.
Point 9.2

Payments in lieu of rent for a lease surrender under the lease terms can be taxed under the premium rules.
Point 9.3

Premiums may actually save tax when received instead of rental streams.
Point 9.6

Capital payments on lease variation or waivers may be taxable as premiums.
Point 9.4

Where a lease was granted at an under-value, further receipts on assignment can be taxable premiums.
Point 9.5

Watch sale and repurchase situations as they can sometimes trigger taxable premiums.
Point 9.7

Taxable gains from capital receipts on lease surrenders can often be reduced by offsetting part of the property's cost.
Point 9.8

9 Premiums received

Point 9.1: *Where a lease is granted for less than 50 years, part of any capital sum received is treated as if it were rent and taxed as income in the year of receipt. The balance of the premium will be assessed as a capital receipt for capital gains purposes.*

Part of any premium charged on the grant of a short lease of 50 years or less will be assessable as income (*TA 1988, s 34; ITTOIA 2005, ss 277–281*). The income element is determined by reducing the premium by 2% for each complete year of the lease less one. The resulting figure will be assessable to tax as additional rental income.

EXAMPLE

A 20-year lease is granted for a premium of £50,000. The Schedule A element of this sum is:

Premium	£50,000
Less: 2% × (20 – 1) × £50,000	(19,000)
Taxable as additional rent	£31,000

In the above example, £19,000 will be treated as the capital element of the receipt, representing the proceeds for the purposes of the capital gains computation.

Point 9.2: *Where a tenant is required to make improvements under a lease, a notional premium can be assessed on the landlord.*

If the terms under which a lease of 50 years or less is granted impose an obligation on the tenant to undertake improvements, the landlord can be taxed as if a premium had been received (*TA 1988, s 34(2)/ITTOIA 2005, s 278*). This will be taxable in the manner set out in Point 9.1 above.

The premium is not based on the amount spent, but on the increase in the value of the interest held by the landlord as a result of the improvements being carried out (*TA 1988, s 34(2); ITTOIA 2005, s 278(3)*). A charge will only arise where the obligation to carry out the work arises under the terms in the lease.

A charge under this provision is rare. The point tends to arise only where the tenant has claimed a deduction for the notional premium (see Chapter 27 in Part C).

Point 9.3:   *A capital payment by a tenant in lieu of rent or for the surrender of a short lease may be taxed as a premium.*

If, when a lease of 50 years or less is granted, there is provision for a future capital payment by the tenant in lieu of rent or for the surrender of the lease, the payment is a deemed premium in the hands of the landlord (*TA 1988, s 34(4); ITTOIA 2005, ss 279, 280*). It will be assessed in the year in which it is payable by the tenant.

The income element of a receipt in lieu of rent will be computed by reference to the period for which there has been a reduction in the rent. The balance will be treated as a capital receipt subject to the rules for the taxation of capital gains.

In the case of a payment on surrender of a lease, the premium is assessed by reference to the length of time the lease had been in existence at the time of surrender.

Where there was no clause in the lease when granted providing for such a payment, no deemed premium arises. In that case, the receipt is taxable as a capital gain but with the possibility of offsetting part of the property cost.

Point 9.4:   *A capital payment by a tenant for the variation or waiver of a short lease could also be deemed to be a premium.*

Any payment to vary or waive the terms of a lease is treated as a lease premium. The element chargeable as income – as distinct from the capital element (see Point 9.1 above) – would be based on the duration of the lease after the waiver or variation takes effect. Periods after the waiver or variation cease to have effect are also ignored. If the relevant duration is 50 years or less, then part of the premium is taxed as rent in the year the variation or waiver takes place (*TA 1988, s 34(5); ITTOIA 2005, s 281*).

EXAMPLE

A 21-year lease, when granted, contains a clause entitling the landlord to terminate the lease after 15 years should he require the property for development purposes. After 12 years, the landlord agrees to accept a sum of £50,000 from the tenant in consideration for waiving this clause.

The £50,000 will be assessed as a premium in the year of receipt. The income element will be based on the period of six years remaining after the waiver comes into effect. The amount taxable as income would, therefore, be:

Premium	£50,000
Less reduction £50,000 × 2% × (6 – 1)	(5,000)
Taxable as income	£45,000

The balance of £5,000 would be assessable to tax as a capital gain.

Point 9.5: *The premium provisions will only apply to a grant of a lease although an assignment can be caught if the original grant was at an under-value.*

The assignment, as opposed to the grant, of a lease is ordinarily outside the premium provisions. There is, however, an anti-avoidance provision applying where a lease of 50 years or less had originally been granted at an under-value. Where the lease is subsequently assigned, the consideration received can be partially taxable as additional rent of the letting business (*TA 1988, s 35; ITTOIA 2005, s 282*).

In the absence of any anti-avoidance provision, premium rules mentioned in Point 9.1 above could be avoided by granting a short lease for a nominal premium to an associated party. The associated party could then assign the lease for full market value.

However, under *TA 1988, s 35; ITTOIA 2005, s 282*, HMRC can assess the assignment consideration in this situation as a premium up to the amount of the market premium forgone on the first grant. There may also be assessments on any subsequent assignment, until HMRC have recouped tax on the deemed market value premium at the time of the original granting of the lease. The income element will be assessable as additional investment income.

EXAMPLE

A Ltd granted its subsidiary B Ltd a 25-year lease of its former offices for £10,000. B Ltd then assigned this lease to a firm of solicitors for £100,000. Since the grant of the lease was at an under-value, the following corporation tax assessments will be raised:

On A Ltd

Premium	£10,000
Less reduction £10,000 × 2% × (25 − 1)	(4,800)
Taxable as income under Schedule A	£5,200

On B Ltd

Deemed premium	£100,000
Less premium paid	(10,000)
	£ 90,000
Less reduction (£90,000 × 2% × (25 − 1))	43,200)
Taxable as income	£46,800

For chargeable gains purposes, A Ltd will be treated as disposing of the property intra-group for a consideration giving rise to neither gain nor loss (*TCGA 1992, s 171*).

B Ltd, on the other hand, will be subject to a chargeable gain. This would not be restricted to the capital element of the receipt. No reduction is available from the £100,000 consideration for any part taxable as income (*TCGA 1992, Sch 8, para 6(2)*). There is, therefore, a significant element of double taxation on this premium.

It should be noted that the parties need not be connected or associated for this provision to apply. It is sometimes recommended that an assignee of a short lease should obtain a certificate from the Inspector of Taxes that the original grant was not at an under-value (*TA 1988, s 35(3); ITTOIA 2005, s 300*).

Point 9.6:   *There may be circumstances where a landlord might benefit from receiving a lump sum premium rather than a rental stream.*

There could be a number of situations where a one-off premium may prove more attractive from a tax viewpoint than future annual rental income. Consider the following instances:

(1)   An individual or company may have a tax shelter in the year, which may not be available to carry forward against future rents. For instance, an individual might have incurred substantial trading losses or have surplus Allowances. A company may be able to claim losses from a fellow subsidiary company by way of group relief. Such tax shelter can be offset against the income element of the premium arising in the year.

(2)   The landlord may have current or past capital losses to offset against the capital element of the receipt.

(3)   A non-resident owner can be exempt from tax on the capital element of the premium (note – tax withholding may be necessary on the income element if paid directly by a tenant to a non-resident – see Point 1.3).

(4)   If the building is to be sold shortly after the grant of a new short lease, any past unused losses may not be offsettable against a capital gain. They may, as a consequence, be lost. If a premium is charged on the lease, these losses can be offset against the income element. The lease would have to reflect a suitably reduced rent payable and the sale consideration of the building would need to be correspondingly reduced, but this should also serve to diminish the chargeable capital gain arising. Accordingly, there can be an overall reduction in the tax liability without affecting the total consideration received by the landlord.

Point 9.7:   *A clause entitling a seller of land to buy back the property at a future date could give rise to an unexpected liability to tax under the premium provisions.*

Selling a property with the right to reacquire it in future could offer a way around the ordinary premium provisions. For this reason, a further anti-avoidance provision seeks to tax the difference between the sale price and lower purchase consideration as a deemed premium (*TA 1988, s 36; ITTOIA 2005, s 284*). The income element is calculated under the normal premium rules and is assessable as income in the period in which the sale occurs. The term of the lease for the purposes of computing the income element is the period between sale and repurchase.

If there is no one particular date but a series of possibilities arising from the sale contract, the repurchase is treated initially as taking place at the lowest possible price under the terms of the sale, if this varies with the date. The vendor then has six years from the reconveyance to make a claim to recover any excess tax paid, once the actual date of the reconveyance is known.

Although an anti-avoidance provision, this could present a pitfall in an innocent transaction. The owner of land may sell a property with the right to repurchase if there is a proposed redevelopment or change of use. For this reason, careful consideration must be given to the deemed premium rules before any repurchase clauses are included in any property sale agreement.

Point 9.8: *If the landlord receives a surrender payment from the tenant where there is no provision for this in the lease, the immediate taxable gain arising can be reduced by offsetting part of the base cost of the property against the receipt.*

If the terms of the lease did not provide for an early surrender payment, the receipt is assessable as a capital gain. The taxable gain is calculated under the 'part disposal rules' (*TCGA 1992, s 42*). Part of the base cost of the property can, therefore, be offset against the sum received in computing the taxable gain.

EXAMPLE

A property with a capital gains base cost of £1,000,000 is let at a market rent. There is no provision in the lease for early surrender.

The tenant wants to relocate premises and agrees to pay the landlord a surrender premium of £300,000. Following surrender, the freehold is valued at £900,000.

£300,000 is a capital receipt against which a portion of the £1,000,000 cost can be offset. This is determined by the fraction A/A+B, where A is the amount received and B is the value of the remaining interest. In this case the fraction is £300,000/(£300,000 + £900,000) or ¼. Therefore, ¼ of £1,000,000, ie £250,000, can be offset against the £300,000 leaving just £50,000 currently in charge to tax.

The base cost of the property for future tax purposes will be reduced by £250,000 to £750,000.

For small part disposals, where landlords receive in aggregate no more than £20,000 in a year, there is no need to carry out an A/A+B calculation; instead, the amount can simply be offset against the base cost carried forward (*TCGA 1992, s 242*).

Where the owner is a company, indexation will accrue subsequently by reference to that lower figure. For individuals, partnerships and trusts, there is no ongoing indexation. These taxpayers should enjoy taper relief at a possibly increasing rate on the higher gain that will arise in the future (see Chapter 35 for taper relief).

CHAPTER 10 – LETTING AS A TRADE

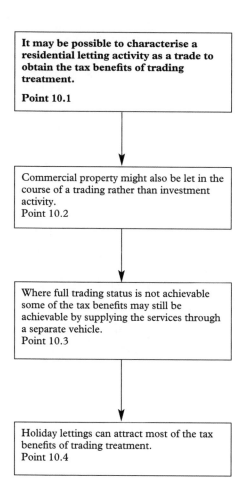

It may be possible to characterise a residential letting activity as a trade to obtain the tax benefits of trading treatment.

Point 10.1

Commercial property might also be let in the course of a trading rather than investment activity.
Point 10.2

Where full trading status is not achievable some of the tax benefits may still be achievable by supplying the services through a separate vehicle.
Point 10.3

Holiday lettings can attract most of the tax benefits of trading treatment.
Point 10.4

10 Letting as a trade

Point 10.1: *Residential letting is normally an investment activity. However, more favourable tax treatment as a trading activity may be available if services and facilities are provided to residents.*

The income tax treatment of letting is similar to that of a trade. However, there are a number of capital gains and inheritance tax reliefs which are available for a trading business but not for an investment activity. In view of this, the benefits of establishing trading treatment in preference to investment can be considerable. Consider the following:

(a) A new relief was introduced for companies from 1 April 2002. This exempts gains on certain disposals of shareholdings in trading companies. Where a company owns at least 10% of the ordinary shares of a trading company, any gain on the sale of those shares is potentially free of tax. It can apply, therefore, to sales of shares in trading joint venture companies as well as subsidiaries.
Further points on the substantial shareholding exemption are set out in Chapter 36 below.

(b) HMRC sometimes seek to restrict any directors' remuneration payable by an investment company. In practice, they do not normally seek to do this for a trading company. This also provides some scope for establishing a pension scheme.

(c) Trading income constitutes relevant earnings against which tax relief is available for personal pension premiums, including the new stakeholder style pensions as well as the old RAPs. A director of a trading company can also claim pension premium relief if there is no company pension scheme, but a director of an investment company cannot.

(d) Trading properties, or shares in a trading company, can be 'relevant business property' attracting 100% inheritance tax exemption (*IHTA 1984, s 105*).

(e) Gains on sales of property used for trading purposes can be rolled over into new trading assets (see Chapter 34).

For disposals before 6 April 2008, business asset capital gains taper relief potentially applies to gains on properties used for a trade or shares in trading properties. After just two years, 75% of any gain can be exempt from tax – resulting in a maximum effective tax rate of only 10% for higher rate taxpayers. The similar rate for investment assets is 24%, available after ten years. However, the Government's 2007 Pre-Budget announcements included proposals for the removal of all taper relief after 5 April 2008. (See the 'Stop Press' note at the beginning of the book.)

In view of the above advantages, the possibility of transforming an investment into a trading activity is often worth exploring.

There are two circumstances where a property owner might benefit from the more favourable taxation treatment as a trader. These are:

(1)   where certain services and facilities are provided to residents;
(2)   where the property qualifies as a holiday letting. This is discussed in Point 10.4 below.

The dividing line between investment and trading can become blurred when services or facilities are provided such that the letting is more like a hotel or guest house operation.

The distinction between a guest house and a pure letting has never been determined either by legislation or in the courts to date. Several cases have confirmed that the activity of letting accommodation and providing limited services, eg laundry, linen and cleaning, did not amount to trade (*Gittos v Barclay (Inspector of Taxes)* [1982] STC 390; *Griffiths v Jackson* [1983] STC 184 and, more recently, *Hatt v Newman* [2000] STC 113).

It is considered that, in addition to cleaning and laundry services, the provision of at least one meal would be necessary to establish a trading activity. Such a meal might be hot or cold, but should be prepared on the premises. A simple breakfast may well suffice for this purpose.

Other tests might be the length of occupation of guests. If the right of occupation is in days or weeks rather than months or years, that is more like a 'hostel' activity. Where longer periods are envisaged and there are multiple accommodation units, the landlord should have the right to move occupants between units at the end of any month. In that way, no occupant establishes exclusive rights over any particular units. Further, landlords should have rights of access over property at all times.

At times, it may even be beneficial to carry on a trade on a temporary basis. For instance, if a trading property is to be sold and the proceeds reinvested in a letting property, no roll-over relief would be available (see Chapter 34 in Part C for replacement of business asset, or 'roll-over', capital gains relief). However, if the new letting activity were a trading activity at least for a short period after the reinvestment, CGT roll-over relief may be available.

There is no provision for claw-back of relief if a trading property merely ceases to be used as such – as long as the property is not a wasting asset (ie is a freehold or a leasehold interest with more that 60 years to run). It must be appreciated that if a property ceases to be used in the trading activity, then any eligibility for future roll-over relief will be affected.

As mentioned in Point 10.3 below, there may be situations where it is not possible to establish the letting as a trade despite a supply of services. In such a situation, having the services supplied through a separate vehicle might preserve some of the benefits of trading treatment.

Point 10.2: *Commercial letting might also be eligible for favourable tax treatment as a trading activity depending on the services and facilities provided to occupants.*

The possibility that residential letting may become a trade is perhaps more evident than commercial letting because of the ready analogy of the hotel and guest house referred to in Point 10.1 above. However, in principle, certain commercial property situations can be run on trading lines and get the benefit of the favourable tax treatments outlined in Point 10.1.

The concept of serviced offices has become quite popular. Owners of properties are offering an increasing range of services to occupants including secretarial, IT and conferencing facilities as well as furniture, equipment, cleaning, telephone and maintenance.

As with residential situations, if occupants do not establish rights over the office units that they use and there is a frequently changing population of users, the potential to claim that a trade is carried on increases.

This opportunity may stretch to other uses of buildings such as smaller warehousing, retail or even factory units where there remains the opportunity for the owner to supply a range of services and facilities to the occupants. It might be more difficult in these situations to get a sufficiently revolving population of occupiers so that some establishment of tenant rights may be unavoidable. In that case, HMRC may regard there to be a 'hybrid' investment and trading activity.

Where services are provided which are ancillary to a letting activity, planning on the lines of Point 10.3 below might be adopted.

Point 10.3: *Where extensive services are supplied, but the activity is still an investment, it may be beneficial to split out the service aspects into a separate trading vehicle.*

Where services are supplied in a situation where a landlord/tenant investment situation exists, there might be some benefit in trying to split out the trading element.

One company might, for instance, let the property under conventional letting terms. Another company – or the shareholders personally – could supply the add-on services at a price which generates an appropriate profit.

The potential advantage is that this could establish a separate business which itself could attract the benefits of trading treatment as set out in Point 10.1 above. Furthermore, insofar as the property rents are not subject to VAT, VAT could be charged on services supplied, which could increase opportunities for VAT recovery on costs incurred by the property owner (see Chapter 18 for a discussion on VAT).

Point 10.4:   *Holiday lettings, although not a trade for tax purposes, attract most of the benefits of trading treatment.*

There is a special tax treatment for qualifying holiday lettings (*TA 1988, ss 503 & 504; ITTOIA 2005, ss 322–326*). Although the income from such lettings continues to be assessed as investment, holiday lettings will enjoy the same benefits as a trading activity (see Point 10.1 above).

To qualify as holiday lettings the following conditions must be met:

(a)   The property must be let as holiday accommodation in the UK.

(b)   There must be a commercial letting with a view to profit.

(c)   The letting must comprise furnished accommodation.

(d)   The accommodation must be available for commercial letting to the public generally as holiday accommodation for periods which amount, in aggregate, to not less than 140 days.

(e)   The period in which the accommodation is so let should amount, in aggregate, to at least 70 days.

(f)   For a period comprising at least seven months (for companies) and 155 days (for non-corporates) the property must not normally be in the same occupation for a continuous period exceeding 31 days. This period need not be continuous, but includes any months in which the property is let as mentioned in (d) above,

Furnished lettings also score one advantage over trading income. As the income is technically assessable as investment income, there are no Class 4 National Insurance contributions payable in respect of the activity.

The property need not be in an acknowledged holiday resort. The conditions could equally be satisfied by a property in the centre of a city. However, it should still, strictly, be used by holidaymakers and tourists to qualify for the special treatment.

Many people in holiday areas let their properties out during the main holiday period on a short-term basis but during the quieter part of the year let on a longer-term basis. These longer lettings – which may be to the same person for more than 31 days – normally would preclude a claim to CGT roll-over relief when the property is subsequently disposed of.

However, provided the letting during the main holiday period satisfies the above conditions, HMRC will regard the whole of the income derived from the property for that year as arising from commercially let furnished holiday accommodation.

CHAPTER 11 – CAPITAL GAINS PLANNING: PROPERTIES HELD AT 31 MARCH 1982

For companies, the taxable gain on a property owned at 31 March 1982 can be reduced by its value at that date where this is more favourable than original cost. For individuals, trustees and personal representatives the 31 March value will have to be adopted post 5 April 2008 if the Government's 2007 Pre-Budget proposals are implemented.

Point 11.1

It is sometimes favourable to make an election for 31 March 1982 values to apply to all assets.
Point 11.2

Where an asset was acquired between 31 March 1982 and 6 April 1988 in circumstances where a roll-over or hold-over claim was made, one half of the gain at the time of transfer can be deducted from any taxable gain on sale. Individuals, trustees and personal representatives may not be able to claim this after 5 April 2008.
Point 11.3

11 Capital gains planning: properties held at 31 March 1982

Point 11.1: *The chargeable gain on a disposal of a property that was owned at 31 March 1982 can be substantially reduced by substituting its value at 31 March 1982 instead of original cost.*

The base cost of any asset held at 31 March 1982 can be revised to its value at 31 March 1982 (*TCGA 1992, s 35*). In many cases where property was acquired before 31 March 1982, this rebasing results in a significant reduction in the gain, which would otherwise have been chargeable to tax by reference to cost.

In the Government's 2007 Pre-Budget announcements there was a proposal to remove the option for individuals, trustees and personal representatives to use cost as an alternative to 31 March 1982 value on the disposal of an asset held at 31 March 1982. If these are implemented, only companies in charge to corporation tax will be able to use cost if it is more favourable in their calculation of capital gains in respect of disposals post 5 April 2008.

There are four situations where the rebasing will not apply (and which are only likely to be relevant to companies after 5 April 2008).

These are:

(a) Where there is a profit by reference to the 1982 value but a loss compared with cost, the disposal will be treated as taking place at no gain/no loss (*TCGA 1992, s 35(4)*).
(b) Where there is a gain by reference to original cost but a loss when using the 1982 value then this is treated as a no gain/no loss disposal (*TCGA 1992, s 35(4)*).
(c) Where the overall loss by reference to cost is smaller than the loss that would arise using the 31 March 1982 value, the lower loss figure applies (*TCGA 1992, s 35(3)*).
(d) Where the person disposing of the asset did not actually own it at 31 March 1982. This rule is relaxed in several specific instances notably where the disposal took place between the members of a group of companies or between companies in the course of a reconstruction.

Following from (d) above, rebasing will not apply where an asset was acquired by way of gift after 31 March 1982 from someone who held it at that date and who may have claimed hold-over relief on the gift. Nor will it apply where there has been a replacement of business assets after 31 March 1982 and roll-over relief has been claimed. However, another relief may be available in these situations (see Point 11.3 below).

A claim can be made for the 31 March 1982 value to apply to all disposals. This can be particularly advantageous where either (b) or (c) above apply (see Point 11.2 below).

Point 11.2:   *Where use of the 31 March 1982 value would result in a loss compared with original cost, or a greater loss, it may be appropriate to consider making an election for the 31 March 1982 valuation to apply. However, such an election will apply to all future disposals of assets held at 31 March 1982.*

To avoid the need to keep records in respect of the cost of, and expenditure on, assets before 31 March 1982, taxpayers are entitled to make an election for all capital gains tax disposals to be computed solely by reference to their assets' 31 March 1982 values (*TCGA 1992, s 35(5)*). Where such an election is made, all pre-31 March 1982 cost figures can be disregarded. As mentioned in 11.1, this planning may only be relevant to companies in charge to corporation tax after 5 April 2008 if the Government's 2007 Pre-Budget proposals are implemented.

The principal advantage of this would be where (b) or (c) in Point 11.1 above applies. An election would enable a capital loss – or larger capital loss – to be available. For instance, the loss may be much lower when we compare the disposal value to original cost, or there could be a small gain. If the 1982 election is made, it would be possible to take advantage of the larger capital loss computed by reference to the 31 March 1982 'base cost'.

Making an election is not a casual matter. It is irrevocable and will apply to all future disposals of assets held at 31 March 1982.

Furthermore, individual companies within a tax group cannot make the election. It must be made by the parent company of the group and this will apply to all companies within the group at the time of the relevant disposal (*TCGA 1992, Sch 3, para 8(1), (2)*).

In view of the above, it is important to review the position for all assets before any election is made. If the historical cost for some properties (including any pre-31 March 1982 enhancement expenditure) exceeds the 31 March 1982 value, the disadvantage of making an election for such properties must be compared with the estimated benefit of the election in respect of others.

If an election is not made, the indexation allowance can be computed on the higher of original cost and the 31 March 1982 value (see Point 12.1). However, where an election is made then this allowance can only be calculated by reference to the 1982 value. The indexation allowance cannot create or enhance a capital loss (see Point 12.3).

The election for the 31 March 1982 value to apply in the case of companies must be made within two years of the end of the accounting period in which the 'first relevant disposal' takes place. The 'first relevant disposal' is the first occasion after 6 April 1988 on which an asset owned at 31 March 1982 is sold (*TCGA 1992, s 35(6)*).

Indexation relief is ignored to the extent that it creates or enhances a capital loss made by a company. See Chapter 12 for a discussion of indexation relief.

Point 11.3: *A special relief is available for properties that were the subject of roll-over relief or gift hold-over relief claims between 31 March 1982 and 6 April 1988. One half of the deferred gain held/rolled over can be exempt from tax.*

As mentioned in Point 11.1 above, rebasing does not apply if the asset was not owned at 31 March 1982. Whilst this seems logical, when introducing the rebasing legislation in April 1988, the Government did accept that this operates unfairly in two situations:

(a) Where the property in question was acquired after 31 March 1982 but business roll-over relief has been claimed on the basis that the proceeds of the sale of an asset owned pre-31 March 1982 have been reinvested in this property (see Chapter 34 for business roll-over relief). Since the new property was not owned on 31 March 1982, tax would ordinarily be payable on any chargeable gain that arose on the property that it replaced without any relief for the pre-31 March 1982 element of the rolled-over gain.

(b) Similarly, between 31 March 1982 and 6 April 1988 there may have been a gift of an asset where the transferor and transferee elected to hold over any capital gain until the asset was sold by the transferee. Since the recipient of the asset will not have owned it on 31 March 1982, he or she could well be liable to tax on the full gain eventually arising notwithstanding the fact that some of the gain could well have been referable to the period prior to 31 March 1982.

In view of the above, the Government introduced a fairly arbitrary relief that can be claimed wherever situations (a) or (b) apply and there is a disposal of an asset after 5 April 1988. The relief involves the total exclusion from the final chargeable gain of one half of the deferred gain (*TCGA 1992, Sch 4*). This relief is due to removed for disposals by individuals, trustees and personal representatives if the Government's 2007 Pre Budget proposals are implemented.

EXAMPLE

In December 1980, A bought an investment property for £100,000. Its value in March 1982 was £150,000.

In 1987, A gave the property to his son B. Both elected to hold over the gain of £200,000 at that time.

In January 2008, when B sold the property, the total gain by reference to A's original cost plus indexation amounted to £1,500,000. Since he did not own the asset at 31 March 1982, B could not substitute £150,000 as the market value of the asset at that date. However, by virtue of the relief in *TCGA 1992, Sch 4,* he was able to deduct £100,000 (ie 50% of the deferred gain of £200,000) from the gain subject to tax.

A claim must be made for the relief, in the case of companies, within two years of the end of the accounting period in which the relevant disposal is made (*TCGA 1992, Sch 4, para 9*). For individuals, alone or in partnership, and trusts, it must be made no later than 31 January in the tax year following that in which the disposal takes place.

CHAPTER 12 – CAPITAL GAINS PLANNING:
THE INDEXATION ALLOWANCE

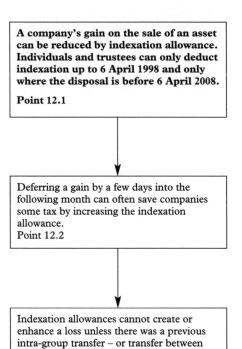

A company's gain on the sale of an asset can be reduced by indexation allowance. Individuals and trustees can only deduct indexation up to 6 April 1998 and only where the disposal is before 6 April 2008.

Point 12.1

Deferring a gain by a few days into the following month can often save companies some tax by increasing the indexation allowance.
Point 12.2

Indexation allowances cannot create or enhance a loss unless there was a previous intra-group transfer – or transfer between spouses – before 30 November 1993.
Point 12.3

12 Capital gains planning: the indexation allowance

Point 12.1: *On the sale of a property, any capital gain realised by a company is reduced by applying increases in the retail prices index to the cost of the asset. Individuals and trustees ceased to be entitled to further indexation allowance from 6 April 1998 and will receive no indexation allowance at all after 5 April 2008 under current Government proposals.*

The chargeable gain on the sale of an asset by a company is reduced by applying the increase in the retail price index since acquisition (or since 31 March 1982 if later) to the asset's base cost (*TCGA 1992, s 53(1)*). The increase can equally be applied to enhancement expenditure from the date the relevant amount became due and payable (*TCGA 1992, s 54(4)*).

For individuals and trustees indexation allowance ceased to be available after 5 April 1998 and was replaced by taper relief (see Chapter 35). Although any allowance accrued up to 5 April 1998 was preserved in the base cost of the property for CGT purposes, this will be lost in respect of any disposals after 5 April 2008 if the Government 2007 Pre-Budget proposals announced in October 2007 are implemented as proposed. (See the 'Stop Press' note at the beginning of the book.)

For assets acquired before 31 March 1982, a corporate taxpayer can ordinarily claim an indexation allowance based on the higher of original cost and the value at 31 March 1982. Individuals, trustees and personal representatives will not have this choice after 5 April 2008 on the basis of the 2007 Pre-Budget proposals. For them, the cost and related indexation will be based solely on 31 March 1982 cost after that date.

EXAMPLE 1

A Ltd bought a property for £200,000 in March 1979 with the expectation of redeveloping it. In March 1982 the property was worth £500,000. The property was sold in February 2007 for £1,000,000.

Unless an election has been made for 31 March 1982 value to apply to all A Ltd's pre-31 March 1982 assets (see Point 11.2), it is necessary to do two calculations:

	[A] 1982 value as base cost £	[B] Original Cost £
Proceeds	1,000,000	1,000,000
Base cost	(500,000)	(200,000)
	500,000	800,000
Indexation allowance £500,000 at 1.575 ×	(787,500)	(787,500)
Chargeable gain	NIL	£12,500

Since there is no gain in calculation [A] but a gain in calculation [B], the former calculation is adopted. Note that in both cases, however, the same indexation figure is used, which in this instance is based on the higher base cost figure of £500,000 (*TCGA 1992, s 55(2)*).

Where the company has made an election for the 31 March 1982 value to apply to all assets (see Point 11.2) this would affect the position in the above example but not the final outcome. There would only be one calculation needed, this would use the market value of the property at 31 March 1982 as the base cost. Note also that the March 1982 value would form the basis for the indexation allowance even if it were lower than the base cost (*TCGA 1992, s 55(2)*).

There will be situations where the use of a March 1982 valuation may not be beneficial. In the above example the value of a property might have dropped since acquisition. Even if this is not the case, substantial enhancement expenditure may have been incurred prior to 31 March 1982 which is not fully reflected in the value of the property at that date. In view of these possibilities, it is important to consider both alternative bases for indexation allowance and obtain a valuation of the property at 31 March 1982 to support any decision on this.

Point 12.2:   *Deferment of exchange of contracts by a few days can save a small amount of tax on the capital gain.*

The indexation allowance is computed by reference to the retail prices index in the month of disposal. Therefore, a sale on 31 March would give rise to a computation by reference to the March index. A sale on 1 April would be by reference to the April index. This offers scope for deferring exchange of contracts a couple of days to attract a higher allowance.

It would be a mistake to assume that the RPI increases evenly every month. In some months the RPI can move ahead rapidly. In others it can actually decrease.

If a sale is scheduled at the end of one of the months where an increase into the next month might be anticipated, a deferral for a couple of days will save tax.

EXAMPLE 2

A property valued at £1 million on 31 March 1982 was sold on 28 February 2007. The indexation allowance would have been £1,574,000 computed as follows:

$$1.574 \times £1m$$

If it had been sold on 1 March, the indexation allowance would have increased to £1,581,000 as follows:

$$1.581 \times £1m$$

A deferral by one day has saved just over £2,000 tax (ie 7,000 at 30%).

Point 12.3:   *The indexation allowance can neither create nor enhance a capital loss. However, if there was an earlier transfer between spouses or group companies, the loss may have been preserved.*

Indexation relief cannot create an allowable capital loss or increase a loss already arising by virtue of the fact that the disposal value is less than cost/31 March 1982 value (*TCGA 1992, s 53(1)*).

EXAMPLE 3

A property owned by X Ltd cost £1m in 1982. In February 2007 it was sold for £1.8m. There was an increase in the retail prices index of 157.4% in this period. Ignoring transaction costs, the capital gains position is:

	£
Sales proceeds	1,800,000
Cost	1,000,000
Gain	800,000
Indexation relief – £1.574m but restricted to gain	800,000
Chargeable gain	NIL

In the above example, the balance of the indexation allowance, £774,000, is lost. It cannot be used against other capital gains.

This restriction was introduced with effect from 30 November 1993.

If the property was acquired from a connected party before this date and HMRC treat this as a disposal at no gain or loss, indexation accrued up to that time is inherited intact. That indexation can be used to create or enhance a usable capital loss on the property (*TCGA 1992, s 56*).

The principal examples of 'no gain/no loss disposals' are transfers between spouses and transfers within a group. If either of these events has occurred before 30 November 1993, some of the effect of these provisions will have been mitigated, as the following example shows:

EXAMPLE 4

In example 3 above assume X Ltd has sold the property having acquired it from a fellow subsidiary, A Ltd, in October 1993. Indexation to October 1993 was 78.5%.

	£
Cost	1,000,000
Indexation relief – to October 1993	785,000

In this situation, the property is treated as being transferred to X Ltd at a value which gives neither a gain nor a loss. Since A Ltd has a base cost of £1.785m (ie £1m plus £785,000 indexation allowance), X Ltd will be treated as acquiring the property for that value and have a base cost of £1,785,000. If the property were sold for £1.7m, it will have an allowable capital loss £85,000 (ie £1,700,000 less £1,785,000). Thus, the full benefit of the £785,000 indexation allowance is preserved.

If the acquisition had been in December 1993 or later, no capital loss could subsequently arise as a consequence of the indexation allowance.

CHAPTER 13 – CAPITAL GAINS PLANNING: DEFERRING A SALE

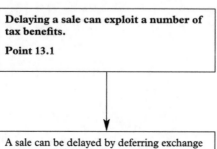

Delaying a sale can exploit a number of tax benefits.

Point 13.1

A sale can be delayed by deferring exchange of contracts, entering into conditional contracts or by certain option arrangements.
Point 13.2

13 Capital gains planning: deferring a sale

Point 13.1: *There are usually tax advantages to be gained from deferring a sale for capital gains purposes from one accounting period or tax year to the next. This is particularly the case if a sale is otherwise planned to take place towards the end of the year in question.*

There are several potential advantages in delaying a chargeable disposal:

(a) In the case of a corporate sale, a deferral may help ensure that any gain qualifies for substantial shareholding exemption where the minimum 12-month ownership rule must be met (see Chapter 36 for substantial shareholding relief).

(b) By pushing the gain into the following tax year, the tax on the capital gain would not be payable until one year later. Accordingly, one year's cash flow advantage of the tax payment can be achieved. This may only involve the deferral of the date of a disposal by a matter of days or weeks if it is due to take place at the end of a fiscal year or period of account.

(c) Delay could attract extra indexation allowance for a company (see Point 12.2).

(d) If an individual or trustee has already used the annual exemption for the tax year, there will be the opportunity of using a fresh exemption available in the following year.

(e) The deferral of a capital gain for one year may also give an opportunity to use any capital losses that arise in the following year. Capital losses can never be carried back but can be offset against gains in the same or future years. If a capital loss is anticipated but may not be realised until a succeeding year, this is added incentive to defer the gain until the same year to ensure that there will be an offset.

(f) As the gain will be aggregated with income arising in the year for tax purposes, deferral may push the gain into a year of low income. This could, for instance, reduce the tax charge from, say, 40% to 20% for an individual.

Up to 5 April 2008, an individual, trustee or personal representative might have secured an extra year's taper relief on deferring a disposal. A chargeable gain on an investment property reduced by 5% annually between years 4 and 10 such that a short delay could trigger an extra year's ownership and a further 2% tax reduction (5% × 40%). However, under the Government's 2007 Pre-Budget proposals, taper relief is scheduled to disappear in large part after 5 April 2008. It will be replaced by a tax rate of 18% on chargeable gains realised by these taxpayers. For some, there will be an incentive to defer a sale until after 5 April 2008 to take advantage of this. Others, who stand to pay more tax under the new regime, would have been considering bringing forward their disposals to before 5 April 2008. (See the 'Stop Press' note at the beginning of the book for a summary of the relevant proposals.)

Point 13.2: *A gain can be deferred from one accounting period or tax year to the next if either exchange of contracts is deferred or there is a conditional contract. Deferring completion will not make any difference to the date of the chargeable disposal.*

The date of disposal for capital gains tax purposes is the date when unconditional contracts are entered into (*TCGA 1992, s 28(1)*). Completion is irrelevant as far as the *date* of disposal is concerned. Interestingly, following a House of Lords decision, it seems possible for a different person to be treated as making the disposal if that person steps into the shoes of the seller before completion. In the case in question, the benefit of a contract to sell land was transferred to an offshore trust before completion (*Jerome v Kelly* [2004] UKHL 25).

Disposals are treated as occurring after the contract date where the parties have entered into a conditional contract (*TCGA 1992, s 28(2)*). In that case, the sale is treated as taking place on the date the condition is satisfied or, if there is more than one condition, when the final condition is satisfied.

EXAMPLE

A Ltd contracts to sell land to B Ltd on 30 December 2007 provided planning permission is granted. At that point the contract is conditional and in its year ended 31 December 2007, there is no disposal for the purposes of corporation tax on capital gains.

The land receives planning permission in February 2008. At that point, the contract becomes unconditional and the chargeable disposal arises in A Ltd's year ending 31 December 2008.

In recent years, parties to property transactions have used the device of cross-options with the object of deferring exchange of contracts until after a specified date, whilst still binding on both parties.

EXAMPLE

A grants an option to B under which B can require A to sell him a piece of land at a specific price on or after 6 April next (the call option). At the same time B grants A an option under which B can be required to purchase this land on or after 6 April next (the put option). Both A and B are in a position to require the other party to enter into a legally binding agreement at any time after the following 6 April.

If put and call options taken together, can be considered to constitute a binding contract to buy and sell at the time they are granted no deferral is achieved. There is less exposure to any challenge, however, where the price of the put option differs from the price of the call option.

An alternative to cross-options is the use of a conditional contract. In a commercial context, it is common to find contracts conditional on obtaining, say, planning permission; landlord's consent to an assignment; or clearance from HMRC. A quoted company may also enter into a major contract conditional on obtaining shareholders' approval at a general meeting to be held after the end of its accounting year.

In these cases, the disposal will not take place until the condition is satisfied. For a contract to be treated as conditional, it is essential that the condition relates to an uncertain future event which is not within either party's power to bring about.

CHAPTER 14 – CAPITAL GAINS PLANNING: SELLING THE COMPANY RATHER THAN THE PROPERTY AND REINVESTMENT RELIEF

Selling shares in a company rather than the company selling the property and distributing the proceeds will normally save tax – particularly if a favourable deal can be struck over the inherent tax on capital gains in the company.

Point 14.1

Selling a property investment company to a UK real estate investment trust (REIT) can provide an exit without any price reduction for the inherent tax on capital gains
Point 14.2

In addition to the price benefit of selling to a REIT, a vendor can indefinitely defer any tax on the share sale by taking shares or even loan stock in the REIT.
Point 14.3

14 Capital gains planning – selling the company rather than the property and the further possibility of selling to a UK REIT

Point 14.1: *Where an investment property is owned by a company, the sale of the shares in the company is usually a more tax-efficient alternative to selling the property and extracting the proceeds from the company. It also minimises stamp taxes for the purchaser.*

Where an investment property is held within a UK resident company, the shareholders could suffer two charges to tax on any appreciation of the property.

The first occasion of charge arises when the company sells the property. Corporation tax on the capital gain would be payable by the company at that stage.

The second occasion of charge arises when the shareholders extract their profit from the company. This might be as remuneration, by way of dividend, or a capital distribution on liquidation of the company.

Remuneration would be assessable to income tax on the recipient who would also suffer employee's National Insurance Contributions (NIC). Employer's NIC would also be payable by the company. For an investment company, there may well be no corporation tax relief for the remuneration paid if the company's tax Inspector considers that it exceeds a reasonable expense of managing the company's affairs.

Dividends are taxable on the recipient shareholders as income and the company will receive no tax relief for the payment. However, no NIC is payable.

On the liquidation of the company, capital distributions received by the shareholders will be assessed to tax as a capital gain in so far as they exceed the nominal value of the shares plus any share premium (or, if higher, the price paid by the shareholder for the shares).

In view of the 'double taxation' effect of extracting the proceeds of a property sale from a company, it is often preferable to sell the company itself. This assumes, of course, that the property is the sole or main asset of the company.

The purchase of a company's shares rather than the property it owns also significantly reduces stamp taxes. The buyer of property would have to pay up to 4% stamp duty land tax (SDLT) on the purchase price of the property. A buyer of shares, however, pays only 0.5% stamp duty on the price of the shares. In practice, this will be less than 0.5% of the value of the property if the value of the company is less than the value of the property (for instance, as a result of company indebtedness). No stamp duty at all will be payable if the shares are in a foreign company. See Point 5.7 for a further discussion on the stamp duty issues on selling a company.

Sometimes a prospective purchaser will require a discount on the share price to reflect the inherent capital gain in the company. However, it then becomes a matter of the negotiating power between the parties as to whether the vendor can reduce the discount and so obtain a benefit from proceeding in this manner.

EXAMPLE

An office building is purchased by a property investment company in 1970 for £500,000. The company, the shares of which are all held by a husband and wife, had no other assets nor liabilities and any net income has been distributed.

The value of the building in March 1982 was £3,750,000. In March 2007 an offer of £10,000,000 was accepted for the property.

The tax payable by the company on the prospective gain in this situation would be around £686,000, illustrated as follows:

Proceeds	£10,000,000
Value at 31 March 1982	(3,750,000)
	7,250,000)
Indexation allowance	
3,750,000* × 1.581	(5,928,750)
Chargeable gain	1,321,250
Tax at 30%	396,375

(NB: After 1 April 2008, a lower rate of 28% applies)

(*Note*: Transaction costs are ignored and it is assumed there has been no enhancement expenditure.)

If, in this example, the shareholders could persuade the prospective purchaser to buy the company instead, any sum received in excess of £9.6m (ie £10m proceeds less the company's inherent tax liability) would increase the net sum due to the shareholders. This amount would be subject to capital gains tax, but would result in a much higher net return to the shareholders than the payment of a dividend or of remuneration. In this pre-April 2008 example, if the shareholders are individuals, trustees or personal representatives, they would also benefit from taper relief, provided that they had held the shares for over three years. After ten years, the maximum taper relief of 40% for non-business assets was available, reducing the effective tax rate to 24% for individuals, trustees and personal representatives. After April 2008, the prospective capital gains tax rate for these taxpayers is 18%. (See the 'Stop Press' note at the beginning of the book for the relevant 2007 Pre-Budget proposals.)

The purchaser would be saving at least £350,000 in stamp taxes by buying the shares in the company (ie 4% less 0.5% of £10m).

Point 14.2: *Selling a property investment company to a UK real estate investment trust (REIT) may present an opportunity to exit without a significant or any price reduction for the inherent corporation tax on capital gains within the company.*

An issue generally for buyers and sellers of UK resident property companies is the underlying taxable capital gains that would be crystallised within the target company when its properties are eventually sold. The tendency is for the price of such companies to be reduced to reflect a discount on the market value of the properties to reflect this inherent tax.

The buyer may, therefore, be reluctant to pay £10 million for a company with £10 million worth of property where there may be potential exposure to say, £2 million corporation tax if the properties were sold at that value. In those circumstances, the prospective buyer may only be prepared to offer £8 million although a higher figure may be negotiated if the buyer has long-term plans to retain the property.

With the introduction of the Real Estate Investment Trust, or 'REIT', in January 2007 there is now a new style prospective purchaser that need not face this issue, because a qualifying REIT is not liable for UK corporation tax on its capital gains.

A REIT is a property investment company or group whose shares (or the shares of the parent company) are quoted on a recognised stock exchange. The listing can be a stock exchange outside of UK, but the company itself must be UK tax resident. If the shares are listed in the UK, it must have a full market listing rather than, for instance, a listing on the alternative investment market (AIM).

The REIT would typically hold all or most of its assets as let investment property. This is because it is a requirement of REIT status that not less than 75% of income and asset value must be derived from let property. The REIT also has a number of other conditions including the need to distribute 90% of its investment income each year to shareholders. There are also requirements in terms of its shareholders and gearing ratios. The Government's intention in creating the REIT was to establish a vehicle though which institutions and the public can invest in property in a reasonably marketable and low-geared manner.

Within any group that meets the requisite REIT conditions, individual companies can generate property income and gains from selling investment property without being subject to UK tax. This will equally apply to any companies which are acquired by a qualifying UK REIT notwith-standing that there may be significant inherent chargeable gains on the target company's property assets at the time of acquisition. There is, however, a conversion cost equivalent to 2% of the market value of the property at the time that the company becomes part of a REIT. Often, that conversion charge is much lower than the inherent corporation tax charge on capital gains and in many situations is proving a relatively modest cost for achieving this exemption.

This means that any acquisitive REIT, by not having discount a price paid for a property investment company to reflect tax in inherent gains, can usually afford to offer considerably more for a UK property company with such gains than another prospective purchaser.

Point 14.3:   *In addition to the price benefit of selling to a REIT, a vendor can indefinitely defer any tax on the share sale by taking shares or even loan stock in the REIT.*

With any corporate sale there is potential for deferring tax on capital gains where the consideration received is in the form of shares or loan stock issued by the purchasing company as opposed to cash. The position is no different where they buyer is a UK REIT.

This may be an attractive proposition for any individual or family looking to exit from a corporately held property or property portfolio, using the opportunity to invest in a possibly bigger property fund where there might be lower long-term risk and higher marketability of the invest-ment. In addition to issuing shares, some REITs may offer this option in the form of fixed-rate preference shares or indeed loan stock. This may also offer the vendors various other permutations including taking some cash and a combination of these types of security.

The deferral of tax in any such situation is always contingent on HM Revenue & Customs being satisfied that the transaction is being carried out for bona fide commercial reasons and not for the avoidance of tax. It may be desirable to take advantage of the advance clearance procedure available under *s 135 TCGA 1992*. Generally, if the reasons behind the structuring of those referred to above or the REIT itself is keen to finance a transaction as far as possible through the use of its own paper, that would normally be sufficient to satisfy this bona fide test.

CHAPTER 15 – ENTERPRISE INVESTMENT SCHEME DEFERRAL RELIEF

> **Any tax arising on the sale of a property investment company can be deferred indefinitely by reinvesting the gain into the shares of a suitable unquoted trading company.**
>
> **Point 15.1**

15 Capital gains planning: Enterprise Investment Scheme deferral relief

Point 15.1:   *It is possible indefinitely to defer tax on the gain on the sale of a property investment company by reinvesting the gain into a suitable unquoted trading company.*

Property investors have never been able to benefit from the capital gains roll-over relief available to traders who reinvest the proceeds of the sale of trading premises into new premises, goodwill and/or other trading assets (see Chapter 34). However, individuals and trustees can defer gains by reinvesting into shares in suitable companies that qualify for the Enterprise Investment Scheme (EIS).

An individual or trustee that realises a gain on the sale of an asset can defer any tax on the gain by subscribing for shares in companies which satisfy conditions for the EIS (*TCGA 1992, Sch 5B*). The company must be unquoted and carry on a trade, but some trades are excluded. The excluded activities are:

(1)   dealing in land, commodities, futures, shares, securities or other financial instruments;
(2)   dealing in goods other than in the course of an ordinary trade of wholesale or retail distribution;
(3)   banking, insurance, money-lending, debt factoring, hire purchase financing or other financial activities;
(4)   leasing or receiving royalties or licence fees;
(5)   providing legal or accountancy services;
(6)   property development;
(7)   farming or market gardening;
(8)   holding, managing or occupying woodlands or other forestry activities;
(9)   operating or managing hotels or comparable establishments;
(10)   operating or managing nursing homes or residential care homes;
(11)   providing services to a commonly controlled company that itself carries on one of the above trades

(*TCGA 1992, Sch 5B, para 1(2); Part 5, ITA 2007*).

The funds raised by the company must be used for a qualifying trade carried on wholly or mainly in the UK by the company or a 90% subsidiary (*ITA 2007, s 183*). The company need not be UK resident.

A further condition relates to the size of the company. To qualify for deferral relief, the company issuing the shares must not have gross assets in excess of £7 million immediately before the shares are issued nor £8 million after. Where the company has subsidiaries, that test is applied to the group as a whole (*TCGA 1992, Sch 5B; ITA 2007, s 186*).

Although the company must be unquoted, companies whose shares are dealt in solely on the Alternative Investment Market (AIM) can qualify.

Finally, the company in question cannot be a 51% subsidiary, or otherwise be under the control, of another company (*ITA 2007, s 139*). Nor can it control another company that is itself not a 'qualifying' subsidiary (*ITA 2007, s 140*).

To qualify for the relief, the individual or trustee must subscribe in cash for shares in a qualifying company up to one year before or within three years after the disposal giving rise to the gain. The shares must be ordinary shares with no preferential rights or rights to be redeemed (*TCGA 1992, Sch 5B, para 1*).

It should be noted that unlike the relief on replacement of business assets (or 'roll over relief') dealt with in Chapter 34, it is sufficient to reinvest only the gain (before taper relief) to obtain full tax deferral under EIS deferral relief. For rollover relief on replacement of business assets, the entire proceeds of sale have to be reinvested for full deferral.

There are provisions for clawback of the relief if certain things happen within three years of the issue of the shares, eg where:

(a)   the acquired shares cease to be eligible shares for EIS relief;
(b)   the company ceases to be a qualifying company;
(c)   the person holding the shares becomes resident and/or ordinarily resident outside the UK (unless the reason for this is a short-term working assignment abroad).

The relief is also clawed back if the person holding the shares or any associate receives value from the company during the four-year period which starts one year before the issue of the shares. The whole of the gain would then be brought into charge, no matter how much or little value was received, subject to the EIS *de minimis* limits on value.

Of course, the deferred gain also comes into charge whenever the shares are disposed of, unless the disposal is a transfer to the disponer's spouse at no gain, no loss.

As presently drafted, there is no doubt that the conditions for EIS deferral relief are restrictive. The EIS rules are complex and contain many pitfalls that can result in denial of the relief. However, if the individual can invest in a qualifying company, there may be the added bonus in future of taking advantage of higher taper relief (see Chapter 35). Where the investment in the company also meets the more restrictive conditions for income Enterprise Investment Scheme relief, the future growth in value can be tax free. Furthermore, the new shares acquired would potentially attract 100% business property relief for inheritance tax purposes should there be a future chargeable gift of them or legacy on death.

CHAPTER 16 – PLANNING FOR LOSSES: CAPITAL LOSSES AND SURPLUS MANAGEMENT EXPENSES

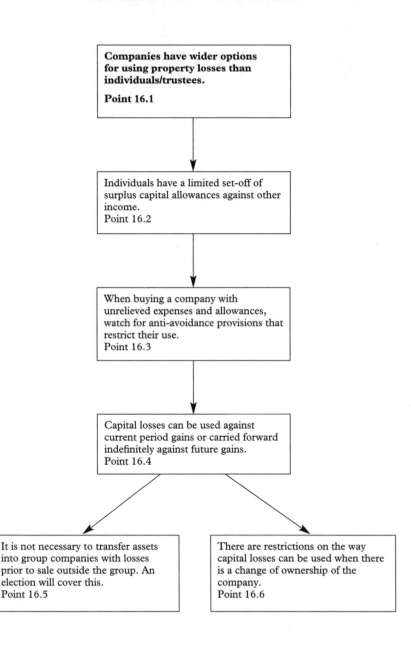

Companies have wider options for using property losses than individuals/trustees.

Point 16.1

Individuals have a limited set-off of surplus capital allowances against other income.
Point 16.2

When buying a company with unrelieved expenses and allowances, watch for anti-avoidance provisions that restrict their use.
Point 16.3

Capital losses can be used against current period gains or carried forward indefinitely against future gains.
Point 16.4

It is not necessary to transfer assets into group companies with losses prior to sale outside the group. An election will cover this.
Point 16.5

There are restrictions on the way capital losses can be used when there is a change of ownership of the company.
Point 16.6

16 Planning for losses: capital losses and surplus management expenses

Point 16.1: *An excess of property expenses over rents will give rise to property losses. For taxpayers other than UK companies, the use of these losses is restricted to current or future property income. For a UK company, a more general offset is available for such losses.*

The income tax regime treats property investment losses differently from corporation tax. Income tax applies to individuals, trustees and non-resident investment companies (ie those non-resident companies not carrying on a trade in the UK through a permanent establishment). Corporation tax applies to UK resident companies.

For individuals, trustees and non-resident investment companies, property expenses (including finance costs and capital allowances) can be deducted from rental income of the property activity. Any surplus expenses are available to carry forward against future property income (*ITA 2007, s 118*). There is no general offset against other income except for some limited scope in respect of surplus capital allowances (see Point 16.2 below). Furthermore, no successor to the property can inherit any entitlement to unrelieved expenses or allowances.

A company is not so restricted in its use of surplus property expenses, including capital allowances. Any losses from its property rental business can be set against its total profits (including capital gains) for the period. Any excess may be surrendered as group relief. Any balance is automatically carried forward to the next period for set-off against total profits so long as the property rental business is still undertaken by the company. This treatment is only available if the letting business is carried on commercially with a reasonable expectation of profit.

Finance costs are treated separately with their own rules for general offset (see Point 3.16 in Chapter 3B). Furthermore, there is also a category of 'management expenses' for which there is also general offset (*TA 1988, s 392A*).

A company can be sold with the purchaser inheriting the entitlement to use unrelieved losses carried forward. However, there are anti-avoidance tax rules that can make it difficult for companies to use these losses under new ownership in certain circumstances (see Point 16.3 below).

Management expenses are the costs of running the company as distinct from the properties. They would include:

- audit and accountancy
- directors' fees

- administrative salaries
- expenses of premises and equipment used in administration of the business.

These expenses, together with surplus finance costs, can also be offset against the company's total income and gains for the period. To the extent that there is an unrelieved surplus, they can be set off against any other group company profits for the year. Surplus management expenses can then be carried forward indefinitely against future income and gains as long as the company remains a 'company with investment business' and under the same ownership.

'A company with investment business' is any company whose business consists wholly or partly in the making of investments (*TA 1988, s 130*). With respect to accounting periods beginning before 1 April 2004, the treatment of management expenses described above was available only for an 'investment company', a much narrower criterion. An investment company is one whose business consists wholly or mainly of holding investments and the principal part of whose income is derived from investments. The new rules consequently represent a considerable relaxation, allowing more companies to qualify.

Surplus finance costs can be carried back to the previous period or carried forward indefinitely to set against non-trading profits including capital gains (see Point 3.16 above).

Point 16.2: *For individuals, there is a limited offset for capital allowances against other income.*

The regime for individuals is much more restrictive than for UK companies. There is no general offset against income or gains.

Individuals and non-resident investment companies can offset losses up to the amount of net capital allowances against other income (but not gains) in the year. Where a loss arises following a claim to capital allowances, it is possible to offset that loss against general income in the same year of assessment or the next. The amount of loss relief will be restricted to the lowest of the following:

(a) the loss;
(b) the other income for the year;
(c) the amount of capital allowances after deducting any clawback of allowances.

(*ITA 2007, ss 121–123*).

If the allowances remain unrelieved, any carry-forward is only against income from the property activity.

Point 16.3: *The ability to deduct past unrelieved expenses and losses against all future profits can make an investment company with these losses attractive to a buyer. However, the availability of these losses can be affected by wide-ranging anti-avoidance rules.*

Anti-avoidance rules can prevent the carry-forward of an investment company's losses in certain circumstances following a change in ownership. These bite where any of the following applies as well as a change of ownership:

- there is a significant increase in the company's capital;
- there is a major change in the nature or conduct of the business within the six years commencing three years before the change in ownership;
- the scale of activities of the company revives, having become small or negligible before the change.

(*TA 1988, s 768B*).

Broadly, a significant increase in capital arises where the value of redeemable loan stock and debt plus shares either doubles or increases by at least £1m (*TA 1988, Sch 28A, para 2*).

Where any of the above three conditions applies, none of the unused management and other expenses incurred before the date of the change of ownership are available to carry forward.

Following a change of ownership, the company's structure and activities should be monitored to ensure that the company does not fall foul of any of the above. The buyer could, for instance, plan on the basis of the losses being used only to have HMRC seek to recover the tax relief several years later because the anti-avoidance conditions have been subsequently met.

The restriction of past losses could also apply to finance costs for which a deduction has been delayed for over 12 months since accrual (see Point 3.17 above for the circumstances in which such late-paid interest is disallowed).

Note that these rules apply to a company that is an 'investment company' (not to any company that is a 'company with investment business' – see Point 16.1 – unless, of course, it is also an investment company).

Point 16.4: *Capital losses can be used against current period gains or carried forward indefinitely against future gains.*

If an individual or company realises a loss on the disposal of a capital asset in a tax year or accounting period, this loss can be offset against any chargeable gain arising in the same year. Unused capital losses can be carried forward against future capital gains but never carried back, except on the taxpayer's death (when a three-year carry back is allowed) (*TCGA 1992, s 2(3)*).

In a year when a chargeable gain is likely to arise, it may be appropriate to review other assets to see whether there might be potential for realising any capital losses. The following opportunities might be available, for example:

(a)   Where assets cease to have any value, a claim can be made to HMRC for any loss to be recognised in the year of claim. Such assets might include investments that have become worthless (including shares in an associated company) or possibly a property interest that has become onerous (*TCGA 1992, s 24*). Such a negligible-value claim can be related back up to two years.

(b)   The outright sale of any asset standing at a loss in the period in which a capital gain is likely to arise. Note, however, that the sale must be to an unconnected party. A capital loss realised on a sale to a connected party can only be offset against gains from disposals to the same person (*TCGA 1992, s 18*).

It has been possible to crystallise losses on quoted shares which are subsequently re-acquired. However, there are anti-avoidance rules to inhibit arrangements where shares are bought and sold for tax mitigation reasons (*FA 2006, s 78*).

Both individuals and companies can carry a capital loss forward. It is important, therefore, that details of unused capital losses are maintained with current tax information.

The carry-forward of capital losses is not affected by changes of ownership in the same way as management expenses and finance costs. However, where a company ownership does change, the future use of the losses may still be severely restricted (see Point 16.6 below).

Point 16.5:   *Within a group of companies, tax shelter may be available for capital gains by using a capital loss or surplus management expense company. It is not necessary, however, to physically transfer assets into such a company prior to sale. It is possible, instead, to make an election treating the asset as if it had been transferred.*

An investment company can shelter chargeable gains by offsetting brought-forward capital losses (Point 16.4 above) or surplus expenses (see Point 16.1 above).

Where a company within a group has incurred capital losses it was common in the past to use that company as a vehicle for acquiring new properties and disposing of valuable properties already held elsewhere in the group. The company became a conduit for the sale of all investment assets held within the group until such time as the losses of that company can be fully used. In the *Finance Act 2000*, a provision was introduced that makes it unnecessary for assets to be physically acquired by, or transferred into, such a company. It is now sufficient for the group company (X) selling the property and the company with losses (Y) to make a joint election that the property should be treated as transferred into and sold by Y. The gain will be treated as realised by Y and can be offset against its losses (*TCGA 1992, s 171A*).

In many cases, this election will be made to use a fellow group company's losses. It might also be used to preserve losses in the actual selling company particularly if there is greater likelihood that these losses will be needed in future in comparison with Y's losses.

The election offers some flexibility in that the disposal can be deemed to have arisen in more than one company. Accordingly, parts of the gain can effectively be allocated between several companies depending on the shelter available in those companies.

The election must be made within two years of the end of X's accounting period in which the property is sold. For the election to be valid, it is necessary for the onward sale to the third party to be to a person not in the same group. Thus no election could be made where there is a sale to a foreign company in the same group. Where such a sale would give rise to a taxable gain, it may still be necessary to route this through any company in the group that may have capital losses available to offset against that gain.

Point 16.6: *There are restrictions on the use of losses within an acquired capital loss company.*

Anti-avoidance provisions can affect the availability of capital losses within a company. Under these, where a company has become a member of a group since 1 April 1987, any losses attributable to the pre-group period ('pre-entry losses') may not be offset against subsequent gains.

These provisions bite in two ways:

(a) If a company already had realised but unused capital losses when it joined a group, those losses can only be offset against gains from property or other assets that the company owned on entry to the group. They cannot be offset against gains on assets subsequently acquired – whether from the acquiring group or from non-group companies (*TCGA 1992, Sch 7A, paras 6 & 7*). Note that a company carrying on a trade can use its losses against assets acquired to be used in the same trade, but this would not apply to an investment situation.

(b) If the company owned an asset on entry to the group which is subsequently sold at a loss, the pre-entry element of the loss can only be used as for pre-entry losses in (a) above (*TCGA 1992, Sch 7A, para 1(2)(b)*).

The pre-entry element of the loss is calculated by time apportioning the total loss since acquisition (or 1 April 1987 if later). Alternatively, it is possible to elect to determine the pre-entry loss by reference to the market value of the asset at any time of entry to the group (*TCGA 1992, Sch 7A, para 5*). This election must be made within two years from the end of the accounting period in which the disposal is made.

These provisions were intended to stop companies sheltering capital gains by buying capital loss companies. However, they will apply in quite genuine commercial situations where groups may need to plan the matching of gains and losses more carefully.

If a group company has actual or potential capital losses, the question of whether or not it has become a group member since 1 April 1987 will be relevant. If it has, pre-entry losses per (a) and (b) above must be identified. These can only be matched with gains as mentioned above.

The rules contemplate the crystallisation of a pre-entry loss elsewhere in the group following a transfer of the asset. This would be similarly restricted. This makes it particularly important to identify pre-entry losses and assets on acquisition of a company.

A pre-entry asset can also include a further asset acquired subsequently which derives its value from the first asset (*TCGA 1992, Sch 7A, para 1(8)*).

There are also rules that prevent a company from offsetting losses against 'pre-entry' gains. In other words, if company A has realised capital losses or has unrealised capital losses on prospective disposals, it cannot buy company B which owns assets with unrealised capital gains and expect to use its losses against B's future gains (*TCGA 1992, Sch 7AA*).

Notwithstanding the rules in place designed to prevent use of capital loss vehicles, further anti-avoidance provisions were introduced with effect from 5 December 2005 designed to counter continuing exploitation of the previous rules (*TCGA 1992, ss 184A–F*).

The efficacy of the arrangements put in place prior to 5 December 2005 has been challenged by HM Revenue and Customs. At the time of writing, there have been two Special Commissioners' decisions with different outcomes. HMRC succeeded in preventing the use of the capital losses in *Five Oaks Properties Limited v Revenue and Customs Commissioners* [2006] STC (SCD) 769. However, in subsequent cases with similar technical issues, the taxpayer companies won their appeal against the HMRC determinations (*Limitgood Ltd v Revenue and Customs Commissioners; Prizedrome Limited v Revenue and Customs Commissioners* [SPC 612]).

Since, 5 December 2005, losses will not be allowed where there has been a change of ownership of a company and broadly there are arrangements designed to secure a tax advantage from tax losses which accrued before the change. There is, accordingly, a tax avoidance motive test which leaves little scope to defeat the rules through exploitation of any technical loophole (*TCGA 1992, ss 184A–F*).

CHAPTER 17 – PLANNING FOR LOSSES: TRANSFER OF PROPERTY TO A DEALING COMPANY

A capital loss can be converted into an income loss by the transfer of a property intra group from an investment to a dealing company.

Point 17.1

Certain points need to be watched in respect of any transfer to minimise the likelihood of challenge by HMRC.
Point 17.2

17 Planning for losses: transfer of investment property to a dealing company

Point 17.1: *Within a group, the existence of established property investment and dealing companies offers the possibility of converting capital losses into trading losses or capital gains into trading profits. The opportunity can be exploited where an investment property is transferred to a dealing company in a situation where the latter has acquired it as part of its trading stock for marketing and sale.*

An investment company transferring a property to a fellow group company would be treated as making a disposal at no gain/no loss for tax purposes (*TCGA 1992, s 171*). A dealing company acquiring the property will be deemed to have done so at the original base cost to the group. On appropriation to trading stock the dealing company has a choice of two alternative values to apply on the transfer of the property into trading stock:

(a) market value (*TCGA 1992, s 161(1)*); or
(b) market value as reduced by any chargeable gain arising or increased by any chargeable loss (election under *TCGA 1992, s 161(3)*).

The election possibility under option (a) can be useful where the sale of an investment property might otherwise give rise to a capital loss. Its effect is to turn the capital loss into a trading loss, which will either be realised on sale or recognised at the end of the accounting period when the property must be written down to market value to comply with generally accepted accounting practice.

A trading loss in most situations is potentially more useful than a capital loss. It can be used in any of the following ways:

(a) offset against the dealing company's taxable profits* arising in the same year;
(b) carried back against the dealing company's taxable profits* in the previous year (assuming the company carried on the trade in that year);
(c) offset against taxable profits* of any other 75% group member in the same year;
(d) carried forward against future profits of the same trade carried on by the dealing company.

* including non-trading income and gains.

The transfer of a property in this fashion could be considered where a capital loss might otherwise have arisen on a direct external sale.

Indexation allowance up to the point of appropriation can be deducted from any gain computed at that point. However, capital losses can no longer arise where the indexation allowance on disposal turns a gain into a loss for tax purposes. Nor can indexation allowance increase capital losses (see Chapter 12 on indexation).

A tax planning opportunity can also arise where there is an anticipated gain on the property. It may be that there is a dealing company within the group that has brought forward trading losses that can now only be carried forward and used against future trading profits in that company. If the property investment company were to sell the property to a third party directly, then any gain arising in that company would be taxable without any prospect of shelter from the past trading losses of the fellow group company.

If the property were transferred into the dealing company and then sold, the effect of the, *s 161(3)* election would be to convert a chargeable gain into a trading profit in the transferee company. The brought forward losses should be available to offset against this trading profit and any tax liability that would otherwise arise could be eliminated.

Although references above are to group situations, the election is also relevant where a company reclassifies a property in its own accounts and can also apply to individuals, partnerships and trustees. When planning on the above lines, consideration must be given to the comments in Point 17.2 below.

Note that no similar election is available where a property is appropriated the other way ie from trading stock to fixed assets. In that situation a taxable profit by reference to market value will arise at that point.

Point 17.2:   *Although the tax planning opportunities referred to in Point 17.1 above arise as a result of specific legislation, the implications of decisions in Furniss v Dawson and Coates v Arndale Properties Ltd have restricted their scope.*

In *Coates (Inspector of Taxes) v Arndale Properties Ltd* [1984] STC 637, there was an attempt to claim a substantial loss on an investment property as a trading loss, following its transfer from an investment company to a dealing company within the group. The property was subsequently transferred on to another group company within a short period. The House of Lords considered that the transaction was fiscally motivated and the only reason for the intra-group sale was to obtain a tax deduction. The Law Lords, accordingly, confirmed the Court of Appeal's view that the dealing company had not acquired the property in question as trading stock.

Notwithstanding the *Coates v Arndale* decision, a dealing company should still be able to acquire a property as trading stock from a fellow group member, but the following points should be adhered to:

(a) The transfer of the property into the dealing company should be made as soon as a decision is made to dispose of the property. If it is left until such time as a buyer is found, HMRC could ignore the transfer to the dealing company.

(b) The transferee company should actually be an established property dealing company with a history of dealing in a similar type of property.

(c) The dealing company should carry out the necessary marketing of the property and incur any further finance charges. Any conversion or rectification of the property prior to sale should be carried out by the dealing company.

(d) The eventual sale should be to a third party purchaser and not to another group company or connected party.

(e) For accounts purposes, the transfer consideration should be at a value which enables the dealing company to make a commercial profit. This will be adjusted in the tax computations since the figure determined in accordance with *TCGA 1992, s 161(3)* (see Point 17.1 above) will be adopted as cost for tax purposes.

The judgment of the Court of Appeal in *New Angel Court Ltd v Adam* [2004] STC 779, confirms this advice. The judges held that the fact that a group of companies wished to obtain a tax advantage was not relevant in deciding whether an asset is acquired as trading stock. What matters is whether there is a trading purpose or not. If the properties transferred to the dealing company were assets of a kind that were sold in the ordinary course of the dealing company's trade and were acquired by that company for the purposes of its trade, that was sufficient. Also, the commercial rationale for the transfer is important in the context of stamp duty land tax where the rules could deny the intra-group exemption for tax motivated transfers.

CHAPTER 18 – VAT PLANNING FOR PROPERTY INVESTORS

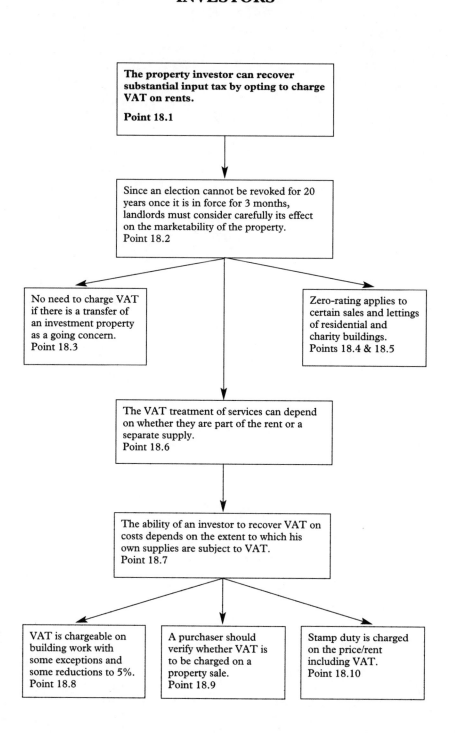

The property investor can recover substantial input tax by opting to charge VAT on rents.

Point 18.1

Since an election cannot be revoked for 20 years once it is in force for 3 months, landlords must consider carefully its effect on the marketability of the property.
Point 18.2

No need to charge VAT if there is a transfer of an investment property as a going concern.
Point 18.3

Zero-rating applies to certain sales and lettings of residential and charity buildings.
Points 18.4 & 18.5

The VAT treatment of services can depend on whether they are part of the rent or a separate supply.
Point 18.6

The ability of an investor to recover VAT on costs depends on the extent to which his own supplies are subject to VAT.
Point 18.7

VAT is chargeable on building work with some exceptions and some reductions to 5%.
Point 18.8

A purchaser should verify whether VAT is to be charged on a property sale.
Point 18.9

Stamp duty is charged on the price/rent including VAT.
Point 18.10

18 VAT planning for property investors

Point 18.1: *The property investor can recover substantial input tax by opting to charge VAT on rents.*

The letting of property is normally an exempt supply for VAT purposes although there are exceptions in certain situations, including where leases are granted for residential property or property used for charitable purposes (see Point 18.4 below).

The implication for a property investor of having exempt supplies is that no related input tax can be recovered. Accordingly, a property investor has to bear the additional VAT cost of any refurbishment or repair work together with any ongoing professional and agents' costs.

A property investor can, however, waive the exemption from VAT on a commercial building at any time. In doing so, it is opting to apply VAT to future rents, grants of leases and sales in relation to that building. In that case, any input tax attributable to the taxable supply would be recoverable from HMRC.

The election can be made by:

- naming individual buildings; or
- opting for all of the elector's buildings without naming them; or
- opting for all the elector's buildings with specially named exceptions; or
- opting for all of the elector's buildings, together with any that he subsequently acquires.

In the case of land, the election can be made for specified land. There are special rules for agricultural land.

There are situations in which an election cannot be made. These are:

- Where a building or part of a building is used as a dwelling or for a 'relevant residential purpose' (see Point 18.4 below).
- Where the building or part of the building is used by a charity for its charitable activities. This does not include property used by a charity for business purposes or an office used by a charity (whether or not in conjunction with a business activity).
- Where land is let to an individual who intends to construct a dwelling on the land or let to a registered housing association.

Sometimes, HMRC must give their express permission before an election to waive exemption can be made. This applies where there have been exempt sales in relation to the property.

Where a property investor owns a property which is divided into units such as a shopping precinct or parade or other commercial complex, one election must cover all the units let therein.

Any election made for agricultural land (including buildings on that land) no longer applies automatically to any adjoining agricultural land owned by the property investor.

As mentioned above, the option to waive the exemption can be made at any time. HMRC do require written notice within 30 days of the effective date.

Where VAT has been incurred on the purchase of a property or on its refurbishment, it is advisable that any letting or grant of a lease immediately after that should be on a fully taxable basis (ie the exemption should be waived). Otherwise there may be no immediate entitlement to recover VAT. If the letting of the property is subsequently made subject to VAT an entitlement to recover VAT will commence under the Capital Goods Scheme. However, VAT recovery will be spread over ten years. See Point 39.7 for a discussion on the Capital Goods Scheme.

The election will apply to any supply involving that property. Accordingly, the property investor must charge VAT on any future sales of the property or grants of further leases in addition to charging VAT on all future rentals.

An election can be revoked but only within three months of its coming into effect or after 20 years.

Point 18.2: *Since an election cannot be revoked for 20 years once it is in force for three months, landlords must consider carefully its effect on the marketability of the property.*

As indicated in Point 18.1 above, the attraction of opting to tax rents is that the property investor can recover input tax on expenditure incurred. However, it may be important to consider the impact of this on future tenants and purchasers of the property.

Where a tenant is a VAT-registered business with fully taxable supplies then that tenant will be entitled to recover all VAT on rents charged. However, there are a number of businesses and organisations with exempt or partly exempt supplies for VAT purposes which will not be in a position to recover fully the VAT. These include banks, buildings societies, betting shops, foreign exchange shops, and insurance brokers. National Health Service Trusts and charities may also be unable to reclaim VAT input tax depending on how they use the premises in question.

Such prospective tenants will attempt to resist the additional rent costs arising from irrecoverable VAT if they can. If the bargaining position of the tenant is strong enough, any property investor that has opted to charge VAT may find that there must be a compensating reduction in the rent charged.

Some leases may specify that VAT cannot be charged or that the rent is inclusive of any VAT. In those circumstances, any waiver of the exemption will shift the burden of tax from the tenant to the landlord.

Apart from the loss of income in these situations, the property investor will also be faced with a reduced capital value of the property asset.

Point 18.3: *The need to charge VAT on the sale of an elected property is avoided where it is a transfer of an investment business as a going concern.*

There is a useful relief in the VAT system which was drafted to facilitate transfers of businesses without VAT consequence but which can be applied to property situations.

Certain transfers of business assets are outside the scope of VAT. Where this is relevant, VAT cannot be charged on the sale. This is quite advantageous to a purchaser who may not otherwise have been in a position to recover all the VAT incurred. It could also be helpful to a seller who may want to avoid an exempt sale which could impact on his own VAT recovery.

The relief is available where there are sales of assets in connection with a transfer of a business as a going concern ('TOGC'). The necessary conditions for this relief are:

(a) The assets are to be used by the buyer in carrying out the same kind of business, whether or not as part of an existing business, as they were used in by the transferor.
(b) The buyer is either already registered for VAT or immediately becomes registered at the time of the transfer. The buyer does not have to be registered if the supplies being made are exempt or below the VAT annual threshold.
(c) If part of a business is being transferred, that must be capable of separate operation.
(d) If the vendor has opted to tax an investment property, the buyer must notify HM Customs, before the time of supply, that it also has opted to tax.

(*Value Added Tax (Special Provisions) Order 1995, SI 1995/1268, article 5(2)*).

The above rules can benefit property investors because property investment is regarded as a business for VAT purposes. Each property within that portfolio is a part of that business capable of being operated as a separate business by the purchaser. A let or partly let property can, therefore, be sold by one investor to another outside the scope of VAT.

An unlet building would not normally qualify under these rules as the business has not been commenced unless a vacant period between lettings by the transferor is involved. The situation may be different if a partly completed building being developed is sold in the course of that development to a buyer who carries on the activity. That could be treated as a sale of the property as a going concern (*Golden Oak Partnership v C & E Comrs* (1992) VAT decision 7212).

Where the tenant is a member of the same VAT group as the landlord, the letting is not treated as a business. Therefore, any sale where the tenant is in the same group as either the seller or the purchaser cannot be a TOGC.

A sale which is outside the scope of VAT is not an exempt supply. It should not, therefore, give rise to any clawback of VAT input tax previously claimed by the seller. However, if the seller did not make any taxable supplies at all in relation to the property, HMRC may seek to argue that the input tax should not have been recovered in the first place.

In 2004 anti-avoidance legislation relating to this type of property transaction was introduced. They target certain VAT avoidance schemes that use the above rules to reduce VAT costs for businesses who cannot recover all the VAT they incur. Where relevant, these rules can both render the sale VATable and simultaneously block VAT recovery for the transferee. They can also create a VAT charge in some situations where shares in a company owning a property are purchased, rather than just the asset itself. As described above, the aim of the legislation is to prevent a VAT free transfer and at the same time deny the purchaser input tax recovery where the rules apply.

Before a transfer can be treated as a VAT-free TOGC, a purchaser is required to make a declaration to the vendor to confirm that its subsequent supplies of the land by the purchaser will not be exempt from VAT. An abuse that this is aimed at is where, say, a holding company buys a property with the intention of waiving the VAT exemption but will be on-letting intra group to a VAT exempt or partially exempt tenant.

These rules are intended to affect only those entities that are participating in VAT evasion arrangements. Essentially the legislation will have an impact where the land or property concerned is a capital item for VAT purposes and any election to waive exemption by the purchaser would be disapplied under existing legislation.

As well as the potential impact on property purchasers, this is also an important issue for vendors because it creates a need to acquire additional information from the purchaser before a VAT-free transfer can be made.

Point 18.4:   *Zero-rating will still apply to sales and lettings of certain new buildings thus avoiding potentially irrecoverable VAT on construction expenditure.*

As mentioned in Point 18.1 above, zero-rating applies in certain situations involving residential property and buildings used by charities.

Eligibility for zero-rating arises in the following cases:

- Where a person has constructed a new building in which a major interest is granted and which is designed for use as a dwelling or for a 'relevant residential' or a 'relevant charitable' purpose.
- There is also a similar treatment if there has been a substantial reconstruction of a protected building (Point 18.5 below). The zero-rating applies to the construction work carried out providing this amounts to 'approved alterations' under the *Planning (Listed Buildings and Conservation Areas) Act 1990, s 6(2)*. It also applies to the initial receipt (ie rent, premium or other consideration) received by the investor from the grant of a major interest in that property by the person constructing it.
- Where a non-residential building is converted into one designed as a dwelling or dwellings. Zero-rating applies to the first grant, assignment or surrender of a major interest by the converter of the building.
- A non-residential building is converted into one intended for use for relevant residential or charitable purposes. Zero-rating similarly applies as for dwellings mentioned above.
- First sale of certain renovated houses.

A major interest for this purpose would be a freehold or grant of a lease in excess of 21 years.

Conversion does not necessarily include refurbishing, altering, extending or reconstructing a building. Furthermore, grants of interests on buildings that have been converted from one type of residential use to another will not qualify.

Use for 'relevant residential purpose' includes use as:

(1) A home or other institution providing residential accommodation for children.
(2) A home or other institution providing residential accommodation with personal care for persons in need of such care by reason of old age, disablement, past or present dependence on alcohol or drugs or mental disorder.
(3) A hospice.
(4) Residential accommodation for students or school pupils.
(5) Residential accommodation for members of any of the armed forces.
(6) A monastery, nunnery or similar establishment.
(7) An institution which is the sole or main residence of at least 90% of its residents.

Use as a hospital, prison or other similar institution does not constitute a relevant residential purpose. Nor would a hotel, inn or similar establishment. Use for a 'relevant charitable purpose' means use by a charity otherwise than in the course or furtherance of a business. It specifically includes, however, use of a property by a charity as a village hall or similar building providing social or recreational facilities for a local community.

To obtain zero-rating, the investor must have commissioned the construction of the building and exercised a measure of control over building, design and planning.

The principal advantage to a property investor of satisfying the conditions for zero-rating is the fact that no VAT is charged on building work. The nature of construction costs and construction work for this purpose is discussed in Point 18.8 below.

Whilst a property investor would be able to recover any input tax incurred on the construction of a dwelling, relevant residential or charitable building, any ongoing costs would not be recoverable as they will relate to exempt supplies. The property investor can no longer recover input tax relating to future repairs or agent's costs for example.

A further point is that only the first receipt will be treated as zero-rated. If a premium is charged in respect of a major interest, eg a 25-year lease, then that will be zero-rated and any subsequent rents would be exempt. If no premium is charged, then the first rental payment only in respect of a lease of over 21 years would be zero-rated.

The first freehold sale by the 'person constructing', the 'person substantially reconstructing' or the 'person converting' as the case may be is zero-rated.

Where any property is both used for a qualifying residential/charitable purpose and has other commercial uses, then the building work will be apportioned between the parts.

Point 18.5:   *Where the property is a protected building used for relevant residential or charitable purposes, or there is a conversion of a building to residential use, zero-rating may still apply if the investor has carried out work amounting to a 'substantial reconstruction'.*

The zero-rating of construction work or the first 'supply' as discussed in Point 18.4 above generally only applies where there is a complete construction of a new building. The requirement is, however, modified in the case of protected buildings.

As a matter of public policy, a number of buildings are protected from demolition for conservation reasons. These buildings are listed by the Department of the Environment, Food and Rural Affairs and by local authorities where they are considered to have continuing historical and architectural interest.

Where buildings and monuments are listed, building work is often prohibited in so far as it affects the façade together with any external features of architectural or historical significance. In addition to planning permission, listed building consent is often also required for specific building work and this could well vary from building to building.

If the building is used as a dwelling or for relevant residential or charitable use, zero-rating will apply where the person granting or selling a major interest in the protected building has carried out or commissioned works of 'substantial reconstruction'. The position as set out in the HMRC VAT Notice 708 under paragraph 10.3 is as follows:

Is the protected building being 'substantially reconstructed'?

A protected building is substantially reconstructed when major work takes place to its fabric, including the replacement of much of the internal or external structure, and either:

– at least 60 per cent of the total cost of the reconstruction (including materials and other items to carry out the work but excluding the services of an architect, surveyor or other person acting as consultant or in a supervisory capacity) could be zero-rated as 'approved alterations' [see section 9.4]; or

– the reconstruction involves 'gutting' the building – that is no more of the original building is retained than an external wall or walls, or external walls together with other external features of architectural or historic interest.

The notice goes on to say:

Apportionment for qualifying parts of buildings

If you sell or let a reconstructed building on a long lease and only part of it will be used for a qualifying purpose, then you must apportion your charge.

Whether or not work amounts to a substantial reconstruction is clearly critical to the VAT status. If the project satisfies this test then the building work will be zero-rated and any VAT on other construction-related costs can be reclaimed. If not, the building work will be standard-rated.

As mentioned in Point 18.4 above only the first grant of a major interest by the person substantially reconstructing will be zero-rated. Furthermore, VAT is only recoverable on the reconstruction expenditure and not on any ongoing costs.

The question whether a project is a substantial reconstruction is a difficult area for the tax specialist alone to comment on. Very often this may be a matter which must be discussed between tax advisers, surveyors and architects at the planning stage before a project can be commenced with any certainty that zero-rating might apply.

Point 18.6: *Where services are provided by a landlord, they may be treated as part of the rent or as a separate supply of services. The best treatment from the landlord's viewpoint may depend on whether the rent charge is standard-rated.*

If a landlord provides services or facilities, the VAT implications will have to be considered. This is a difficult area where HMRC practice has tended to prevail. In this connection, HMRC distinguish between two categories of service provision, ie:

(1)   Normal services provided under the lease for which all tenants pay in addition to the rent. Whether or not separate charges are made for these, they are regarded as part of the consideration for the grant of a lease. If this consideration is exempt, charges in respect of these services will be exempt. If the consideration is standard-rated, these charges will be standard-rated (see HMRC Notice 742, section 11 *et seq*). Typically, such services include cleaning, maintenance, repairs and insurance.

(2)   Services provided separately to individual tenants and for which different charges may be involved depending on usage. This may involve heating, lighting, telephone and fax. The range of services will be greater for serviced offices and certain residential accommodation, possibly including receptionist, secretarial and computer facilities. As separate supplies, these are all standard-rated.

Where a landlord has waived the VAT exemption and is letting to commercial tenants, VAT will be charged on rents in either scenario so the treatment is of little consequence. The landlord will still be able to fully recover input tax.

The main impact of the distinction lies where the landlord has not waived the exemption. In that case, services provided in category 1 will give rise to additional exempt outputs. If the landlord is incurring VAT on supplies it receives, that VAT is irrecoverable.

A way around this might be to arrange for a separate management company to render the services. If that company is registered for VAT, it will be able to charge VAT on the services and recover the input tax it itself incurs.

See Point 18.7 below for a further discussion on recovering input tax.

Point 18.7:   *If a property investor's supplies are all exempt then no input tax can be recovered. If, on the other hand, supplies are partly standard-rated and partly exempt, input tax will be attributed as far as possible to the related supply (including future supplies) and will be recoverable or irrecoverable accordingly.*

The position on the recovery of input tax can be summarised as follows:

(a)   inputs directly attributable to taxable supplies can be reclaimed in full;

(b)   inputs which are directly attributable to exempt supplies are normally irrecoverable;

(c)   input tax which is common to the business generally (eg overheads) should be apportioned on a reasonable basis between exempt and taxable supplies to determine the recoverable element.

This approach does give rise to some important VAT implications for property investors. In the first place, it will be noted that inputs should be associated as far as possible with related supplies. For the property investor, this may mean looking at each property separately. If rents or premiums received in respect of a particular building are standard-rated, then all input tax relating specifically to that building, eg on repair work or management fees, should be recoverable. Similarly, if a building is generating exempt supplies, then all the related input tax is irrecoverable.

Where the option to tax rents is exercised (see Point 18.1 above) input tax can be recovered. Where a new building is constructed and zero-rating will partly apply (because the property is partly residential, for instance) then if the remainder of the property will give rise to exempt supplies an apportionment will be necessary.

HMRC have clarified the rules for VAT recovery in the case of intended developments and speculative property investors in Business Brief 14/04 dated 14 May 2004.

For intended transactions, HMRC would previously only allow VAT recovery where the property developer or investor had actually notified an option to tax to Customs. Only then was the intention to make taxable supplies clear. HMRC now accept that a taxpayer can have an intention to make taxable supplies before an option is in place, although clear documentary evidence of this intention is essential. Of course, the best documentary evidence is still a valid option to tax notification letter.

For speculative property transactions, HMRC have confirmed that VAT on initial costs can be treated firstly as an overhead of the business. Once the nature of the project is determined, suitable adjustments to VAT recovery can be made. It follows that claims may be appropriate where VAT has been attributed incorrectly in the past.

HMRC may agree an alternative method of apportionment if it produces a fair and reasonable result.

There are *de minimis* limits below which there will be no restriction in VAT input recovery. In this connection, input tax which relates directly or indirectly to exempt supplies will be recoverable if it is less than £625 a month on average and it does not exceed 50% of all the input for that period (VAT Regulations 1995, Reg 106).

Point 18.8: *Where new property is being built for either residential or charitable use or where there is a conversion from non-residential use, VAT should not be charged on most of the construction cost. Other building work will be standard-rated or subject to VAT at 5%.*

As mentioned in Points 18.4 and 18.5 above, certain building work in connection with new residential property or property used for charitable purposes will be zero-rated.

Building work, including work on qualifying properties, will be standard-rated unless it falls in one of the following categories:

(a)   supplies of services in the course of the construction of a building (or part of a building) designed as a dwelling or number of dwellings (*VATA 1994, Sch 8, Group 5, Item 2(a)*);

(b)   supplies of services in the course of the construction of a building (or part of a building) intended for use solely as a dwelling or for a 'relevant residential purpose' or a 'relevant charitable purpose' (*VATA 1994, Sch 8, Group 5, Item 2(a)*). See Point 18.4 above for relevant residential and charitable use;

(c)   'approved alterations' to a protected building designed to remain as or became a dwelling or number of dwellings or intended for use solely for a 'relevant residential purpose' or a 'relevant charitable purpose' after the reconstruction or alteration (*VATA 1994, Sch 8, Group 6, Item 2*). See Point 18.5 above for a discussion on protected buildings;

(d)   supplies or services in the course of the construction of any civil engineering work necessary for the development of a permanent park for residential caravans (*VATA 1994, Sch 8, Group 5, Item 2(b)*).

In addition, building work for a 'relevant housing association' which involves the conversion of a non-residential building or part of a non-residential building for residential use can also be zero-rated (*VATA 1994, Sch 8, Group 5, Item 3(a), (b)*).

In each case, the services of an architect, surveyor or any person acting as consultant or in a supervisory capacity are standard-rated unless subsumed into a 'Design and Build' contract.

A certificate must be produced to the builder stating the extent to which the building is to be used for relevant residential or charitable purposes. Sample certificates are illustrated in the HMRC Notice 708 'Buildings and Construction'.

The question of whether or not the construction of a new building (or substantial reconstruction of a protected building) has taken place is crucial to the issue of whether VAT is charged upon the building work. HMRC have issued guidelines in their Notice 708. These summarise their views on the position and are set out below:

A zero-rated building is constructed when the following applies:

1.   It is designed as a dwelling or number of dwellings, it is built from scratch, and, before work starts, any pre-existing building is demolished completely to ground level. Cellars, basements and the 'slab' at ground level may be retained.

2.   The new building, which is intended for use solely for a relevant residential or charitable purpose, makes use of no more than a single façade (or a double facade on a corner site) of a pre-existing building. The pre-existing building is demolished completely (other than the retained facade) before work on the new building is started and the facade is retained as an explicit condition or requirement of statutory planning consent.

3. A semi-detached building is built intended for use solely for a relevant charitable purpose.

4. An existing building is enlarged or extended and the enlargement or extension creates an additional dwelling or dwellings.

5. An annexe to an existing building is built and it is intended the annexe, or a part of it, be used solely for a relevant charitable purpose.

6. A garage is built, or a building is converted into a garage and it is constructed or converted at the same time as, and intended to be occupied with, a building designed as a dwelling or number of dwellings.

7. A building is built that is one of a number of buildings constructed at the same time on the same site and it is intended to be used together with those other buildings as a unit solely for a relevant residential purpose

(HMRC VAT Notice 708 Buildings and Construction, section 3.2).

The notice gives common examples of work you cannot zero-rate such as:

- a 'granny' annexe which cannot be used, or disposed of, separately from a main house;
- a detached enclosed swimming pool in the grounds of a new house;
- a detached building in the grounds of an existing care home which extends the facilities of the home.

There are also notes on determining the position where party walls are involved. For instance, in determining whether a building has been demolished, you can ignore the retention of party walls forming part of a neighbouring property that is not being developed. Therefore, a building is constructed when there is an infill in a row of terraced houses provided the pre-existing houses are demolished completely (apart from the party walls at the end of the infill site) and any retained facade is retained as a condition or requirement of planning consent.

When redeveloping neighbouring houses in a terrace, the party wall between the houses being redeveloped will also need to be demolished before there is the construction of a building for VAT purposes.

The enlargement of, or extension to, an existing building can be zero-rated to the extent that the extension or enlargement contains an additional dwelling provided:

- the new dwelling is wholly within the enlargement or extension; and
- the dwelling is 'designed as a dwelling'.

So, for example, a new eligible flat built on top of an existing building can be zero-rated.

If the new dwelling is partly or wholly contained within the existing building, work cannot be zero-rated under these rules. It may be possible to reduce the rate of charge as a 'changed number of dwellings conversion' (see section 7 of Notice 708). Also, the sale or long lease of the new dwelling may be able to be zero-rated as a converted non-residential building (Section 5 of Notice 708).

(HMRC VAT Notice 708 Buildings and Construction, section 3.2).

Any departure from these guidelines must be on the expectation that HMRC will take a different view, leaving the investor to challenge the position through the courts. A prudent builder will always charge VAT at the standard rate where a possible liability is suspected. Since 1 June 2002, building work on an annex used by a charity is only standard rated to the extent that some or all of it is used for business purposes. Previously, all work was standard rated if there was any element of business use.

Since 11 May 2001, the following supplies have been chargeable at the reduced rate of 5%:

(a)   converting a non-residential property into one or more single-household dwellings;

(b)   changing the number of single-household dwellings in a building;

(c)   converting a single-household dwelling or a house in multiple occupation into a care home or for other qualifying residential use;

(d)   converting a house in multiple occupation into a single-household dwelling;

(e)   converting a single-household dwelling into a house in multiple occupation;

(f)   services supplied in the course of renovating a single-household dwelling that has remained empty for at least three years;

(g)   building materials and certain other goods incorporated by a builder into a building in the course of supplying services under (a) and (b) above.

A single-household dwelling is a dwelling intended for occupation by a single household (ie a single individual, a couple or a family).

The following situations have also been subject to the reduced rate since 1 June 2002:

(a)   converting a non-residential property into a care home (or other qualifying building used solely for a 'relevant residential' purpose);

(b)   converting a non-residential property into a multiple occupancy dwelling, such as bed-sit accommodation;

(c)   converting a building used for a 'relevant residential' purpose into a multiple occupancy dwelling;

(d)   renovating or altering a care home (or other qualifying building used solely for a 'relevant residential' purpose), that has not been lived in for three years or more;

(e)   renovating or altering a multiple occupancy dwelling that has not been lived in for three years or more; and

(f)   constructing, renovating or converting a building into a garage as part of the renovation of a property that qualifies for the reduced rate.

The reduced rate can also apply to certain grant-funded heating installations and energy saving materials.

Point 18.9: *Before entering into an agreement to acquire a property, a purchaser should verify whether VAT is to be charged.*

An investor negotiating the purchase of a property may need to take into account the possibility that VAT will also have to be paid on the agreed price. This is likely to be the case in three situations:

(a) Where a new freehold building is acquired within three years of completion. In this case, VAT at the standard rate is chargeable by the vendor unless the 'going concern' rules apply (see Points 26.1 and 26.4).

(b) The vendor had waived the exemption in the course of letting the property. As stated in Point 18.1 above, the option to tax can be revoked within three months of its coming into effect. The next opportunity to do so will be 20 years after the waiver came into effect. In the meantime, VAT must also be charged by the person who opted to tax his interest on any subsequent sales or grants of interests in the property unless the sale is part of a transfer of a business as a going concern (see Point 18.3 above).

(c) The vendor may be a developer or dealer that opts to charge VAT before making what would otherwise be an exempt sale. The vendor could be concerned in this instance to recover VAT that may have been incurred on the acquisition of the property and any building work carried out.

If the purchaser intends to charge VAT on the letting of the property once it is acquired, there may be no financial consequence of having to pay VAT on the purchase. In such a case, the investor would want to give immediate notification to HMRC of the intention to tax rents to ensure that it will be able to reclaim the input tax.

Where there is no intention to opt to tax rents, any VAT incurred on the purchase will represent a significant additional cost of purchasing the property.

Even where the investor is in a position to reclaim all the VAT, it could take two to three months to recover the tax from HMRC. For a £5 million purchase, therefore, the buyer will need additional funding of £875,000 for that period and should be prepared to incur finance charges accordingly.

As mentioned above and in Point 18.3, some sales will be outside the scope of VAT as transfers in the course of a transfer of a business as a going concern. No VAT should be charged, or paid where this applies.

Point 18.10: *Stamp duty land tax is charged on the VAT-inclusive price of a property. In the case of a lease grant, extra SDLT can arise if the letting is subject to VAT.*

Stamp duty land tax (SDLT) is a tax paid by the purchaser of a property or an incoming lessee on the grant of a new lease.

In the case of a purchase of a freehold or a lease, the duty is payable on the purchase price paid including any VAT which is chargeable. If no election has been made to waive the exemption on the property, and the sale is completed without VAT arising, there is a corresponding saving in SDLT.

With regard to grants of leases, the position is somewhat different. In these cases, the SDLT liability depends on the length of the lease and the rent passing. If the exemption has been waived in respect of the rent, SDLT is assessed on the rent plus VAT.

This can be avoided if there is a specific prohibition in the lease on the landlord charging VAT.

See also Point 5.3 on SDLT and VAT.

Part B Property Dealers and Developers

CHAPTER 19 – TAX RELIEF FOR REDUCTIONS IN PROPERTY VALUES

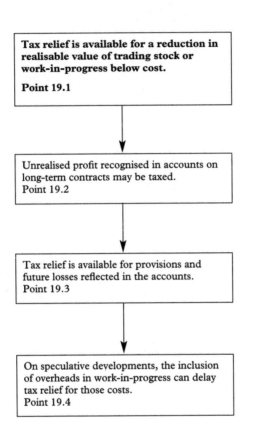

Tax relief is available for a reduction in realisable value of trading stock or work-in-progress below cost.

Point 19.1

Unrealised profit recognised in accounts on long-term contracts may be taxed.
Point 19.2

Tax relief is available for provisions and future losses reflected in the accounts.
Point 19.3

On speculative developments, the inclusion of overheads in work-in-progress can delay tax relief for those costs.
Point 19.4

19 Tax relief for reductions in property values

Point 19.1: *If at the end of an accounting period the market values of particular properties are lower than their cost, a provision to reduce the cost to net realisable value should be allowable for tax purposes.*

The profits of a trade for tax purposes are those which, subject to adjustments required by law, are computed in accordance with generally accepted accounting practice. This may involve UK or international financial reporting standards depending on the entity in question and the choice of accounting method (*FA 1998, s 42/ITTOIA 2005, s 25*).

The proper valuation of trading stock for accounting purposes, other than long-term construction work-in-progress (see Point 19.2 below) is the lower of cost and net realisable value (ie market value less selling costs). This is a test which should be applied to each individual property rather than globally (see *IRC v Cock, Russell & Co Ltd* (1949) 29 TC 387).

Where the market value of a property forming part of trading stock is below cost, the lower value should be reflected in the accounts. The drop in value will, therefore, need to be provided for and this stock provision will reduce taxable profits accordingly.

In such instances, tax relief is effectively available on an unrealised loss. If the property subsequently recovers its value, then the loss will be reversed in a later period. In the meantime, there will have been a deferral of the earlier period's tax liability. The reversal can only bring the carrying value of the asset to cost and cannot result in any excess being taxed at that point. For accounting and tax reasons, therefore, it is important to recognise losses on trading stock as early as possible.

Point 19.2: *Unrealised profit may have to be recognised on a long-term construction project to comply with accounting standards and this profit is taxable.*

The valuation principle of 'lower of cost and market value' does not necessarily apply to work-in-progress in the course of a long-term contract. 'Long-term' contracts are those which start and finish in different accounting periods.

According to the Statement of Standard Accounting Practice on stock and work-in-progress (SSAP 9), an appropriate proportion of accrued profit on long-term contracts must be recognised as soon as work is sufficiently advanced for a likely profit to be determined. If at the end of an accounting period a project is, say, three-quarters complete, any projected profit on the contract should be estimated at that stage and three-quarters of this reflected in the accounts. With accounts being prepared several months after the year end, the company and its auditors will often have the benefit of hindsight in arriving at such estimates.

SSAP 9 may dictate what is acceptable for the preparation of accounts but does this mean that HMRC are entitled to tax profit on this basis?

It is an established principle of tax law that profit cannot be taxed until realised (*Willingale v International Commercial Bank Ltd* [1978] STC 75; *BSC Footwear Ltd v Ridgeway* (1971) 47 TC 495). However, in HMRC's view, the valuation of long-term work-in-progress under SSAP 9 involves the recognition of profit which has been realised at the balance sheet date (following *Pearce v Woodall-Duckham Ltd* (1978) 51 TC 271). Since 6 April 1999, tax law has explicitly required the profits of a trade, profession or vocation to be computed for tax purposes in accordance with generally accepted accounting practice (GAAP) or International Accounting Standards (IAS) where appropriate, subject to any adjustment then required by tax law (eg disallowance of depreciation and so on) (*FA 1998, s 42*). Generally, therefore, if the accounts recognise a profit, that profit is also recognised for tax purposes. By the same token, if GAAP or IAS requires a loss to be recognised before it is incurred, that loss should also be recognised for tax. See Point 19.3 below.

Point 19.3:   *HMRC allow relief for anticipated losses.*

It is certainly prudent accounting practice to reflect losses in accounts as early as possible. For example, under SSAP 9, a loss on a contract should be recognised in full once foreseeable and the work-in-progress valuation reduced to net realisable value for balance sheet purposes. For contracts which are likely to absorb a considerable part of the company's capacity in future periods, the work-in-progress should be further reduced for estimated administration overheads to be incurred.

In the past, HMRC believed there was a rule of tax law that neither profit nor loss could be anticipated. In their view, this overrode UK generally accepted accounting practice (GAAP) if the application of GAAP resulted in the anticipation of a profit or loss.

HMRC was forced to change their minds on this following the decision in *Herbert Smith v Honour* [1999] STC 173. This is now a leading case on the interaction between tax law and accounting practice. It concerns the allowability of a provision made where an existing contract becomes onerous. In the *Herbert Smith* case, it was a lease on vacant business premises. The judge held that:

1.   it was not open to the Revenue to replace a treatment which accorded with GAAP – and indeed was the only such treatment – with one that did not;

2.   there was no general rule of law that prohibited provisions made on the grounds of prudence, where the provision was required by GAAP.

In view of this decision, HMRC announced in a press release on 20 July 1999 that they now accept that there is no tax rule which denies provisions for anticipated losses or expenses.

This position is clearly reflected in the HMRC Business Income Manual, which states:

> *Herbert Smith* establishes that where accounts are drawn up on generally accepted accountancy principles there is no overriding rule of tax law which denies relief for losses or expenses which will only be paid in the future. (para BIM 11090)

Now provisions are allowable so long as:

*   they are in respect of allowable revenue expenditure;
*   they are required by GAAP (or IAS);
*   they are estimated with sufficient accuracy;
*   they do not conflict with any specific tax rule as to whether the expense is allowable or governing the time at which the expenditure is allowed.

With regard to the last point, this would prevent deduction for relief for instance for employee/director's remuneration payable more than nine months after the year end (HMRC Bulletin 44, December 1999).

Point 19.4:   *On speculative developments, the inclusion of indirect expenses in the cost of work-in-progress rather than charging them to profit and loss account will delay tax relief.*

Normally, profits on speculative developments will only be recognised when the property is sold. The proper treatment of direct costs attributable to the development is to debit them to work-in-progress. This would, therefore, include the cost of the land plus any direct labour and material used in the construction.

With regard to indirect costs, ie overheads and finance charges, there is a choice of treatment for the developer. They can be included in work-in-progress if they specifically relate to the development. Alternatively, they can be charged directly against profit.

If overheads and interest charges are included in work-in-progress in the balance sheet, no deduction is taken for these items in the profit and loss account until that stock is actually sold. If the developer has no taxable profits during the project period then there is no tax effect unless, in the case of a company which is a member of a group, there is potential for group relief surrender.

CHAPTER 20 – RECLASSIFICATION OF TRADING STOCK AS INVESTMENT PROPERTY

Reclassification of trading stock as a fixed asset may crystallise taxable income – or generate an allowable loss.

Point 20.1

Where a property is acquired and/or developed with the prospect of its being let for a number of years on completion, there are benefits to its being classified at the outset as an investment.
Point 20.2

20 Reclassification of trading stock as investment property

Point 20.1: *A reclassification of trading stock as a fixed asset or its transfer to an investment vehicle must be carefully considered as it will result in a tax liability on any unrealised gain on the property.*

If a property trading entity were to reclassify any of its properties as investments, there would be an immediate deemed disposal under *TCGA 1992, s 161*. As a result, a taxable trading profit would arise at that time by reference to the market value of the property. The tax would become payable even though the property had not been sold and no profit realised. Therefore, any individuals, partnerships or companies who reclassify a property in this manner could face an outflow of cash to pay a tax bill without any inflow of cash from the sale proceeds of the property. A similar problem would also arise if the properties are transferred to an investment entity, including the case of a transfer between two group companies.

Where a property has been acquired as trading stock, this classification will probably not be disturbed unless there is a formal decision by the proprietors/directors to change its status at any particular time.

The courts appear reluctant to accept that a property acquired as trading stock has ceased to be trading stock merely because it has been let for a number of years rather than sold (*J & C Oliver v Farnsworth* (1956) 37 TC 51; *Speck v Morton* (1972) 48 TC 476). For the court's attitude to deemed appropriation generally see *Taylor v Good* (1974) 49 TC 277 and *Simmons v IRC* (1980) 53 TC 461.

Trading stock should retain that classification, therefore, in the absence of any of the following actions:

(a) reclassification of the property in the balance sheet from trading stock to fixed assets; or

(b) transfer of the property out of a trading entity into an investment entity (this will also be the case if the transfer is between two companies in the same group – *TCGA 1992, s 173*); or

(c) formal resolution or board minute that the property in question is to be held as an investment.

Before any of the above actions are taken, it is important to consider if there is likely to be a tax liability by reference to the property's market value. Timing will also be relevant in the light of the possibility of any tax shelter (eg group relief, losses in year) in the year of appropriation.

Of course, if the market value is below carrying value at the time of appropriation this would give rise to a trading loss which can be set against other profits in the year or group relieved. Such a loss would arise in any event at the end of the accounting period (assuming the value remains depressed) by virtue of the accounting requirement to reduce carrying value to net realisable value – see 19.1 above.

On appropriation from trading stock to investment, no election is available to defer any tax on the gain as there is with the reclassification the other way round – see Chapter 17 above.

Point 20.2:   *Where a site is acquired on which it is intended to construct a property which will be retained for investment purposes, it could save future tax if the acquisition was made by an investment company rather than by a property trading entity.*

On acquisition, the future tax position may hang on how a property is classified. If it is treated as trading stock, then on a subsequent sale or appropriation the profit will be taxed as income. Sometimes substantial value may be added to a property during construction as a result of work carried out and increased property values. An appropriation of the property at the end of this period could be costly.

If it is recognised at the outset that any site in the process of acquisition is likely to be retained for some period, it may well be advisable to bring that property into an investment company, rather than a development company, from the start. This can have very positive advantages:

(a)   It removes the problem of appropriation to investment property in future. Within property groups there is often an incentive to classify investment properties as such since it improves the group's balance sheet and asset backing.

(b)   For companies, the cost of an investment property and subsequent improvement expenditure can be increased by an annual indexation allowance for tax purposes based on increases in the retail prices index (see Chapter 12).

(c)   With an investment property, the lessor would be entitled to claim capital allowances in respect of any element of plant and machinery included in the cost. This would not be the case for trading stock since any expenditure would not be 'capital expenditure' for capital allowances purposes. Once the property is appropriated, it would be possible to claim capital allowances but at that stage the market value of the fixed assets may have depreciated. Furthermore, if the property has been let before that date, the company may have lost an opportunity to claim capital allowances in an earlier period.

(d)   Finance costs debited to stock are not deducted until the sale of the property. In the case of investment property, costs can be deducted as incurred in line with accounts.

(e)   Up to 5 April 2008, where the property is owned by an individual or individuals, a gain on a sale of the property attracts a significant element of business asset taper relief if the property has been let to a trading entity for a reasonable period post development. The Government's 2007 Pre-Budget report included proposals to remove taper relief after 5 April 2008 although, following representations from interested parties, a more modest entitlement to claim this may be retained (see the 'Stop Press' note at the beginning of the book).

CHAPTER 21 – TAX PLANNING ON THE TRANSFER OF TRADING STOCK

> There may be tax planning opportunities in transferring a stock of properties from a property trading company to another property trading vehicle. If the parties are connected, they can elect for cost to apply, thus realising any profit in a more favourable entity.
>
> Point 21.1

21 Tax planning on the transfer of trading stock

Point 21.1: *The transfer of trade to an associated entity offers the opportunity of transferring trading profit to an entity with a lower tax rate, unless the trade is run by a company which is within the UK transfer pricing regime*

As a general rule, any trading stock sold or transferred to an entity must be at market value. This is a general principle laid down in *Sharkey v Wernher* (1955) 36 TC 275 and, subsequently, reinforced in *Skinner v Berry Head Lands Ltd* (1970) 46 TC 377. As a result of these cases, whenever the sale or transfer of stock does not arise in the course of a genuine commercial transaction, then market value must be substituted for the consideration actually paid.

There is an exception to the above rule where stock is disposed of on the cessation of a property dealing or development trade which is then carried on by another party. The transfer price for tax purposes depends on whether or not the two parties are connected (*TA 1988, s 100(1)/ITTOIA 2005, s 176*).

Where a property dealer or developer ceases trading and transfers stock to a connected entity which succeeds to the trade, the parties can elect for cost – or, if higher, the transfer price – to apply instead of market value (*TA 1988, s 100(1C)/ITTOIA 2005, s 178*). That value is brought in as the cost of the stock for tax purposes of the buyer (*TA 1988, s 100(1E)*). This election can only be made if cost and transfer price are both less than market value (*ITTOIA 2005, s 180*).

For a definition of connected parties see Point 3.17. Where the parties are not connected, any transfer price agreed between the parties is accepted as the sale price for tax purposes (*ICTA 1988, s 100(1A)*). If the property is sold at below cost, the seller will incur a loss which can be treated as a trading loss for tax purposes. This could lead to some useful tax planning except that it is most unlikely that a seller would be prepared to sell a property to an unconnected purchaser at below market value.

Where the seller and buyer are connected, there is no similar opportunity to crystallise a tax loss. However, there is the possibility to move a potentially taxable profit to an entity where there might be scope for shelter. Consider the following possibilities:

1. A partnership where the individuals pay tax at 40% might transfer to a company where the rate might only be 20% (ie the small companies rate – which is increasing to 21% in financial year 2008 and to 22% from financial year 2009).

2. A company might transfer the trade to a company which has trading losses that can shelter the gain.

3. The buying company, although trading in the UK, might enjoy a lower tax rate or nil rate of tax by virtue of being resident in a jurisdiction with a favourable tax treaty with the UK. For instance, an Isle of Man or Channel Islands company may pay no local tax on UK property trading profits at all following corporation tax reform in those jurisdictions. Within the EC, a Cyprus company may only pay tax at say 10%, on UK property trading profits. In each case, that is subject to the proviso that the company has no permanent establishment in the UK. Consideration may have to be given to the possible application of UK anti-avoidance rules (see Chapter 1 for further discussion of the anti-avoidance issues)

It should be borne in mind that the transfer of any assets at an undervalue might be construed as a distribution for tax purposes (*TA 1988, s 209(4)*). This could have income tax consequences notably for UK resident individuals and trustee shareholders of the transferring company.

There could also be implications for the transferring company under company or insolvency law particularly if it subsequently becomes insolvent.

An election for this paragraph to apply must be made no later than two years after the end of the chargeable period in which the trade ceases in the case of companies subject to corporation tax. For other trading entities the relevant deadline is 31 January following the income tax year.

Note that if the trade is carried on by an enterprise which is 'large' within the European Commission definition, any sales should be at market value to comply with our transfer pricing rules (*TA, Sch 28 para 1(2)*). The transfer pricing rules will override the provisions of, *s 100* in these situations (*TA, s 100 (1ZA)/ITTOIA 2005, s 173*). In cases of blatant tax avoidance, HMRC may also seek to apply the transfer pricing rules to smaller entities.

The House of Lords' decision in *Furniss (Inspector of Taxes) v Dawson* (1984) 55 TC 324 could provide authority for HMRC to consider whether the transfer of stock was merely a step in a series of predetermined transactions. However, HMRC might have difficulty in pursuing such an argument if there was a commercial reason for the cessation of trade and the transfer of stock. One such reason might be the desire to incorporate a trading activity. Another reason could be to centralise future property dealing situations within one particular company.

CHAPTER 22 – TAX RELIEF FOR FINANCE COSTS

Generally, finance costs will be fully deductible on the same basis as they are treated in the accounts.

Point 22.1

The expensing of finance costs rather than their inclusion in stock or work-in-progress accelerates their deduction for tax purposes.
Point 22.2

Watch debt releases in the hands of company borrowers as this can give rise to taxable income.
Point 22.3

Both individuals and companies can offset excess finance costs against other income and gains.
Point 22.4

A company's relief for delayed payments of interest may be deferred. This can offer tax planning possibilities.
Points 22.5 & 22.6

Tax relief for finance costs can be restricted if the arrangements are uncommercial or a company is thinly capitalised.
Point 22.7

Tax must be deducted from interest payments by individuals to non-residents and in some circumstances by companies.
Point 22.8

The introduction of rules for 'alternative finance' has improved tax relief for financing structures which are compliant with Islamic law.
Point 22.9

22 Tax relief for finance costs

Point 22.1: *Generally, all interest and other costs incurred on property finance from third parties will be fully tax deductible on the same basis as they are treated in the accounts.*

Finance costs are, generally speaking, deductible as trading expenses from taxable trading profits on the same basis as they are reflected in the accounts.

In the context of a property trader, the differences in the treatment of companies and individuals are less significant than with investors. As a general rule, any expenses and incidental costs related to finance are going to be deductible as trading expenses. However, there are some differences, which are mentioned in Points 22.3 to 22.8 below.

Foreign companies (which are not tax resident in the UK) trading in the UK through a permanent establishment would be subject to the same rules as any UK company. Therefore, a foreign company that is trading in the UK through a permanent establishment is subject to UK corporation tax on its profits. On the other hand, a foreign company which trades in the UK but does not have a permanent establishment here would be subject to UK basic rate income tax on those profits. A non-UK tax resident investment company, is similarly only subject to basic rate income tax on its property income.

The costs are deductible for tax purposes on the same basis as they are reflected in the accounts. The rules require interest or other expenses of a loan relationship to be brought into account only if they are recognised in determining the company's profit or loss for the accounting period concerned in accordance with generally accepted accounting practice (GAAP) or where relevant, International Accounting Standards (IAS). They will be recognised in this way if they are accounted for in the company's:

(i)   profit and loss account/income statement; or
(ii)   its statement of recognised gains and losses; or
(iii)   its statement of changes in equity; or
(iv)   in any other statement of items brought into account in computing its profits and losses,

except for those items recognised in order to correct a fundamental error (*FA 1996, ss 85A, 85B*).

In most cases, this will require the accounts to be drawn up under an amortised-cost basis (which is broadly similar to the previous accruals method).

These rules have been recast to apply to accounting periods beginning after 31 December 2004 to accommodate the adoption of international accounting standards. Previously, an authorised accounting method, normally the accruals method, had to be used.

The actual payment dates or due and payable dates do not themselves influence the timing of the deduction – other than for certain connected-party loans (see Point 22.5 below).

The amortised-cost basis (and the previous accruals method) would similarly apply where there are either stepped or 'balloon' payments of interest. This may mean smaller payments in earlier years and larger amounts later. For the payer, the effect would be to 'flatten' out the cost on an accruals basis with higher amounts tax relieved in the earlier years. A lender, on the other hand, would be taxed on accelerated income.

Borrowers will similarly receive relief for any discount paid on discounted securities on an accrued basis. At the extreme, where finance is provided by way of zero coupon loans, accrued interest will be allowed each year although the interest is not paid until the security is redeemed. An exception is where the holder of the security and the borrower are connected and the lender is not taxed on the accruals basis.

If the borrower and lender are connected, there are several issues such as the timing of the allowability of accrued costs where the interest payments are deferred (see Points 22.5 and 22.6 below).

A company is connected with another person in any accounting period if at any time in that period the other person is a company and:

(a)   one controls the other; or
(b)   both companies are under the control of the same person

(*FA 1996, s 87(3)*).

Control can be exercised by holding shares or otherwise possessing voting power. A person may also exercise control by means of any powers conferred on him by articles of association or any other documents (*FA 1996, s 87A*). In all cases, control means the power to secure that the affairs of the company are conducted in accordance with that person's wishes. In the case of a partnership involving one or more companies, the assumption is that any powers, rights or property vesting in the partnership can be exercised by the partners separately according to their profit-sharing ratio. Banks or financial traders are generally excluded, since control by shares or voting power is not taken into account if a sale of the shares would give rise to a trading receipt.

Point 22.2:   *If finance costs are expensed to the profit and loss account, tax relief is obtained earlier than if the costs are included in stock or work-in-progress in the balance sheet.*

The normal rule provides for a deduction for any finance costs that are charged to the profit and loss account. In such a case, costs that are included in the cost of trading stock in the balance sheet would not be allowed until the property is sold.

There is a specific allowance for capitalised finance costs of capital assets (see Point 3.11). This provision does not, however, help property traders and developers who include interest in the value of stock and work-in-progress in the balance sheet.

This may not be an issue where any loss crystallised by this accounting treatment of expensing costs is merely going to be carried forward. On the other hand, where the company or group has other current period taxable profits, the recognition of costs and losses in that period can shelter these. At worst, this improves cash flow. At best, it may be an opportunity to use losses now in the face of a possibility that there may not be profits in the future to use these against.

Point 22.3: *Watch debt releases in the hands of company borrowers as they can be taxed.*

In the same way that costs and expenses reflected in the profit and loss account are allowed for tax purposes, so will any credits be taxed under the debt rules for companies.

Distressed property situations have been resolved in the past by an arrangement between the lender and borrower under which some or all of the debt is forgiven. A credit to a company's profit and loss account as a result of such a release gives rise to taxable income if the parties are not connected. This can also be the case if the credit is directly to reserves.

See Point 3.13 in Chapter 3B for a further discussion on debt releases together with Point 3.14 on ways to get around the problem.

Point 22.4: *Where a borrower has raised finance for a property dealing and developing trade, surplus finance costs can reduce other income or gains chargeable to tax.*

Where funds have been borrowed for trading purposes, the related finance costs will be deductible on an accrued basis as trading expenses. The costs are part of the borrower's normal trading expenses.

For individuals (including individuals in partnerships), surplus expenses can be relieved as follows:

- against other income arising in the same year of assessment (*ITA 2007, s 64*);
- if there is still an unrelieved loss, against income of the preceding year (*IITA 2007, s 64(2b)*);
- any loss still unrelieved can be offset against any chargeable gains for the year (*ITA 2007, s 71*);
- unrelieved losses can be carried forward against future trading income (*ITA 2007, s 83*).

In the first four tax years of assessment of a trading business, the possibility of offset is yet greater. The loss can be offset against income for up to the three years preceding the year of assessment in which the loss is made (*ITA 2007, s 72*).

There is also provision for 'terminal loss relief' where a loss is sustained in the final 12 months of trading, which supplements the reliefs mentioned above. Under the terminal loss rules, the loss can be offset against any profits from the trade in the three years ending immediately before the commencement of the 12-month period up to the date of discontinuance (*ITA 2007, s 89*).

For a company, expenses can be offset in the following ways:

- against other profits (including other income and gains) of the company in the same year (*TA 1988, s 393A*);
- surrender by way of group relief against the total taxable profit of any UK company within the same group in the same year *TA 1988, s 402*);
- carry-back up to one year against total profits of the same company (*TA 1988, s 393A*);
- carry-forward indefinitely in the company against profits from the same trade (*TA 1988, s 393*);
- carry-back up to three years as a terminal loss in the last period of trading (*TA 1988, s 393A (2A)*).

Point 22.5:   *Where the borrower is a company, and the lender is both connected and not within charge to corporation tax on the full amount of any interest, the interest must be paid within 12 months of the year end to get a tax deduction in the year of accrual.*

The fact that the borrower is connected to a lender does not prevent a deduction for accrued interest. Generally, where the lending is between UK companies, the treatment is no different for the borrower than if the loan was with an unconnected lender (except that the 'fair-value-accounting' basis cannot be used to account for the loan relationship). Furthermore, there is nothing to prevent individuals and partnerships of individuals from getting a tax deduction for accrued interest where the actual payment is deferred.

However, if the borrower is a company and a connected lender is not subject to UK corporation tax on the full amount of the accrued interest, the borrower will not receive a deduction in a year in which the interest accrues unless it is paid within 12 months of the year end (*FA 1996, Sch 9, para 2*). The deduction will be allowed in the accounting period when the interest is subsequently paid.

For the definition of 'connected' see Point 22.1 above.

UK companies are taxable on accrued interest. Therefore, this provision is only likely to be relevant where the lender is an individual, a partnership of individuals, a foreign investment company or a trustee connected to the company that are taxed on a received basis.

This point clearly has to be watched since a borrower might find its tax liability retrospectively increased, having failed to pay its accrued interest by this deadline. Alternatively, a fellow group company that has relied on group relief could find that the losses it has claimed from the borrower have disappeared.

Anyone buying a company from a group where such relief is being relied upon would need to ensure that there is an appropriate warranty in place in the purchase agreement. By the same token, anyone buying a company with past relief for unpaid interest might be required to ensure that the company it buys pays the interest by the requisite date.

Point 22.6:   *The mismatch between the accruals basis of relief under the corporate debt regime and the received basis of taxation for certain lenders offers a cash flow tax planning opportunity. An individual or non-UK resident company can exploit this when lending to a connected UK company.*

Where the lender is not liable to UK corporation tax in full on the accrued interest, yet is connected to the borrower, the borrower will not be entitled to a tax deduction for interest accrued in a year if the interest is not actually paid within 12 months of the year end (*FA 1996, Sch 9, para 2*). Instead, the deduction will be allowed in the accounting period when the interest is subsequently paid (see Point 3.17).

There are three other specific situations in which relief is deferred until the interest is actually paid. These are where at any time in the accounting period:

(a)   the debtor is a 'close company' and the person standing in the position of creditor is:
  • a 'participator' in the debtor company;
  • the 'associate' of such a participator; or
  • a company that the participator controls or in which the participator has a 'major interest';
(b)   the person standing in the position of creditor is a company and the debtor has a major interest in the creditor company or the creditor company has a major interest in the debtor company;
(c)   the loan is made by pension trustees and:
  • the debtor company is the employer of scheme members; or
  • the debtor company and the employer are connected; or
  • the employer is a company and the debtor company has a major interest in that employer or the employer has a major interest in the debtor company.

(*FA 1996, Sch 9, para 2*)

A person standing in the position of creditor can be the creditor himself or any person who is indirectly the creditor through a series of loan relationships or money debts.

A close company for the purposes of this rule is, broadly speaking, any UK or foreign company that is under the control of fewer than six 'participators' or any number of directors. A 'participator' is a person owning a share or an interest in the income and/or capital of the company. The term extends to a person with a right to acquire such a share or interest.

In certain circumstances even a company fully listed on the Stock Exchange can be close (*TA 1988, s 415*).

A company has a 'major interest' in another company if, essentially, it and another person together control the other company and both it and the other person have no less than 40% of the total holdings, rights and powers in that other company (*FA 1996, Sch 9, para 20*).

Individuals, trustees and non-resident investment companies are outside the corporate debt regime. Individuals will suffer full UK tax in the year the interest is received. The taxability of a non-resident company will depend on the jurisdiction in which it is resident.

In many cases, that gives rise to an opportunity to exploit a potential cash flow tax advantage. See the example in Point 3.19 in Chapter 3B for an illustration of this.

Point 22.7:   *Tax relief for finance costs in relation to loans directly or indirectly from connected parties may be restricted if they are uncommercial or where a borrowing company is thinly capitalised.*

See Points 3.20 and 3.21 for a discussion on these possible restrictions on tax relief for interest and related costs.

Point 22.8:   *Individuals must generally deduct tax from interest payments to non-residents. For companies, there has been a more general requirement to deduct tax, but this is no longer necessary where the payee is another UK company or an exempt body. Payment may also be made without deducting tax if the payee is an associated company in another EU member state (subject to HMRC approval).*

See Points 3.6 and 3.7 in Chapter 3A regarding the obligation on individuals to deduct tax on interest payments to non-residents. This also applies to trustees although it is rare for trustees to be directly engaged in property trading as opposed to investment.

Points 3.23 to 3.28 deal with the tax deduction issues for companies. As mentioned in Point 22.1 above, these will also apply to non-resident companies which are taxed as companies when trading in the UK through a permanent establishment.

Point 22.9:   *The introduction of rules for 'alternative finance' has enabled tax relief to be obtained for costs incurred in relation to financing structures which are compliant with Islamic law.*

See Point 3.29 in Chapter 3B for an outline of the typical structures that have been accommodated by changes in the UK tax rules as introduced by Finance Acts in 2005, 2006 and 2007.

CHAPTER 23 – ACQUIRING A TRADING COMPANY WITH TAX LOSSES

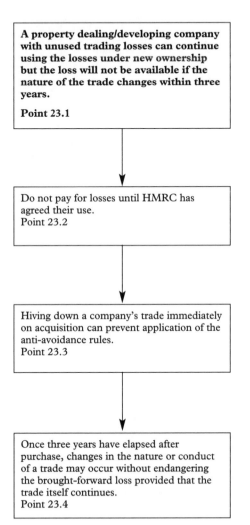

A property dealing/developing company with unused trading losses can continue using the losses under new ownership but the loss will not be available if the nature of the trade changes within three years.

Point 23.1

Do not pay for losses until HMRC has agreed their use.
Point 23.2

Hiving down a company's trade immediately on acquisition can prevent application of the anti-avoidance rules.
Point 23.3

Once three years have elapsed after purchase, changes in the nature or conduct of a trade may occur without endangering the brought-forward loss provided that the trade itself continues.
Point 23.4

23 Acquiring a trading company with tax losses

Point 23.1: *The acquisition of a land dealing or development company with unused past trading losses can offer future tax shelter providing anti-avoidance provisions cannot be applied.*

A property developing or dealing company which has incurred trading losses would normally be able to carry forward the losses against future profits from the same trade. However, once there is a change in the ownership of the company, the carry-forward of unused losses will be denied if there is a major change in the nature or conduct of the trade carried on by the company at any time within a three-year period (whether before or after the change in ownership). There will also be a disallowance of losses carried forward if the trading activity has become small or negligible and before any revival of the trade there is a change in the ownership of the company (*TA 1988, s 768*). Similar rules may also apply to prevent the carry forward of property letting losses (*TA 1988, s 768D*).

A change in ownership is determined by comparing the position at any two points in time within a three-year period. If between those two points a different person or different set of persons owns more than 50% of the ordinary share capital, ownership has changed (*TA 1988, s 769*).

The concept of a major change in the nature and conduct of a trade is potentially quite wide. Where land development becomes land dealing (or vice versa), this would probably amount to a change in the conduct of trade. Furthermore, a change from one type of building to another (eg from residential to commercial) may well come within the provisions. More narrowly, this may even occur if the change is from houses to residential flats. Another example of a situation caught by the provisions might be where a developer moves away from contract work into speculative property development.

A situation where trading activities have become small or negligible is much easier to identify although there are no definitions either in turnover or asset terms given by the legislation. It has been suggested that the reduction in activities must arise from the company's policy. If there have been attempts at maintaining activity at the normal level (as evidenced by the size of its staff and the holding of stock), but local or national economic conditions have depressed sales, it might be argued that the company's trade has not become small or negligible.

The problem with the anti-avoidance provisions arises from the uncertainty as to how wide their scope actually is. In any situation where a company can be turned round from losses to profits it is possible that some element in the conduct of trade has changed. However, this may well not have been the case if losses have arisen in the past from inadequate contract pricing; bad workmanship and disputes; poor financial control; or external factors such as high interest rates, market stagnation or cost escalation. HM Revenue and Customs have published a statement of practice with examples of situations which they would not regard as major changes in the nature of trade (HMRC SP 10/91).

Point 23.2:   *In view of the possible exposure under the anti-avoidance provisions it is inadvisable to pay for the future benefit of a company's losses on acquisition.*

If part of the consideration is geared to the expected use of such losses, it should only be payable as and when the Inspector has agreed to the offset of losses against future profits. In practice, this is likely to be several years after the acquisition.

Point 23.3:   *Hiving down the target company's trade immediately on acquisition can circumvent the anti-avoidance rules.*

The acquisition of a target company from a third party inevitably means that the ownership of that company will change. If it has unused losses, it will then be necessary to avoid a major change in the nature or conduct of the trade if those losses are to be preserved.

There is a possible way to minimise this exposure. Immediately upon the acquisition of the target, its trade, assets and liabilities should be transferred down to a newly established subsidiary (Subco). Since Subco is taking over the trade from its parent, trading losses are also passed down and are available against future profits of the transferee company arising from the same trade (*TA 1988, s 343*).

The difference is now that Subco, unlike its parent company, will not have changed ownership at any point. Therefore, it would need more than a change in the nature or conduct of the trade – or the trade's becoming small – to deny Subco's future use of the losses. It would require a change of trade.

If essentially the same trade is being carried on, ie of property dealing or development, this extra step of hiving down the trade to avoid forfeiting losses is worthwhile.

An arrangement such as this designed to get around anti-avoidance legislation must be carefully implemented with the involvement of professional advisors.

On any hive-down of trade, there is a separate danger of losing all or part of past losses. The loss available to carry forward will be reduced by the extent to which the 'relevant liabilities' – outstanding liabilities of the parent when the trade was transferred but which are not transferred to

Subco – exceed the 'relevant assets' at the time of the transfer (*TA 1988, s 343(4)*).

In view of this, it helps to address any 'net relevant liability' situation of the target prior to acquisition so that this issue would not arise on a hive-down straight after acquisition.

A further problem area is stamp duty land tax. The SDLT intra-group exemption is conditional on the transfer being for commercial reasons and not forming part of an arrangement with tax avoidance as its whole or main objective (*FA 2003, Sch 7, para 2 (4A)*). In this connection, it should help if there are significant commercial objectives in the transfer such as to facilitate refinancing or achieving the separation of the property into a clean new company.

Point 23.4:   *Once three years have elapsed from the date of purchase of a loss company, changes in the nature or conduct of the trade can occur. However, to benefit from brought-forward losses, it is still necessary to carry on the same trade.*

The real benefits from the use of a tax loss company arise from longer-term planning. As mentioned in Point 23.1 above there is a potential disallowance of losses carried forward if there are changes in the nature or conduct of the trade within three years of the change in ownership.

Once the three years have expired, the stringent conditions of *TA 1988, s 768* cease to be relevant. At that stage, trading reforms can be implemented which should not affect the carry-forward of past losses. It is, therefore, not uncommon for groups acquiring companies with substantial losses to delay their more radical plans for three years to ensure the continuing availability of brought-forward losses. In the interim period, trading should be carried on in a similar fashion to the pre-acquisition period.

Apart from the anti-avoidance provisions, the future use of trading losses is still subject to the general rule that they can only be set against profits from the same trade (*TA 1988, s 393(1)*). This could be a problem if, for instance, land dealing or speculative building supersedes land development activity. Thus in any situation where past losses are being relied on to shelter future profitable activity, it is always necessary to consider whether the new activity is a different trade to that previously carried on. However, once the critical three-year period for, *s 768* has passed, a subsequent HMRC challenge would be restricted to denying use of losses against particular profits not arising from the same trade. Therefore, the losses could still be used in future against profits from the same trade as long as the company continues that trade.

CHAPTER 24 – SELLING SHARES IN A PROPERTY TRADING COMPANY AND ANTI-AVOIDANCE PROVISIONS

Sales of trading companies may be tax-free or benefit from the reduced capital gains tax rate from 5 April 2008 depending on the seller's tax status and whether anti-avoidance rules apply.

Point 24.1

The company sale agreement should require the purchaser to ensure that the properties will be sold in the ordinary course of trade to prevent application of the anti-avoidance provisions.
Point 24.2

Where vendors are relying on favourable capital gains treatment, clearance can be sought from HMRC that they will not apply certain anti-avoidance rules.
Point 24.3

24 Selling shares in a property trading company and anti-avoidance provisions

Point 24.1: *For some vendors, any gain on sale will be exempt from tax. In other cases, an improved tax position can arise from a new lower tax capital gains tax rate of 18% post 5 April 2008.*

For companies selling shares in trading subsidiaries, the tax landscape has altered dramatically since 1 April 2002. Provided that certain conditions are met, capital gains from the sale of such shareholdings are exempt from corporation tax (*TCGA 1992, Sch 7AC*). For individuals, trustees and other tax payers not subject to corporation tax, there is no corresponding exemption, but the normal rules of capital gains tax will apply, which may result in an 18% effective tax rate post 5 April 2008 if proposals in the Government's 2007 Pre Budget report are implemented – see 'Stop Press' note at the beginning of the book.

In certain circumstances, anti-avoidance rules may come into play, even where avoidance is not a motive, or the main motive, for the transaction (see Point 24.2 below).

For companies, the exemption ('the substantial shareholdings exemption') applies where:

(a)   a trading company or a member of a trading group sells a 'substantial shareholding' in;

(b)   a trading company or the holding company of a trading group or subgroup; and

the shareholding has been held for a continuous period of at least 12 months in the two years immediately preceding the disposal.

A substantial shareholding is one of 10% or more.

See Chapter 36 for further points on the substantial shareholding exemption.

Where the vendor of the shares is not a company, the normal capital gains tax rules apply. Nevertheless, for certain classes of shareholder, any gains will be free of UK tax. Apart from exempt owners such as pension funds and charity trustees, this will also apply to non-residents, unless they are trading in the UK through a branch or agency and the shares are an asset of that trade.

Non-domiciled individuals may be able to sell tax-free if the company owning the property is incorporated outside the UK. The proceeds of sale would need to be received and retained outside the UK. HMRC do, however, have available anti-avoidance rules through which they can seek to tax such gains where relevant. These are referred to in Points 24.2 and 24.3 below.

In other cases, the owners may have available tax shelter through losses in the year of sale. With the prospective abolition of taper relief after 5 April 2008, all capital gains after 5 April 2008 in the hands of individuals, trustees and personal representatives will be subject to a lower capital gains tax of 18%. It is possible that some business asset taper relief (reducing the effective tax to as low as 10%) may be retained for relatively modest gains. See the 'Stop Press' note at the beginning of the book for a summary of the relevant proposals in the Government's October 2007 Pre-Budget report.

Where a company is sold and the sale consideration takes the form of shares or loan notes in the buying company, it is often possible to defer any taxable gain arising. The gain on sale is rolled-over into the new shares/loans acquired so that the gain will only crystallise when these are sold/redeemed (*TCGA 1992, s 135*).

The treatment of loan notes differs depending on whether they are qualifying corporate bonds (QCBs) or non-qualifying corporate bonds (non-QCBs). A QCB is broadly a normal commercial loan note issued by a company. Its issue in exchange for shares crystallises the chargeable gain at that point in time but defers its being brought into charge to tax until the loan note is sold or redeemed (*TCGA 1992, s 116*).

A non-QCB is also a corporate loan note, but has one or more specified features that distinguish it from a QCB. These are a right to subscribe for further loan notes; being denominated in or redeemable in a foreign currency; a right to convert into shares; or entitlement to a return linked to the business's results (*TCGA 1992, s 117*). With a non-QCB, the gain is not merely held over but the gain does not crystallise until sale or redemption.

This share for share or share for loan note deferral relief is only available where the sale is for bona fide commercial reasons. HMRC may refuse the relief where there is any indication that the tax benefits for the seller have been the driving factor for the structure of the transaction. It is advisable to obtain advance clearance from HMRC that they are satisfied that the sale is for bona fide commercial reasons and not tax driven (*TCGA 1992, s 138*).

In the absence of HMRC clearance, any gain arising on a sale in consideration for shares or loan stock could crystallise and become taxable at that point instead of being held over or rolled over into the new shares/securities acquired. That would mean tax would be payable on the transaction for that tax year even though cash has not been received.

Point 24.2: *When selling the shares of a dealing or development company it is advisable to incorporate in the sale agreement the condition that the properties held by the company as trading stock are disposed of in the normal course of its trade.*

Whenever a gain of a capital nature is realised either directly or indirectly from property, HMRC can invoke *ITA 2007, s 752* and subsequent sections (or *TA, s 776* for companies) to tax that gain as income. The sections potentially apply where:

(a) land, or any property deriving its value from land, is acquired with the sole or main object of realising a gain from disposing of the land; or

(b) land is held as trading stock; or

(c) is developed with the sole or main object of realising a gain from disposing of the land when developed;

and any profit of a capital nature is obtained from the disposal of the land (*ITA, s 752 (2)/TA 1988, s 775(2)*).

These sections do not apply to the profits directly derived from the purchase and sale of properties by a dealer or developer. Since such profits arise from trading they would not be gains of a capital nature.

The sale of the shares in a property dealing or developing company, however, could give rise to a gain of a capital nature within *ss 752* and *776*. There is, therefore, a possibility that the profit on sale is assessed to tax not as a capital gain, but as income in the year of sale. Furthermore the gain for *s 752* purposes would not attract any indexation allowance or, in the case of individuals and trustees benefit from the new proposed capital gains tax rate of 18% for those taxpayers. Similarly, *s 776* cannot be sheltered through substantial shareholdings exemption or offset of capital losses.

There is an important exemption in *ITA 2007, s 766* (for individuals and trustees) and *TA 1988, s 776(10)* (for companies). This provides that the sections shall not apply where there is a disposal of shares in a company:

(a) which holds land as trading stock; and

(b) all the land so held is disposed of in the normal course of trade; and

(c) all opportunity of profit in respect of that land arises to that company.

The section was applied in the case of *Chilcott v IRC* [1982] STC 1 where the taxpayer sold shares in a property company on the specific condition that the land stock should be sold in the normal course of its trading. *Section 776* was held not to apply in that case by virtue of *s 776(10)* (now *ITA 2007, s 766* for individuals).

Since the sale of any property-owning company is potentially a situation within *s 752*, it is advisable to incorporate the condition in the sale contract that the stock will be sold in the normal course of trade. This would help the vendor rely on the exemption in, *s 766/s 776(10)* as well as forming the basis of any damages claim if the purchaser ignored the undertaking and a *s 752/776* liability consequently arose in the vendor.

This exemption from *ss 752/776* is only available where there is a straightforward sale of shares. If the transaction is part of a larger scheme or arrangement, it will not apply.

It should be noted that although there is a procedure for obtaining clearance that *s 752* does not apply (*ITA 2007, s 770/ICTA, s 776*), this does not apply where land is held as trading stock.

Point 24.3: *Notwithstanding the ss 752/766 position, before any sale of shares, formal clearance should be obtained from HMRC that the anti-avoidance rules relating to transactions in securities will not apply.*

Where shareholders realise gains on the sale of a company, the possibility that the gains will be subject to income tax cannot be ruled out. In *IRC v Wiggins* [1979] STC 244 it was established that the anti-avoidance provisions of *TA 1988, s 703* (for corporation tax), or *ITA 2007, s 713* (for income tax), may apply. These sections seek to tax gains from certain 'transactions in securities' to income tax in prescribed situations may well apply if the proceeds of sale reflect the value of underlying stock. By selling the company, the shareholders have effectively avoided the additional tax that would have become payable if the stock had been realised and the proceeds distributed.

There is, however, a formal clearance procedure under which confirmation of the *TA 1988, s 703/ITA 2007, s 682* position can be obtained in advance (*TA 1988, s 707/ITA, ss 701 & 702*). HMRC is required to respond within 30 days to any application for formal clearance, which is normally in the form that they either are or are not satisfied that the anti-avoidance provisions should be applied.

If complete information is supplied with a clearance application and clearance formally given, the transaction can proceed without fear of any liability under these anti-avoidance sections. For this reason, an application for clearance is a common procedure in advance of most share sales.

As mentioned, HMRC are reluctant to give clearance where they consider that the sale is a device to extract tax-free funds. Sales where vendor shareholders retain shares through the buying company after the sale normally attract extra scrutiny from HMRC.

This clearance is separate from the clearance mentioned in Point 24.1 above in respect of share for share and share for loan note sales, although requests for the two clearances may be submitted in a single application. A clearance under *TCGA 1992, s 138* confirms that HMRC accept that new shares or loan stock issued by the buying company in exchange for the shares in the company acquired are treated as the same asset as the old shares. It is as if there had been a reorganisation of the target company's shares. As a result, a gain on the sale of shares can be held over or (in the case of certain loan stock) not crystallised for tax purposes until the new securities are sold or redeemed.

A sale involving the issue of shares or loan notes in the buying company normally proceeds after obtaining clearances under both *TA 1988, s 707/ITA 2007, s 701* and *TCGA 1992, s 138*. It is possible in a transaction to receive clearance under one head but for clearance to be refused for the other.

CHAPTER 25 – CONSTRUCTION INDUSTRY SCHEME

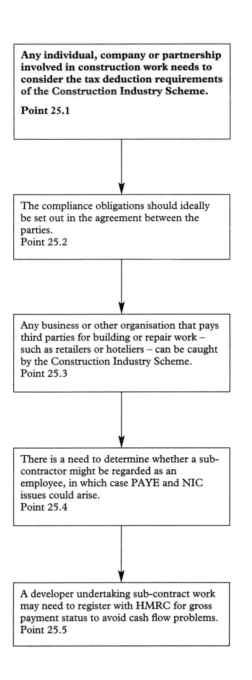

Any individual, company or partnership involved in construction work needs to consider the tax deduction requirements of the Construction Industry Scheme.

Point 25.1

The compliance obligations should ideally be set out in the agreement between the parties.
Point 25.2

Any business or other organisation that pays third parties for building or repair work – such as retailers or hoteliers – can be caught by the Construction Industry Scheme.
Point 25.3

There is a need to determine whether a sub-contractor might be regarded as an employee, in which case PAYE and NIC issues could arise.
Point 25.4

A developer undertaking sub-contract work may need to register with HMRC for gross payment status to avoid cash flow problems.
Point 25.5

25 Construction Industry Scheme

Point 25.1: *Any individual, partnership or company that carries out or engages in construction work needs to consider the implications of the Construction Industry Scheme. Failure to withhold tax from payments where required under the scheme could result in a contractor being liable to account for the tax.*

The Construction Industry Scheme (CIS) is designed to minimise tax evasion in the building industry. It does this by putting the onus on a 'contractor' to withhold one of two prescribed rates on account of income tax from payments to a 'sub-contractor' in respect of any works of construction carried out – unless the sub-contractor has successfully registered for gross payment status with HMRC and the contractor has verified that status. The tax deduction is not applied to payments in respect of materials and VAT.

The current CIS came into operation on 6 April 2007. Please see earlier editions of this work for details of the scheme in operation up to 5 April 2007.

The prescribed rates of tax withholding are 20% for verified sub-contractors on deduction and 30% for unmatched (unknown to HMRC) sub-contractors for 2006/07.

Any contractor who fails to fulfil this obligation could be liable to HMRC for the amount of tax which should have been deducted. A genuine belief that the sub-contractor in question has properly accounted for receipts to HMRC and paid any related income or corporation tax will not necessarily prevent the contractor from still being liable for the withholding tax.

The first thing a contractor must do is check the employment status (see Point 25.4). If satisfied the sub-contractor is not an employee instead of checking certificates contractors must now, using information provided by the sub-contractor, verify their deduction statuses by contacting HMRC. This may be done on the telephone, over the internet or by EDI. EDI is the Electronic Data Interface that large contractors who register with HMRC can use to check the status of sub-contractors and is a useful way of dealing with large numbers of verifications. HMRC provide a verification number and a deduction rate which a contractor should use until HMRC say otherwise or there is a gap between payments of more than two years. Contractors must provide sub-contractors on deduction with a statement that includes the amount deducted and the relevant unique verification number provided by HMRC.

CIS returns should be made monthly and show the sub-contractor's details and the amounts paid and deducted. Additionally, the return includes a declaration that employment status has been considered (see Point 25.4) and that all sub-contractors have been verified.

HMRC may charge penalties for late returns, incorrect returns for deductions omitted from the return and for failures to provide statements to sub-contractors and provide records to HMRC.

Point 25.2:   *It is advisable for there to be a contractual requirement for a sub-contractor to provide the information required for verification as a pre-condition to the making of any payment.*

The necessary information includes, the sub-contractor's name, unique taxpayer reference, national insurance number and company registration number. Additionally it would be advisable to include a contractual requirement for sub-contractors to provide information required to establish their employment status.

As mentioned above, the contractor can be liable for tax and fines if these procedures are not followed.

Point 25.3:   *It is not just builders or developers who are caught by this scheme. Any business or other organisation that pays third parties for building or repair work – such as retailers or hoteliers – can be caught by the Construction Industry Scheme.*

The scheme has to be operated by 'contractors' in relation to the sub-contractors whom they pay. The sub-contractors can, in turn, then become a contractor in respect of payments they make. The result can be a chain of 'contractors' for the purpose of the legislation.

Any person carrying on business which includes construction operations is a contractor for the purposes of the legislation (*TA 1988, s 560(2)(a)*). Construction operations for this purpose are set out in Appendix IV.

The definition of a 'contractor' is extended to include non-construction businesses and certain other bodies or persons spending more than £1 million per annum on average over three years on construction operations (see Point 38.1).

There is a potential trap here for, say, chains of retailers or hotels who might easily spend more than £1m per annum over a three-year period on refurbishment and repair work. In those cases, HMRC investigation teams looking into a group's PAYE compliance will almost inevitably extend their enquiries to payments to sub-contractors.

Whilst the compliance on major projects is generally monitored by the project managers involved, smaller jobs involving jobbing builders, plumbers, electricians etc are often overlooked. If, for instance, a hotel pays a plumber without inspecting documentation as required, HMRC can collect any non-deducted tax from the hotel and may also seek interest or a fine.

Point 25.4:   *As a new obligation under the scheme, contractors must also distinguish between self-employed individuals and those that HMRC regard as employees. For these latter persons, PAYE and National Insurance contributions may apply to payments.*

Often individuals are treated as self-employed by the person for whom they work when, in fact, they have many of the characteristics of employees. In those cases, HMRC will try to recategorise the individual as an employee and collect back tax and National Insurance from the 'employer' going back up to six years.

Typically, the self-employed deal with a number of non-associated customers, have their own premises and have their own resources of finance, staff and tools etc. Where those features are missing, HMRC will look for an employer/employee relationship for tax purposes, whether or not that is the case under employment law. Pointers for them include:

- Whether an individual works virtually full-time for a company or is otherwise economically dependent on the company.
- Does the individual have his own business premises?
- Does the individual have his own staff?
- Is the individual at risk for his time and capital?

Where the answer to the first question above is yes, and the answer to the remaining questions is no, there is a strong presumption in favour of an employer/employee relationship. If agreement cannot be reached with HMRC, the parties have to contemplate the time, expense and uncertainty of a hearing before the General or Special Commissioners, and beyond that, the courts. Any tribunal will look at the facts and circumstances of each case. The factors mentioned above and others (listed in the HMRC Factsheet 'Are your workers employed or self employed? – Advice for contractors' Form CIS 349) will be persuasive but not decisive in the decision. It is important to remember also that what the parties may agree among themselves (eg the contract may state that the worker is self-employed and responsible for his or her own tax etc) will be of little weight if the facts point the other way.

A different situation prevails if the individual worker is engaged indirectly through the medium of a service company or partnership ('the intermediary'), ie where the contract for the individual's services is concluded between the client and the intermediary that retains the individual's services. In such circumstances, if the facts are that the individual would be treated as an employee of the client if he or she had contracted directly with that client, then the so-called 'IR 35 rules' come into play. Under these rules (contained in *ITEPA 2003, Pt 2, Ch 8*), the intermediary will be liable for PAYE and National Insurance as if the payment from the client to the intermediary for the individual's services had been made by the intermediary to the worker as employment income, whether or not any such payment has been made (often, using the example of a service company, the individual will draw a small salary from the intermediary and receive the rest of the payment as a dividend).

If IR 35 applies and the Construction Industry Scheme applies to payments by the client to the intermediary, the intermediary is treated as having received the payment gross (ie without taking any tax deduction into account) when the amount of the deemed payment under the IR 35 rules is calculated. However, by concession, a company may set CIS deductions against IR35 tax and NIC due providing it makes a formal claim for a CIS deduction repayment by 31 January following the tax year.

Under proposed managed service company legislation subject to a number of conditions, the IR 35 rules would not apply. If the MSC rules did apply it may be possible for any PAYE/NIC debt to be attached to other parties including it seems the client. However, at the time of writing it is not clear how HMRC will apply these rules in practice.

Point 25.5:   *If a developer undertakes contract work, gross payment status may be essential to avoid a cash flow problem.*

Where the developer is potentially a sub-contractor and where work is being carried out for a 'contractor' (which may include persons outside the construction industry – see Point 38.1) gross payment status may be essential.

In the absence of gross payment status a withholding on payments must be applied and this will represent a payment on account of the developer's final tax liability. In the meantime, the developer is faced with a loss of cash flow.

This means for 2006/07, for instance, a 20% or 30% withholding of tax (which is on the VAT-exclusive amount less materials) potentially leaves the developer with insufficient cash to pay for materials, staff, its own sub-contractors and income tax payments on account. However, sub-contractor companies – but not individuals or partnerships – may reduce their monthly payments to HMRC or PAYE/NIC and CIS deductions by the amount withheld. Consequently, few cash-flow difficulties arise for companies.

A developer anticipating the possibility of sub-contractor status on future projects should obtain and maintain gross payment status. In this connection, sub-contractor status may not always be obvious. However, an easement introduced on 6 April 2007 means that 'reverse premiums' eg payments from developers to tenants for fit out works are not caught by the scheme.

Gross payment status involves a detailed application procedure and is only issued to those individuals, partnerships and companies that meet the criteria. In that connection there are three tests to satisfy before HMRC will grant gross payment status. These are:

(a)   The business test – essentially that the company is carrying on a construction business in the UK or providing workers for such a business. It also has to have its business bank account in the UK.

(b)   The turnover test – income net of VAT and materials must be at least £30,000 per year in the case of sole traders. For companies and partnerships, it is £30,000 multiplied by the number of directors or partners as the case may be. For larger businesses there is the alternative test of a minimum of £200,000 turnover.

(c)   The compliance test – to satisfy this, the personal and business tax affairs of the proprietor must be up to date for the preceding 12 months.

Notwithstanding the fact that the provisions were introduced to deal with small firms and individuals, it is also necessary for large firms to be able to demonstrate to HMRC history of regular compliance with their corporation tax returns and payments.

Where gross payment status cannot be obtained, all contracts which might result in the development entity becoming a sub-contractor should be approached with caution. An unexpected withholding could well upset cash and profit budgets on a job.

CHAPTER 26 – VAT POINTS FOR PROPERTY DEVELOPERS

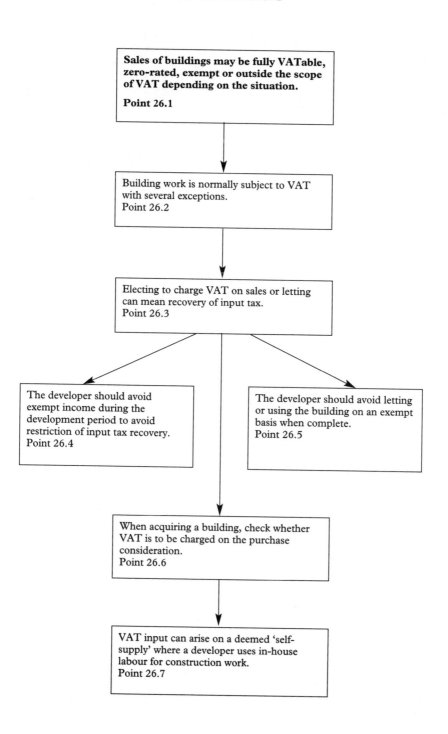

Sales of buildings may be fully VATable, zero-rated, exempt or outside the scope of VAT depending on the situation.

Point 26.1

Building work is normally subject to VAT with several exceptions.
Point 26.2

Electing to charge VAT on sales or letting can mean recovery of input tax.
Point 26.3

The developer should avoid exempt income during the development period to avoid restriction of input tax recovery.
Point 26.4

The developer should avoid letting or using the building on an exempt basis when complete.
Point 26.5

When acquiring a building, check whether VAT is to be charged on the purchase consideration.
Point 26.6

VAT input can arise on a deemed 'self-supply' where a developer uses in-house labour for construction work.
Point 26.7

26   VAT points for property developers

Point 26.1: *Sales of commercial buildings within three years of completion are VAT standard-rated supplies. Sales of new properties for residential or charitable use may be zero-rated. Any other sales would be exempt supplies subject to the option to tax unless outside the scope of VAT because of the 'going concern rules'.*

There are several possible VAT situations in connection with property related supplies. These can be summarised as follows:

Zero-rated

(1)   The sale by the developer of the freehold of a building (or part of a building) which is designed as a dwelling or where the purchaser is to use the property for a relevant residential or charitable purpose (see Point 18.4 for 'relevant residential' or 'charitable use'). Also, the first sale of a renovated building that has not been used for any residential purpose for at least ten years.

(2)   The sale by the developer of the freehold of a building (or part of a building) which is designed as a dwelling or is to be used as in (1) above which is not new but is a substantially reconstructed protected building (see Point 18.5).

(3)   The grant by the developer of a lease of more than 21 years in a building which is either new or a substantially reconstructed protected building where the design or use is as in (1) above. Only the initial consideration will be treated as the zero-rated output. This may be a premium payable on grant or the first rent payment if there is no premium.

(4)   The grant of a lease of over 21 years or a freehold interest by a person converting a building from a non-residential building (or a non-residential part of a building) into a dwelling or dwellings or a property intended solely for a relevant residential use.

Standard-rated

(5)   The sale of a freehold by the developer of a non-residential building within three years of its completion.

(6)   The sale of a freehold commercial building more than three years after its completion if the developer has elected to waive the exemption for supplies arising from that building. In the absence of such an election, any such sale would constitute an exempt supply (see (9) below and Point 18.1 for the option to tax).

(7)   The grant of a lease of a commercial building by a developer who has opted, as in (6), to waive the exemption in respect of the

building. In this situation VAT must be added to any premiums and rents charged.

(8)   The assignment or surrender of a lease of a commercial building by a person who has elected to waive the exemption.

Exempt

(9)   All freehold sales, assignments, surrenders, grants of leases and licences other than the specified situations in (1) to (8) or (10).

Outside the scope of VAT

(10)   Sales of properties where there is a transfer of the business as a going concern (see Point 18.3).

The recovery of input tax, which could be substantial where there are major construction, refurbishment or repair works, will only be possible if property sales or grants are either zero-rated or standard-rated for VAT purposes. The developer's strategy should be to avoid exempt supplies. This may involve electing to tax lettings or sales as discussed in Point 26.3 below. Alternatively, a sale which is outside the scope of VAT such as in (10) above may avoid irrecoverable VAT.

Point 26.2:   *Building work is subject to VAT at the standard rate with a few limited exceptions. These include the new construction of a building for residential or charitable use, work on approved alterations to a protected building to be used for these purposes or the conversion of a building to residential use.*

See Point 18.8 for a discussion of standard-rated and zero-rated building work, as well as the reduced 5% rate applying to certain conversions etc since 11 May 2001.

As a reminder, the 5% rate applies to the following supplies:

(a)   converting a non-residential property into one or more single-household dwellings;

(b)   changing the number of single-household dwellings in a building;

(c)   converting a single-household dwelling or a house in multiple occupation into a care home or for other qualifying residential use;

(d)   converting a house in multiple occupation into a single-household dwelling;

(e)   converting a single-household dwelling into a house in multiple occupation;

(f)   services supplied in the course of renovating a single-household dwelling that has remained empty for at least three years;

(g)   building materials and certain other goods incorporated by a builder into a building in the course of supplying services under (a) and (b) above.

A single-household dwelling is a dwelling intended for occupation by a single household (ie a single individual, a couple or a family).

Since 1 June 2002, the following situations have also been subject to the reduced rate:

(a) converting a non-residential property into a care home (or other qualifying building used solely for a 'relevant residential' purpose);

(b) converting a non-residential property into a multiple occupancy dwelling, such as bed-sit accommodation;

(c) converting a building used for a 'relevant residential' purpose into a multiple occupancy dwelling;

(d) renovating or altering a care home (or other qualifying building used solely for a 'relevant residential' purpose), that has not been lived in for three years or more;

(e) renovating or altering a multiple occupancy dwelling that has not been lived in for three years or more; and

(f) constructing, renovating or converting a building into a garage as part of the renovation of a property that qualifies for the reduced rate.

The reduced rate can also apply to certain grant-funded heating installations and energy saving materials.

Point 26.3: *The developer should consider whether to elect to tax in situations where the sale or letting of a commercial property might otherwise be an exempt supply. This would give the developer the opportunity to recover any VAT incurred.*

The situations where a supply in connection with a commercial property is exempt for VAT purposes are highlighted in Point 26.1 above. In these situations, a developer can make an election to waive the exemption in respect of any specific property unless the building is a dwelling or used for relevant residential or charitable purposes (see Point 18.4).

The advantage for a property developer in making standard-rated as opposed to exempt supplies is that input tax incurred will be recoverable. Given that substantial VAT is likely to be involved in any construction or refurbishment project, this represents an important opportunity to recover this VAT. The VAT could not be recovered if the supplies in relation to a building remain exempt. Irrecoverable VAT could also arise on the deemed 'self-supplies' of construction services as discussed in Point 26.8 below.

The discussion in Point 18.1 regarding the option to tax in relation to a property investor is also relevant to a property developer as is the cautionary message in Point 18.2. The election, once made, can only be revoked within three months of its being made or once 20 years have expired after making the election. Subject to that, it applies to all future supplies of the property. Thus, if a letting is taxable, so will be any subsequent lease grants. If the person making the election owns the freehold, then VAT would also have to be charged on any sale of a freehold unless the 'going concern' rules apply (see Point 26.6 below). Furthermore, stamp duty land tax is also chargeable on the VAT element of the sale consideration or lease premium (see Point 5.3).

Point 26.4:   *Any exempt income during the development period can prejudice the entitlement to VAT recovery.*

VAT recovery will also be affected if the developer has exempt income during the period of construction or refurbishment. This might arise, for instance, if the person constructing it uses a site on an exempt basis in this period. This could happen with any exempt or partially exempt organisation such as a charity, hospital, educational establishment or financial institution.

Alternatively, the site may be let on an exempt basis to users during the construction period.

Strictly, if there are only exempt supplies in a period, none of the VAT incurred during that period is recoverable. However, HM Customs and Excise can agree a reasonable level of VAT recovery taking into account prospective taxable supplies (VAT Regulations 1995 (SI 1995/2518), reg 102). As far as possible it is advisable to establish a basis for recovery with HM Customs and Excise at the outset. Otherwise, the developer may be budgeting for a higher level of VAT recovery than HM Customs are prepared to allow. See Point 18.7 for a discussion on VAT recovery in respect of speculative and intended property developments.

The developer should also be prepared for an impact on the VAT recovery if there is a subsequent change in plan that affects the anticipated periods of exempt and taxable supplies.

Point 26.5:   *The developer should try to avoid exempt letting or exempt use of the property at the outset.*

If a developer's first lease grant is on a VAT-exempt basis, any VAT reclaimed on the construction or refurbishment work can be clawed back by HM Revenue and Customs. For that reason the developer should ensure that the initial lease grant is either zero-rated, in the case of residential or charitable property (see Point 26.1 above), or waive the exemption for commercial property.

A similar problem arises if the new property is used in an exempt activity before there is any taxable supply (*C & E Comrs v University of Wales College of Cardiff* [1995] STC 611).

If the exempt letting is only temporary and the developer can demonstrate a definite intention to grant taxable interests or standard-rate rents, some recovery of VAT input tax is still possible. The procedure would involve agreeing with HM Revenue and Customs an appropriate basis for apportioning the VAT incurred between taxable and exempt supplies (*C & E Comrs v Briararch Ltd; C & E Comrs v Curtis Henderson Ltd* [1992] STC 732). There will, inevitably, be some loss of VAT in that situation.

Point 26.6: *When acquiring a building, check whether VAT is to be charged on the purchase consideration.*

The question of VAT becoming chargeable on the purchase price is discussed in Point 18.11 and reference should be made to that section.

There is the possibility that a property sale is outside the scope of VAT if it is in connection with the transfer of a business as a going concern (TOGC). This topic is dealt with in Point 18.3 above in relation to property investors. In some cases, the sale of a partially completed new development to a developer who carries on the project can be treated as a TOGC (*Golden Oak Partnership v C & E Comrs* (1992) VAT decision 7212).

As far as the seller is concerned, a TOGC does not create the same problem with VAT input recovery that an exempt supply would do. The buyer in turn avoids having to pay VAT. However, this treatment is not optional. Where VAT is chargeable on a sale, this will also result in an increased stamp duty land tax liability for the purchaser (see Point 18.10).

Point 26.7: *When using in-house labour to construct a property, there is a deemed VAT charge on the self-supply of construction services. Normally this is recoverable except where the building is wholly or partially let or occupied on an exempt basis.*

Where any construction work is undertaken in-house by a developer (or a member of the developer's VAT group) there is a deemed self-supply of construction services unless the open-market value of the services is less than £100,000. VAT is charged on the market value of these services.

This represents a potential pitfall for the developer who enlarges or extends a building and grants a lease without electing to charge VAT on any rents or premiums due.

Part C Trading Premises

CHAPTER 27 – PREMIUM RELIEF ON THE ACQUISITION OF A SHORT LEASE

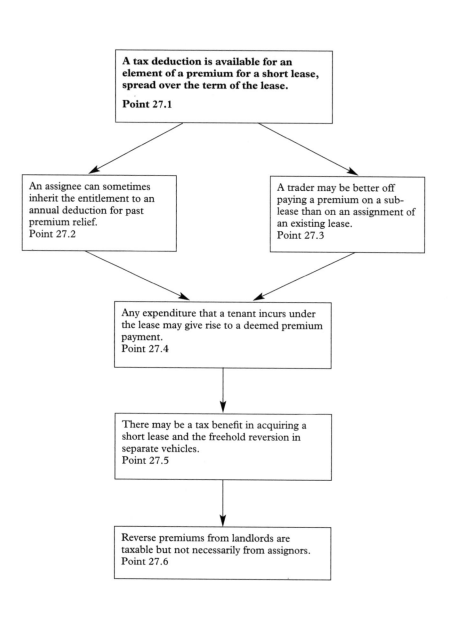

A tax deduction is available for an element of a premium for a short lease, spread over the term of the lease.

Point 27.1

An assignee can sometimes inherit the entitlement to an annual deduction for past premium relief.
Point 27.2

A trader may be better off paying a premium on a sub-lease than on an assignment of an existing lease.
Point 27.3

Any expenditure that a tenant incurs under the lease may give rise to a deemed premium payment.
Point 27.4

There may be a tax benefit in acquiring a short lease and the freehold reversion in separate vehicles.
Point 27.5

Reverse premiums from landlords are taxable but not necessarily from assignors.
Point 27.6

27 Premium relief on the acquisition of a short lease

Point 27.1: *Where a trader pays a premium on the grant of a short lease for business premises, an annual tax deduction can be claimed against trading income in respect of the 'income element'.*

On the grant of a lease of less than 50 years, the recipient of any premium paid will be assessed to tax on part of the total amount as if it were income rather than capital (see Chapter 9 in Part A). Where the premium is paid by a trader, an annual deduction can be claimed for this 'income element' spread over the life of the lease (*TA 1988, s 87(2)* for corporation tax and *ITTOIA 2005, ss 60 & 61* for income tax).

The 'income element' is the total premium reduced by 2% for each year of the lease except the first.

EXAMPLE 1

A trader pays £100,000 premium on the grant of a 20-year lease. The income element is £62,000 (£100,000 less 2% × (20 − 1) × £100,000). The annual deduction against the trader's profits will be this amount spread over the life of the lease ie £3,100.

It will be noted that whereas the recipient of a premium will be assessed to tax on the whole sum in the year of receipt, the lessee's relief must be spread over the full term.

Point 27.2: *Premium relief is not limited to tenants paying a premium on the grant of a lease. An assignee of a lease can continue claiming the annual deduction which had been available to the assignor, providing the property continues to be used for trading purposes.*

The annual premium deduction referred to in Point 27.1 above is available to any trader occupying the property for the duration of the lease. Thus, another trader taking an assignment of the lease will inherit the previous leaseholder's entitlement to a tax deduction, assuming the property is used for trading purposes. This will also be the case if the previous tenant was not entitled to a deduction. As long as, on the original grant of the lease, a premium was partly assessable as income (whether or not it was actually chargeable), a deduction will be available during the life of the lease to any successor in title using the property for trading purposes.

The relief gives rise to the practical problem of determining whether any premium was originally paid and to what extent it was assessable on the landlord. These are matters which should be ascertained, as far as possible, at the time of grant or assignment. Generally, details of any premium paid originally should be shown on the lease agreement or gleaned from Land Registry documents.

Point 27.3: *In view of premium relief, a trader may be better off paying a premium on the grant of a sub-lease rather than on an assignment of the existing lease. There could well be situations where the assignor would be amenable to such an arrangement.*

EXAMPLE 2

A five-year lease is to be assigned for £100,000. No relief would be available on the expenditure of £100,000 except in so far as it formed part of the base cost of the lease for capital gains tax purposes. This would be depreciated to zero over its life. If, as an alternative, a sub-lease is granted for 4 years and 11 months on the payment of a premium of £105,000, £98,700 would be treated as the revenue element (ie £105,000 less 2% × (4 − 1) × 105,000). The trader would therefore be entitled to a monthly deduction of £1,673 over the 59 months of the lease.

Property vendors might be reluctant to enter into such an arrangement as it would involve them in being taxed as a deemed recipient of income (under Schedule A) rather than to capital gains tax on part of their receipt. Although, generally, capital gains and income are subject to tax at the same rate, it may be a useful arrangement for, say, a pension fund which would be exempt from charge to tax. Certain other vendors may also be prepared to enter into the arrangement if they have losses available to offset against any taxable profit arising.

A disadvantage from the grantor's point of view is that it leaves behind a residual interest (in this case, one month). For this reason it might be appropriate to offer somewhat more than the assignment price to compensate for this as in the example. Alternatively, the residual interest might be assigned to the lessee or an associate for a nominal sum at a later stage.

Another point to factor in to this planning is stamp duty land tax. The amount of SDLT payable will differ depending on whether a lease grant or lease assignment route is chosen. See Chapter 5 for further details on SDLT.

Point 27.4: *A premium may not just be a cash payment to the landlord. Any expenditure which the tenant is obliged to incur under the terms of granting a lease could give rise to a premium relief deduction for the tenant.*

Where the terms under which the lease is granted impose an obligation to carry out any improvements, a deemed premium will arise. The measure of the premium is not the cost of the work, but the increase in the value of the recipient's interest as a direct result of the work. This amount would be taxable on the landlord in accordance with the premium rules and there would be the corresponding deduction for the tenant if occupied for the purpose of a trade.

This point could easily be overlooked by a tenant who might be faced with a disallowance of the expense of any improvement work. Clearly, there is a practical problem of determining the increase in the landlord's interest. However, as long as the situation is identified, it should be possible to liaise with the landlord or the Inspector of Taxes to ensure the appropriate relief is obtained.

Point 27.5: *The availability of annual deductions for premiums paid does offer some scope for tax relief on the acquisition of long leasehold and freehold property. This can be achieved by acquiring a short lease and the reversionary interest separately.*

A trader, anticipating the acquisition of freehold or long leasehold premises, might take advantage of premium relief by carrying out the transaction in two stages:

1. taking a grant of a short lease on the payment of a full market premium;
2. purchasing the residuary interest through a separate entity.

If we take the example of the proposed acquisition of a freehold for £1m, a five-year lease could perhaps be granted for £250,000. The freehold could then be conveyed to, say, another group company for £750,000. Using the formula referred to in Point 27.1 above, the deemed income element would be £230,000, which would be allowable as a trading expense at a rate of £46,000 per year for five years to the leaseholder.

The arrangement has disadvantages from the view point of tax on capital gains. The short lease is a wasting asset for capital gains purposes and, after five years, no part of the £250,000 paid would be reflected in the base cost of the freehold. Accordingly, the capital gains cost on the property would be £750,000 rather than £1,000,000 and indexation allowance would only be given on the former figure.

Many trading companies may not be affected by the possibility of extra tax on capital gains. In practice, this can often be deferred indefinitely by claiming relief for replacement of business assets (see Chapter 34).

A further capital gains disadvantage can arise here from the fact that the company owning the freehold will not be occupying it for trading purposes. Thus, the property will not technically be an asset qualifying under the capital gains roll-over provisions. However, relief is nevertheless available in the following situations:

1. a property is owned by an individual and occupied by his family trading company (*TCGA 1992, s 157*); or
2. a property is owned by a partner and used by the partnership (*TCGA 1992, s 152* – see Statement of Practice D11); or
3. a property is held by a property holding company within a group and occupied by a fellow group company (*TCGA 1992, s 175*).

In the above situations, therefore, the availability of roll-over relief need not be jeopardised by this arrangement. Accordingly, the scheme could provide the opportunity for short-term revenue deductions for a trading entity, whereas the extra tax on capital gains might be deferred indefinitely.

Point 27.6:   *Premiums received by tenants from landlords as inducements to enter into a lease ('reverse premiums') are taxable. Tax can be deferred depending on the accounting policy adopted or if the receipt is a contribution to fixtures and fittings. Inducement payments from assignors should not be taxable.*

Where a tenant receives a payment from a prospective landlord as an inducement to enter into a lease, this is taxable as part of the normal income and profits of the tenant (*FA 1999, Sch 6, para 2; ITTOIA 2005, s 101*).

In taxing the receipt, HMRC will follow the tenant's accounting treatment for the item, in assuming it is in accordance with generally accepted accounting practice. If this involves bringing the receipt into the balance sheet and then crediting it to the profit and loss account over, say, the five years to the first rent review, only the amount so credited each year is taxable.

An alternative treatment is available if the receipt is a contribution toward fixtures and fittings. Where these are eligible for capital allowances as plant or machinery (see Chapter 6), the allowances are restricted to the expenditure net of the contribution. That means that the contribution is effectively brought into taxable profit over a period through capital allowances at a rate (after March 2008) of 20% each year on a reducing balance basis. After seven years, around 80% of the amount would have been brought into tax with most of the remaining 20% taking a further 12 years or so to be subject to tax.

Whilst there is specific legislation with regard to inducement payments given to existing tenants by landlords, there are no rules for similar payments from assignors of leases – unless the assignors are connected with the landlord (*FA 1999, Sch 6, para 1(1)(c)* – see HMRC Bulletin 44, December 1999). These receipts are capital in nature and, in the absence of special rules, are not taxable as income. Since an asset (ie the lease) is only owned as a consequence of receiving the amount, there is no capital sum derived from an asset or its disposal. So capital gains tax is not in point either. Therefore, as long as it is a pure inducement payment, an amount paid to a prospective tenant to take an assignment of a lease should not be taxable on the tenant.

What needs to be avoided as far as the tenant is concerned, where the payment is on an assignment, is any reference to the assignor's contributing to the new tenant's fit-out. In that situation, there would be effective taxation of the receipt through disallowance of capital allowances on the related element of expenditure.

CHAPTER 28 – TAX RELIEF FOR FINANCE COSTS

Generally, finance costs will be fully deductible on the same basis as they are treated in the accounts.

Point 28.1

Companies should try to get professional fees on property projects allocated as far as reasonable to the funding aspects. These and other finance costs will be allowable even if capitalised in the accounts.
Points 28.2 & 28.3

Watch debt releases in the hands of company borrowers as this can give rise to taxable income.
Point 28.4

Individuals and companies can offset excess finance costs against other income and gains.
Point 28.5

A company's relief for delayed payments of interest may be deferred. This can offer tax planning possibilities.
Point 28.6

Tax relief for finance costs can be restricted if the arrangements are uncommercial or a company is thinly capitalised.
Point 28.7

Tax must be deducted from interest payments by individuals to non-residents and in some circumstances by companies.
Point 28.8

The introduction of rules for 'alternative finance' has improved tax relief for financing structures which are compliant with Islamic Law
Point 28.6

28 Tax relief for finance costs

Point 28.1: *A trader that obtains conventional finance from an unconnected lender for property investment is entitled to a tax deduction for the related finance costs. The deduction for the interest and other costs is normally given on the same basis as they are treated in the accounts.*

Finance costs are, generally speaking, deductible from taxable trading profits on the same basis as they are reflected in the accounts.

The treatment differs depending on whether or not the borrower is a company. If it is, there are a range of deductions permissible as set out below. For an individual or trustee, the deduction is limited to finance costs of a revenue nature. Therefore, in principle, 'capital' costs such as legal, accounting and bank fees relating to the borrowing would not be allowable. There are also differences as mentioned in Points 28.2 to 28.8 below.

With traders, as distinct from the position with investors discussed in Chapters 3A and 3B, foreign companies would be subject to the same rules as any UK company. A foreign company that is trading in the UK through a permanent establishment is subject to UK corporation tax on its profits, unlike a non-resident investment company, which is subject to basic rate income tax.

A company that obtains conventional finance from an unconnected lender for the finance of property trading would be entitled to a deduction for the following costs:

- interest payable;
- premium/discount payable on redemption of the loan;
- losses arising from the repurchase of debt;
- costs of obtaining loan finance including the issue expenses incurred in connection with quoted debt;
- abortive expenditure and expenses incurred in connection with a loan facility which is never drawn;
- termination costs/costs of repaying loan finance;
- any other payments made under the terms of a loan including payments to reimburse a lender's costs

(*FA 1996, s 84(3)*).

HMRC have also confirmed that the costs incurred in varying the terms of a loan are allowable (HMRC Tax Bulletin, October 1996).

The costs are deductible for tax purposes on the same basis as they are reflected in the accounts under generally accepted accounting practice. The rules require the basis adopted to be the amortised-cost basis (analogue to the former accruals basis) or a fair-value accounting basis (analogous to the former mark-to-market basis) (*FA 1996, ss 85A, 85B*). Either basis is acceptable where:

- it conforms to generally accepted accountancy practice (or, as appropriate, International Accounting Standards) for that item. Different loan relationships may involve different practice; and
- there is proper provision for allocating payments under loan relationships or from related transactions between accounting periods.

Unlike in the past, the actual payment dates or due and payable dates do not themselves influence the timing of the deduction – other than for certain connected-party loans (see Point 28.6 below).

The amortised-cost basis (and the former accruals method) would similarly apply where there are either stepped or 'balloon' payments of interest. This may mean smaller payments in earlier years and larger amounts later. For the payer, the effect would be to 'flatten' out the cost on an accruals basis with higher amounts tax-relieved in the earlier years. A lender, on the other hand, would be taxed on accelerated income.

Borrowers will similarly receive relief for any discount paid on relevant discounted securities on an accrued basis. At the extreme, where finance is provided by way of zero-coupon loans, accrued interest will be allowed each year although the interest is not paid until the security is redeemed. The exception is where the holder of the security and the borrower are connected and the borrower is not taxed on the accruals basis.

If the borrower and lender are connected, there are several issues such as the timing of the allowability of accrued costs where the interest payments are deferred (Point 28.6 below).

Point 28.2:   *For UK corporate borrowers funding purchases of property or related capital projects, fees should be allocated as far as reasonable to the funding.*

The purchase of trading premises – or indeed any capital asset – gives rise to costs that may not be deductible from taxable profit. Such costs are generally of a capital nature ie they relate to an item which confers a benefit for far longer than just the current accounting period. As such, they cannot be expensed for tax purposes against the profits of this or any other year.

Where a property attracts an element of capital allowances (see Chapters 29 to 33), the professional costs might be apportioned wholly or partly over the relevant aspects of the property and included in the related capital allowance claim. At best, however, this will only confer a deduction which must be spread over a number of years.

If the fees relate to the funding, then they are part of the finance costs for which a deduction can be claimed. It is, therefore, worthwhile liaising with professionals supplying their services in relation to a property acquisition, reconstruction or refurbishment to ensure they allocate an appropriate portion of their fees to the related funding exercise.

Point 28.3: *If a UK company capitalises interest in the balance sheet, tax relief can still be claimed in that year where the finance is in respect of capital assets.*

The normal rule provides for a deduction for any finance costs which are charged to profit and loss account.

Where interest is included in the value of a fixed asset in the balance sheet, a UK company can claim a deduction for tax purposes (*FA 1996, Sch 9, para 14*). This would include, therefore, interest on finance for purchases and development of trading premises.

The interest relief is available in the accounting period for which the related debit is 'given' (*FA 1996, Sch 9, para 14(2)*). The best interpretation of this is that the relief is available on an accruals basis.

HMRC regard the relief as including all expenses that are revenue as opposed to capital in nature. Thus, whilst interest may be allowable, fees in respect of the finance for a property purchase would not be deductible unless and until charged to the profit and loss account or income statement.

Point 28.4: *Watch releases of debts as they can give rise to a tax liability in the hands of a corporate borrower.*

See Points 3.13 to 3.15 for the tax implications of having debt released by an unconnected lender.

Point 28.5: *Where a borrower has raised finance for a property used in a trade, excess finance costs can reduce other income or gains chargeable to tax.*

Where funds have been borrowed for trading purposes, the related finance costs will be deductible on an accrued basis as trading expenses. The costs are part of the borrower's normal trading expenses.

For individuals (including individuals in partnerships), surplus expenses can be relieved as follows:

- against other income arising in the same year of assessment;
- if there is still an unrelieved loss, against income of the preceding year;
- any loss still unrelieved can be offset against any chargeable gains for the year and against chargeable gains of the previous year, if a claim for setting the loss against income of that year is possible and has been made (*ITA 2007, s 71*);

- unrelieved losses can be carried forward against future trading income.

(*ITA 2007, s 64* and subsequent sections).

In the first four tax years of assessment of a trading business, the possibility of offset is yet greater. The loss can be offset against income for up to three years preceding the year of assessment in which the loss is made (*ITA 2007, s 72*).

There is also provision for 'terminal loss relief' where a loss is sustained in the final 12 months of trading, which supplements the reliefs mentioned above. Under the terminal loss rules, the loss can be offset against any profits from the trade in the three years ending immediately before the commencement of the 12-month period up to the date of discontinuance (*ITA, s 90*).

For a company, expenses can be offset in the following ways:

- against other profits (including other income and gains) of the company in the same year (*TA 1988, s 393A(1a)*);
- surrender by way of group relief against the total taxable profit of any UK company within the same group in the same year (*TA 1988, s 402*);
- carry-back up to one year against total profits of the same company (*TA 1988, s 393A(1d)*);
- carry-back up to three years against total profits for losses incurred in the last 12 months of trading (*TA 1988, s 388*);
- carry-forward indefinitely in the company against profits from the same trade (*TA 1988, s 393(1)*).

Point 28.6:   *Where the borrower is a company and the lender is both connected and not taxed on the accruals basis, the interest must be paid within 12 months of the year end to get a tax deduction in the year of accrual.*

The fact that the borrower is connected to a lender does not prevent a deduction for accrued interest. Generally, where the lending is between UK companies, the treatment is no different for the borrower than if the loan were with an unconnected lender, except that a fair-value basis cannot be used to account for the loan relationship. Furthermore, in a trading situation there is no restriction on the availability to individuals and partnerships of individuals of a tax deduction for accrued interest where the actual payment is deferred.

However, if the borrower is a company and a connected lender is not subject to tax on an accruals basis, the borrower will not receive a deduction in the year in which the interest accrues unless it is paid within 12 months of the year end (*FA 1996, Sch 9, para 2*). The deduction will be allowed in the accounting period when the interest is subsequently paid.

Since UK companies are taxable on accrued interest, this provision is only likely to be relevant where the lender is an individual, a partnership of individuals, a foreign-based company not subject to UK corporation tax or a trustee connected to the company.

There are four specific situations in which relief is deferred until the interest is actually paid. These are where at any time in the accounting period:

(a) the borrower company and the lender are connected;

(b) the borrower is a 'close company' and the lender is a 'participator' in the borrower; an 'associate' of such a participator or a company that the participator controls or in which the participator has a 'major interest'.

A close company is, broadly, any UK or foreign company that is under the control of fewer than six 'participators' or any number of directors (*TA 1988, s 414*). A 'participator' is a person, generally a shareholder, although the term extends to a person with a right to acquire such a share or interest (*TA 1988, s 417*). For what constitutes control see *TA 1988, s 416*.

In certain circumstances even a company fully listed on the Stock Exchange can be close (*TA 1988, s 415*).

A company has a 'major interest' in another company if, essentially, it and another person taken together control the other company and both it and the other person have no less than 40% of the total rights, powers and holdings in that other company (*FA 1996, Sch 9, para 20);*

(c) the lender is a company and the borrower has a major interest in the creditor company or the creditor company has a major interest in the borrower company;

(d) the loan is made by pension trustees and:

(i) the borrower company is the employer of scheme members; or

(ii) the borrower company and the employer are connected; or

(iii) the employer is a company and the borrower company has a major interest in that employer or the employer has a major interest in the borrower company.

This point clearly has to be watched since a borrower might find its tax liability retrospectively increased where it fails to pay its accrued interest by this deadline. Alternatively, a fellow group company that has relied on group relief could find that the losses it has claimed from the borrower have disappeared.

Anyone buying a company from a group where such relief is being relied upon would need to ensure that there is an appropriate warranty in place in the purchase agreement. By the same token, anyone buying a company with past relief for unpaid interest might be required to ensure that the company it buys pays the interest by the requisite date.

A company is connected with another person in any accounting period if at any time in that period:

(a)   the other person is a company and one controls the other; or

(b)   the other person is a company and both companies are under the control of the same person.

(FA 1996, s 87(3))

Control can be exercised by holding shares or otherwise possessing voting power *(FA 1996, s 87)*. A person may also exercise control by means of any powers conferred on him by articles of association or any other documents. In all cases, control means the power to secure that the affairs of the company are conducted in accordance with that person's wishes. In the case of a partnership involving one or more companies, the assumption is that any powers, rights or property vesting in the partnership can be exercised by the partners separately according to their profit-sharing ratio *(FA 1996, s 87)*. Banks or financial traders are generally excluded, since control by shares or voting power is not taken into account if a sale of the shares would give rise to a trading receipt.

The mismatch between the accruals basis of relief under the corporate debt regime and the receipts basis of taxation for certain lenders offers a cash flow tax planning opportunity. An individual or non-UK resident company can exploit this when lending to a connected UK company.

Individuals, trusts or non-resident investment companies are outside the corporate debt regime. Where an individual, trustee or non-resident company is liable to UK tax on interest it is normally on a received basis.

In many cases, that gives rise to an opportunity to exploit a potential cash flow tax advantage. See the example in Point 3.19 in Chapter 3B for an illustration of this.

Point 28.7:   *Finance costs are allowable on funds borrowed from associated and connected persons. This includes lenders based overseas. However, transfer pricing rules will restrict deductibility where loans are not commercial or borrowed by companies that are thinly capitalised.*

See Point 3.5 (for individuals, trustees and non-resident companies) and Points 3.20 and 3.21 (for UK companies) for a discussion on the need for arm's length terms in any borrowing arrangement and the possibility of disallowance for companies with excessive debt to equity ratios.

Point 28.8:   *For payments of interest to anyone other than a UK bank, it is always advisable to check whether there is an obligation to deduct tax.*

HMRC can collect tax from borrowers who make payments of interest in a number of situations.

There is a different regime for individuals on the one hand and UK companies on the other. For the former category, the issues are covered in Points 3.6 and 3.7 in Chapter 3A. For UK companies, this is covered by Points 3.23 to 3.27 in Chapter 3B.

See Points 3.6 and 3.7 in Chapter 3A regarding the obligation on individuals (including individuals in partnerships) to deduct tax on interest payments to non-residents. This relates to trustees as well, although it is rare for trustees to be involved in trading activities directly.

Points 3.23 to 3.28 deal with the tax deduction issues for companies – which for traders includes non-resident companies trading in the UK through a permanent establishment as explained in Point 28.1 above.

Point 28.9: *The introduction of rules for 'alternative finance' has enabled tax relief to be obtained for costs incurred in relation to financing structures which are compliant with Islamic law.*

See Point 3.29 in Chapter 3B for an outline of the typical structures that have been accommodated by changes in the UK tax rules as introduced by Finance Acts in 2005, 2006 and 2007.

CHAPTER 29 – CAPITAL ALLOWANCES ON PLANT AND MACHINERY

Capital allowances are available on machinery and plant fixed to a building occupied for trading or other qualifying purposes. For new builds, reconstruction and purchase of second-hand property it pays to identify eligible items.

Point 29.1

A buyer of second-hand property can claim allowances. There is a need to ascertain what previous claims have been made, if any, and also the opportunity to agree a claim with the seller.
Points 29.6, to 29.9

Expenditure on integrated fixtures from April 2008 attracts a lower, 10% rate of allowance and must be separated from general expenditure on plant and machinery.
Point 29.2

There is a reduced allowance to the extent that the trader has received a contribution or grant.
Point 29.12

In some property situations, it is also necessary to separately identify long-life assets which from April 2008 also attract a 10% writing-down allowance (formerly 6%).
Points 29.3

Allowances are claimable when expenditure is incurred.
Point 29.10

100% capital allowances are available on expenditure in several situations.
Point 29.4

Maximising claims involves proper descriptions and cost allocations particularly of electrical and plumbing work and also in relation to floors, walls, ceilings and professional fees.
Point 29.5

Surplus allowances can usually be offset against other income or gains.
Point 29.11

Lessees can claim allowances on their expenditure and in respect of capital sums paid on grant/assignment.
Point 29.13

It is better to claim repairs where possible.
Point 29.14

Allowances are available on irrecoverable VAT.
Point 29.15

29 Capital allowances on plant and machinery

[*Note* – At the time of writing, there are proposed reforms to the regime for capital allowances on plant and machinery which are outlined in a Government Consultative Document issued in July 2007. The proposals in that document are summarised in this chapter. Final details of the changes will not be available until some time after the consultation period ends in October 2007]

Point 29.1: *A trader can claim capital allowances on expenditure in respect of plant and machinery that is fixed to a building occupied for trading purposes.*

Capital allowances are available on capital expenditure incurred by a person carrying on a 'qualifying activity' on plant and machinery acquired for that purpose (*CAA 2001, s 11*). A trade is a qualifying activity (*CAA 2001, s 15(1)(a)*).

Up to 1 April 2008 (for companies within charge to corporation tax) and fiscal year 2007/08 (for other taxpayers subject to income tax), annual allowances at a rate of 25% apply to the tax written-down value of the of the plant unless the items of plant and machinery are long-life assets (see Point 29.3).

After these dates, there have been changes to the capital allowance regime and the rates of allowances as announced in the 2007 Budget. As a result of these changes, the main rate of writing-down allowances reduces from 25% to 20%. In the year of transition straddling April 2008, a hybrid rate will apply to the pool of expenditure. Using the example of a company with a 31 December year end, this will mean that one quarter of its year falls in the period when the 25% writing down allowance applies. The remaining three quarters will fall in the period when the 20% rate. The result is a hybrid rate of 21.25% (ie 3/12ths of 25% plus 9/12ths of 20%) which is applied to the pool of expenditure at the end of the year. In practice, the hybrid rate is calculated by the number of days in each period.

See Point 29.10 for a summary of the rules for identifying when expenditure is actually incurred for these purposes.

There will also be a new separate category of certain 'integral fixtures' within a building. It is proposed that these will attract a reduced annual writing down allowance of 10%. The Government's proposals regarding integral fixtures were set out in a consultative document issued jointly by HM Revenue and Customs and the Treasury on 26 July 2007 (see point 29.2 below).

100% 'Enhanced Capital Allowances' or ECAs can be claimed on expenditure on qualifying energy efficient plant – see Point 29.4.

Up to April 2008, increased first-year allowances have been available on plant and machinery (except cars and leased assets) where the trader is classified as a 'small or medium-sized enterprise'. To come within this category, a business needs to be within two of the following three criteria (*CAA 2001, s 47(2)(a)*; *Companies Act 1985, s 247*):

- turnover of not more than £22.4 million;
- of not more than £11.2 million; and
- 250 or fewer employees.

The rate of allowance is 40%, although this is increased to 50% for small businesses for a one-year period which ends in April 2008.

These first-year allowances are replaced from April 2008 by a new Annual Investment Allowance under which the first £50,000 of expenditure on machinery and plant can be written off (see Point 29.4).

Point 29.2:   *Expenditure from April 2008 on 'integral fixtures' must be separated from other plant and machinery as this attracts a lower, 10%, rate of annual allowance. This may include some items for which allowances were not previously available.*

The Government announced in the 2007 budget that there would be a new category for certain fixtures which are considered as integral to the structure of a building and which it regards should be eligible for a lower, 10%, rate of annual writing down allowance. The announcement was followed by a consultative document which went a little further in outlining its thinking on this. At the time of writing, the consultation period had not expired and the Government was still contemplating the simplest way to define the assets within this category.

Unless the Government finally opt for a general definition of 'integral fixtures', there is likely to be a short but specific list of items that would only be eligible for this lower allowance. In that case, the probability is that this would include items such as lifts, escalators, air conditioning, heating and ventilation equipment. This would cover the more significant areas of plant expenditure within a construction or refurbishment project.

Whilst this new lower rate category, combined with the reduction of rates on other plant from 25% to 20%, will reduce overall capital allowance relief, there may be some new benefit. In that connection, some expenditure which previously was not eligible for writing-down allowances as plant or machinery, might now attract the 10% allowance under this category, The items the consultative document tentatively refers in that regard include:

- general electrical and power systems;
- cold as well as hot water systems;

- certain fixed, non-moveable parts of building structures which are energy efficient (the consultative document gives the examples of brise soleil and active facades).

On the transition to the new regime, the consultative document proposed that the new 10% rate applied to expenditure from April 2008 (1 April for companies in charge to corporation tax, 6 April for individuals and other entities subject to income tax). Qualifying expenditure and ongoing capital allowance pools before that date are unaffected by the introduction of this new category.

The full 10% allowance will be due in the first transitional period. Therefore, a company with a 31 December year end that incurs the expenditure on the integral fixtures in June 2008 receives a full 10% allowance in the year to 31 December 2008.

Since expenditure relating to integral fixtures incurred prior to the regime continues to attract 20% allowances, this suggests that buying a property company with its ongoing pool of integral fixtures may be more beneficial than buying the property. In the first scenario, the company can carry on claiming writing-down allowances at a rate of 20% a year. If the property were acquired, only 10% allowances might be available on that expenditure.

See Point 29.10 for a summary of the rules for identifying when expenditure is actually incurred for these purposes.

Point 29.3: *In some property situations, it is also necessary separately to identify long-life machinery and plant which from April 2008 also attract a 10% allowance.*

Writing-down allowances for certain 'long-life' plant and machinery are available at a reduced rate which is 10% from April 2008 and 6% per year before then (*CAA 2001, ss 90–104*).

The reduced allowance relates to items where there is a reasonable expectation of a useful economic life of at least 25 years when they are first brought into use. These provisions do not apply where the plant and machinery in question is a fixture in a building used as a retail shop, showroom, hotel or office or for a purpose which is ancillary to any of these (*CAA 2001, s 93*).

Typical items of plant installed as fixtures of buildings would not have an expected useful life over 25 years and many of the more common commercial buildings have been excluded in any event. Where buildings are used for purposes that are not excluded – the leisure and nursing home sectors being notable examples – the category of 'long-life' assets could be relevant. However, as mentioned in Point 29.2 above, a similar 10% rate is being introduced for certain other fixtures in a building from April 2008.

Point 29.4:   *100% capital allowances are available for energy-saving/environmentally beneficial plant, renovating/converting property which is brought into use for business purposes and also, from April 2008, for the first £50,000 expenditure under the new annual investment allowance scheme.*

100% allowances – which provide the opportunity for a complete write-off of costs in the year in which they are incurred – can be claimed in the following situations:

(a)   Expenditure is incurred on new qualifying energy-saving or environmentally beneficial plant and machinery. The government publishes details of the products that will qualify for these enhanced capital allowances (or ecas) in an energy technology product list (ETPL). The ETPL can be accessed on the internet at website www.eca.gov.uk (*CAA 2001, ss 45A–45C; 45H–45J*). Note that under the 2007 Budget proposals, companies that cannot fully benefit from these allowances, eg due to losses, should be able to opt instead for a tax refund. Details of this proposal have not been finalised at the time of writing. This opportunity is only to be made available to companies.

(b)   A 100% allowance has been available since 11 April 2007 for the cost of converting or renovating property situated in an 'assisted area' to bring it back into business use. Although the relief was introduced in the *Finance Act 2005*, its introduction was delayed pending EU consent and the consequent need to reduce the areas in which the property could be situated (see Point 33.11 in Chapter 33).

(c)   The first £50,000 of expenditure on plant and machinery incurred by a business from April 2008 under the annual investment allowance scheme. This proposed relief includes qualifying expenditure on integral fixtures (Point 29.2) and long-life assets (Point 29.3). As envisaged at the time of writing it is aimed at all sizes of businesses and replaces the previous system of special first-year allowances to small and medium-sized enterprises from April 2008.

The intention is that only one £50,000 allowance is available for a group of companies each year. The provisions will also seek to prevent associations of companies from gaining a multiple entitlement to the allowance by fragmenting their expenditure between a number of companies.

In contrast, individuals who carry on more than one business will receive a £50k allowance for each business.

100% allowances are also technically available where plant and machinery is installed in a qualifying enterprise zone building although, following the expiry of the zones, the situations where this can now be relevant will be rare

There is also a 100% allowance on the renovation or conversion of vacant or underused space above certain premises to residential use. This is primarily aimed at unused space above shops and similar commercial property which was formerly used as a dwelling.

Proposals were announced in the 2007 Budget to extend the relief to the clearance of derelict or long-term unused land.

Point 29.5: *Whether the expenditure is on the construction of a new building, reconstruction work at an existing building or the purchase of a second-hand building, it pays to identify the items on which capital allowances could be due.*

See Points 6.1 to 6.4 in Part A for a discussion of what constitutes plant and machinery in a building. Appendix I lists some of the more common items within a building and the extent to which they qualify for allowances. Further consideration is now necessary following the implementation of the 2007 Budget changes in relation to 'integrated fixtures'. Note that expenditure on some of the items of plant listed there will, from April 2008, be regarded as integral fixtures and be part of a separate pool attracting just 10% writing-down allowances (see Point 29.2). Furthermore, some expenditure in certain buildings will be on 'long-life assets' which also attracts a 10% writing-down allowance (Point 29.3), which will go in the same capital allowances pool.

The above legislation, in specifying which items constitute plant, needs to be read in conjunction with case law where the distinction between plant and non-plant has been explored in a number of cases (see Points 6.3 and 6.4 in Part A).

There has been much debate over what expenditure does qualify as plant. Electrical and water installations can be problematic with HMRC seeking to disallow normal services to the building. There is a discussion on this in Point 6.3 in Part A above.

Expenditure on items such as floors, walls and ceilings are generally disallowed since these items are normally associated with the setting of the business rather than apparatus used in the trade. However, sometimes allowances are lost because of inappropriate description or allocation of the amounts involved. See Point 6.4 for further discussion of this.

As mentioned in Point 29.2, some items which formerly attracted no allowance may come under the new category of integral fixtures.

Finally, an element of professional fees should be allowed – see Point 6.8.

Point 29.6:   *A buyer of second-hand property with fixtures that qualify as plant and machinery can potentially claim significant allowances. Steps should be taken to establish eligibility and the likely quantum of allowances.*

Tax relief arising from capital allowances on the purchase of a property enables the buyer to recoup a part of the cash outflow.

In some cases, 40%–50% of the purchase price of modern buildings has been attributable to fixtures and equipment eligible for allowances. From April 2008, some of these items will be 'integral fixtures' (see Point 29.2), attracting writing down allowances at a lower rate of 10%. The actual entitlement to allowances will be influenced by the following factors:

(a)   Whether the plant allowances attach to the interest being purchased. The freeholder is normally the person owning the plant and entitled to allowances. However, in the past, an election may have been made in favour of a long lessee (see Point 6.8 in Part A). Alternatively, the allowances may arise from expenditure by the lessee, such as the retail tenant that fits out empty premises. Clearly, whether the freehold or a leasehold interest is bought, it is important to establish the capital allowances background to that interest.
Note that lessees can claim allowances in respect of fixed plant in a building even though as a matter of law these items belong to the freeholder (see Point 6.8).

(b)   For properties bought after 24 July 1996, what was the previous claims history and is the seller looking to do some deal on the allowances (see Points 6.12)

(c)   For properties not affected by (b), what 'reasonable value' can be attributed to the plant (see Point 6.14)

(d)   Whether the plant or machinery is an integral fixture or long-life asset (Points 6.5 and 6.6) and therefore subject to a reduced 10% annual allowance (formerly 6% in the case of long-life assets) – see Point 29.3

(e)   Whether there might be eligibility for 100% allowances on any expenditure (Point 29.4)

29.7:   *A buyer of property must ascertain what eligible expenditure the seller or any previous seller owning the property claimed after 23 July 1996.*

See Point 6.12 in Part A for an explanation of this point.

Point 29.8:   *The buyer and seller can elect to adopt a specific value for the plant and machinery for capital allowances purposes on the transfer of a property.*

See Point 6.13 in Part A for a discussion on this point.

Point 29.9: *Where Points 29.7 and 29.8 do not apply there is no statutory restriction on the amount eligible for allowances by reference to the vendor's cost. The amount eligible is then determined by estimating a just apportionment of the purchase price.*

There will be no statutory restriction on the available allowances if everyone who has owned that property at or since 24 July 1996 has done so without making any claim to allowances in respect of the plant.

See Point 6.14 for an illustration of the position.

Point 29.10: *The allowances are claimable in the chargeable period in which expenditure is incurred.*

Capital allowances are claimable when expenditure is incurred.

Once a trade is commenced, future expenditure is treated as incurred when there is an unconditional obligation to pay (*CAA 2001, s 5(1)*). This might be when an invoice is issued or a binding agreement signed.

On long-term construction contracts, stage payments are normally made periodically on production of an architect's certificate. When the obligation to pay becomes unconditional on the production of a certificate, expenditure is treated as incurred in an accounting period or period of account if the certificate is issued not more than one month after the end of the period.

Where payment is due more than four months after the obligation to pay becomes unconditional, the expenditure is treated as incurred on the date(s) it is due to be paid (*CAA 2001, s 5(5)*). The issue of an invoice or signing of a contract designed to bring forward the capital allowances claim to an earlier accounting period or period of account than would have been the case in a normal commercial transaction is countered by an anti-avoidance provision (*CAA 2001, s 5(6)*).

Point 29.11: *Traders can use surplus allowances in a number of ways but the rules differ depending on whether or not the claimant is a company.*

Where capital allowances exceed income, individuals and companies can use the resulting trading loss in a number of ways. These have already been set out in Chapter 28 in relation to finance costs and reference can be made to Point 28.5 on this.

Point 29.12:   *If a trader receives a contribution towards capital expenditure, capital allowances will usually be restricted.*

A contribution or grant that a trader gets toward the installation of plant or machinery will normally restrict the amount eligible for capital allowances accordingly (*CAA 2001, s 532*).

Where the contribution is made by a landlord as an inducement to enter into a lease, this may result in a more favourable treatment than a pure inducement payment (see Point 27.6).

Where the payer is not the landlord – for instance the assignor of the lease – a pure inducement payment unattached to any specific works/assets may well not give rise to any tax liability in the trader's hands.

Point 29.13:   *Lessees can claim allowances in respect of fixed plant in a building even though as a matter of law these items belong to the freeholder.*

Lessees are entitled to allowances on fixed plant in the following circumstances:

(a)   Where a lessee incurs expenditure on fixed plant for use in a trade (or other qualifying activity), capital allowances can be claimed on that expenditure (*CAA 2001, s 176*).

(b)   Where a lessee takes an assignment of a lease and pays a capital sum which wholly or partly represents expenditure on fixed plant, the lessee can claim allowances on that element of the payment in respect of the plant (*CAA 2001, s 181*). A claim can only be made if either no one has previously been entitled to claim the allowance or the receipt is brought into the vendor's capital allowances computation. Thus if a remaining sub-tenant has claimed allowances the new landlord cannot claim for any capital sum paid in respect of the tenant's fixtures. Similarly, the lessee cannot become entitled to allowances on assets on which the freeholder is entitled to claim.

(c)   A lessee can claim allowances where a capital sum is paid on the grant of a lease and the sum wholly or partly includes expenditure in respect of fixed plant (*CAA 2001, s 184*). However, if the lessor would otherwise have been entitled to the allowances, both the lessee and the lessor must make an election within two years of the commencement of the lease if the lessee is to claim the allowances (*CAA 2001, s 183*). If no election is made, the lessor might be entitled to the allowances.

No election is necessary if the lessor would not have been entitled to allowances. An election cannot be made where the lessor and the lessee are connected or the sole or main object would be the obtaining of allowances.

Point 29.14: *It is worthwhile scrutinising expenditure to see whether it may strictly qualify as repairs and maintenance since this can be fully deductible in the year it is incurred.*

When an item of plant is installed or completely replaced, the related expenditure will be treated as capital and eligible for capital allowances. However, if the expenditure is in respect of the overhaul of plant or the replacement of parts, then this should qualify for 100% deduction as repairs or maintenance.

It may be advisable to consider the exact nature of work carried out or to be carried out to determine whether expenditure that might appear to be capital is, in fact, revenue. For instance, if air conditioning work involves the removal of defective ducting rather than the replacement or renewal of a whole system, that might be shown as repairs. Similarly, if heating expenditure related to the replacement of worn radiators, then it would be repairs as opposed to capital expenditure. However, if the nature of the work changes the nature of the original asset then that would not be a repair – such as in the recent case of plastic inner piping inserted within an old cast iron main (*Auckland Gas Co Ltd v IRC* [2000] STC 527).

A related point is that when reviewing a refurbishment programme, it may well be sensible to consider repairing assets where this is a possibility rather than replacing them (see Point 4.1 in Part A regarding repairs as distinguished from capital expenditure).

Note that to obtain a deduction in a year, the relevant expenditure will need to be reflected in the profit and loss account rather than capitalised in the balance sheet. If the expenditure is capitalised, the tax treatment will follow the accounting treatment with a deduction delayed unless and until amounts are written off as expenses through the profit and loss account.

Point 29.15: *If irrecoverable VAT is incurred on a building purchase – or building/installation work – the expenditure eligible for capital allowances in relation to plant and machinery is increased accordingly.*

If a trader cannot fully reclaim VAT on property expenditure, the irrecoverable VAT increases the related cost for direct tax purposes.

Where VAT incurred on plant expenditure is wholly or partly irrecoverable, the amount eligible for capital allowances will include the irrecoverable amount. Furthermore, if adjustments are required under the Capital Goods Scheme, resulting in changes to VAT recovery over a ten-year period, the qualifying capital allowance expenditure will vary accordingly (*CAA 2001, s 235*).

See Chapter 39 for further points on VAT and Point 39.7 for the Capital Goods Scheme.

CHAPTER 30 – CAPITAL ALLOWANCES ON INDUSTURIAL BUILDINGS

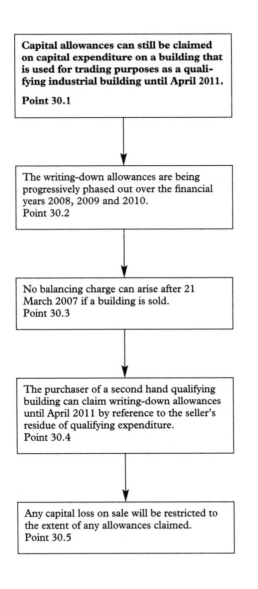

Capital allowances can still be claimed on capital expenditure on a building that is used for trading purposes as a qualifying industrial building until April 2011.

Point 30.1

The writing-down allowances are being progressively phased out over the financial years 2008, 2009 and 2010.
Point 30.2

No balancing charge can arise after 21 March 2007 if a building is sold.
Point 30.3

The purchaser of a second hand qualifying building can claim writing-down allowances until April 2011 by reference to the seller's residue of qualifying expenditure.
Point 30.4

Any capital loss on sale will be restricted to the extent of any allowances claimed.
Point 30.5

30 Capital allowances on industrial buildings

Point 30.1: *Capital allowances can still be claimed in respect of capital expenditure incurred on a building which is used for trading purposes as an 'industrial building or structure'. However, these allowances are being phased out in the period to April 2011.*

A taxpayer owning a relevant interest in a qualifying industrial building can claim allowances on qualifying expenditure incurred in relation to that interest (*CAA 2001, s 271*). These allowances are being phased out in the period to April 2011 as mentioned in 30.2 below.

To be an 'industrial building', a building must be used for the purposes of a trade in one of the ways prescribed in, *s 274* of the *Capital Allowances Act 2001*. These are set out in Appendix III.

The expenditure in question must be capital expenditure for the taxpayer. Repairs and maintenance costs which would normally be allowable as revenue items would not qualify. Nor would expenditure incurred by a property dealer or developer in respect of a building held as trading stock. This may also preclude a taxpayer claiming an allowance where the building is bought and sold within a short period.

Allowances claimed by the taxpayer are in respect of the 'relevant interest' held. The owner of a freehold may, for instance, have incurred expenditure on the construction of the building. A tenant, in turn, could incur capital expenditure carrying out other construction or improvement work which would constitute qualifying expenditure in relation to the leasehold interest. The concept of the relevant interest for IBA purposes used to be important when there was a possibility of a balancing charge or allowance arising on a disposal. Such balancing adjustments ceased to arise after 21 March 2007 (see Point 30.3) although they continue to apply to disposals of Enterprise Zone properties (see Chapter 33).

Ordinarily, a leaseholder could not claim allowances for expenditure by a freeholder. However, this rule is relaxed where:

(a) a lease is granted for more than 50 years; and
(b) the lessor and lessee elect that the lessee may claim IBAs; and
(c) the lessor and lessee are not connected; and
(d) the lessor is not granting the lease and making the election in order to obtain a balancing allowance.

(*CAA 2001, ss 290, 291*).

Point 30.2:   *Writing-down allowances are available on capital expenditure on qualifying industrial buildings, although the rate of allowance is diminishing from 4% in financial year 2007 to nil from April 2011.*

Expenditure on a qualifying industrial building attracts an annual 4% writing-down allowance in 2007/08. After that, the allowances reduce to 3% in 2008/09, 2% in 2009/10 and finally 1% in the last year 2010/11. These are the amounts available on the construction or purchase of new unused buildings. The position, together with the allowances that can be claimed on the purchase of second-hand buildings is set out in Point 30.4 below.

The situations in which qualifying expenditure arise (and will continue to do so up to April 2008) are:

(a)   Where a new building is purchased unused from a developer who has sold the building in the course of his development trade, allowances are claimable on the purchase price of the building less the element of cost attributable to the land or fixed plant and machinery (*CAA 2001, ss 272(1), 296*).

(b)   Where a new building is purchased unused from anyone other than a developer, allowances are claimable on the lower of the purchase price and the actual cost of construction. Unlike situation (a), therefore, allowances could not be claimed on any element of profit incorporated in the vendor's sale price (*CAA 2001, s 295*).

(c)   Where the building is being constructed by the taxpayer or there is an existing building to which structural work is being carried out, the cost of construction work will qualify for allowances (*CAA 2001, s 294*).

(d)   Where a second-hand building is acquired, the purchaser may claim allowances by reference to the residue of expenditure of the vendor (see Point 30.4 below).

If part of the building is not used for a qualifying purpose (eg space is occupied as offices or showrooms), there can be a pro-rata restriction of the allowances. No restriction will apply unless the expenditure on the non-qualifying part exceeds 25% of the whole (*CAA 2001, s 283*).

There may be items of expenditure which relate to plant and machinery as distinguished from the structure of the building. Since such items attract a higher rate of writing-down allowance (see Chapter 29), these items should be separately identified where possible.

Writing-down allowances are only available in an accounting period or period of account where the building is actually in a qualifying use at the end of the period.

Point 30.3: *Allowances claimed on an industrial building are permanent as no clawback of IBAs can now arise on the sale of the building.*

Until 21 March 2007, where the relevant interest in a building was sold, a balancing charge could arise. Only where buildings had been kept a certain length of time after the allowance entitlement first arose – usually 25 years – would a balancing adjustment be avoided. If the sale price was above the tax written-down cost of the property a taxable balancing charge arose. If the arm's-length sale price was below that figure, a further allowance – or balancing allowance – could be claimed.

The changes to the IBA regime announced in the 2007 Budget resulted in an immediate abolition of all balancing adjustments with effect from 21 March 2007 (*FA 2007, s 36*). From that date, anyone buying a second-hand building merely stepped into the seller's shoes and carried on claiming allowances subject to new transitional rules (see Point 30.4 below).

The disbanding of the balancing adjustment as at 21 March 2007 did not apply to sales which were already subject to a contract entered into before that date (*FA 2007, s 36(7)*). The rules also do not extend to Enterprise Zone disposals where balancing adjustments can still arise (*FA 2007, s 36(3)* – see Chapter 33).

The changes now mean that it is no longer necessary to plan to avoid a clawback by selling a lesser interest (eg a 999-year lease out of a freehold or a 100-year lease out of a 125-year lease).

Point 30.4: *The purchaser of a second-hand building can claim writing-down allowances by reference to the vendor's 'residue of expenditure' up to April 2011.*

The position of a person buying a used industrial building will depend on whether the purchase occurred before or after 21 March 2007. The position as indicated by the Government's consultative document can be illustrated with two examples:

EXAMPLE 1

A building cost £600,000 in January 1997, excluding any land element. It was sold in January 2007 (ie before 21 March 2007) for £1 million. It has been used as a qualifying industrial building throughout the period.

In this scenario £600,000 less ten years of 4%, gives rise to a tax written down value of £360,000 as at January 2007 when the building was sold for £1 million, all £240,000 allowances are clawed back. The residue of expenditure inherited by the buyer is £600,000.

On purchase, the buyer (a company with a 1 January to 31 December accounting year) would have been entitled to write off £600,000 over the balance of the 25-year ownership ie 15 years (as the previous owner had it for

10). That works out at 6.66% per year, which would be the rate of allowance in the year to 31 December 2007.

The year to 31 December 2008 straddles the financial year 2008, which starts for companies within charge to corporation tax on 1 April. For that financial year, the IBA entitlement falls by one quarter. Accordingly, the entitlement falls to 5% for financial year 2008. Straddling that financial year means that a quarter of the year attracts the 6.66% rate and three-quarters of the year the 5% rate, leading to a hybrid rate of 5.4%.

In the year to 31 December 2009, the original allowance falls by a half, reducing the hybrid rate to 3.75%.

The next year to 31 December 2010 sees the allowance fall by a further quarter to 2.08%.

The final year the purchaser will get allowances to will be to 31 December 2011 in which it will be entitled to three months at 2.5% taking it up to 31 March 2011. The hybrid rate for that year becomes .42%.

The position changes if the building were sold in April 2007. Using similar details as for example 1 above, we will assume that the previous owner brought the property into use ten years earlier in April 1997.

EXAMPLE 2

On purchase, the buyer is immediately within the new rules. The allowance in the year to 31 December 2007 will be 4%. This can only be applied to the seller's written-down amount of £360,000 as no balancing adjustment is now brought into account.

The year to 31 December 2008, straddles the financial year 2008, which starts for companies within charge to income tax on 1 April. For that financial year, the IBA entitlement falls by one quarter to 3%. The hybrid rate for the year to 31 December 2008 becomes 3.25% (one quarter of 4% and three quarters of 3%)

In the year to 31 December 2009, the allowance falls by a further quarter, reducing the hybrid rate to 2.25%.

The next year to 31 December 2010 sees the allowance fall by a further quarter to 1.25%.

The final year of allowances will be to 31 December 2011. The purchaser will be entitled to three months at 1% taking it up to 31 March 2011. The hybrid rate for that year becomes .25%.

The residue of expenditure, to which the above allowance rates apply, will reduce further if the building has not been in qualifying use throughout its life.

Note that the above examples are based on interpretation of the Government's proposals in its July 2007 consultative document and the position may be subject to revision once final legislation is published.

Point 30.5: *A chargeable capital gain can arise on the sale of an industrial building but an allowable capital loss cannot, to the extent that capital allowances have been given.*

Any excess of sale price of a building over cost (or value at 31 March 1982 if higher) plus indexation allowance (where appropriate) would give rise to a capital gain chargeable to tax under capital gains tax rules. A loss, on the other hand, may not necessarily constitute an allowable loss to the extent that capital allowances have been claimed of that amount (*TCGA 1992, s 41(2)*).

Since no allowances are available on land, capital loss treatment would be available for any loss sustained in relation to the land element.

Indexation relief can neither create nor enhance a capital loss on any disposal and so will not figure in the calculation. See Point 12.3 for a discussion of this.

As explained in Point 12.3, it still may be possible to claim a capital loss on a disposal where it arises from indexation allowance accruing before 30 November 1993 following an earlier acquisition on a no gain/no loss basis (eg intra-group sale or transfer between spouses).

CHAPTER 31 – CAPITAL ALLOWANCES ON QUALIFYING HOTELS

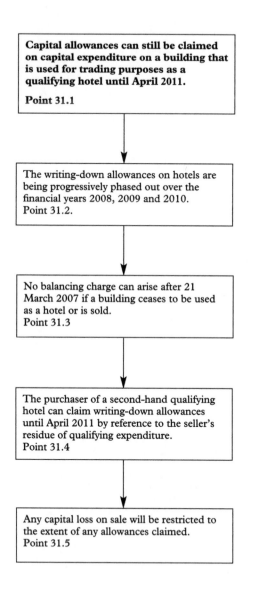

Capital allowances can still be claimed on capital expenditure on a building that is used for trading purposes as a qualifying hotel until April 2011.

Point 31.1

The writing-down allowances on hotels are being progressively phased out over the financial years 2008, 2009 and 2010.
Point 31.2.

No balancing charge can arise after 21 March 2007 if a building ceases to be used as a hotel or is sold.
Point 31.3

The purchaser of a second-hand qualifying hotel can claim writing-down allowances until April 2011 by reference to the seller's residue of qualifying expenditure.
Point 31.4

Any capital loss on sale will be restricted to the extent of any allowances claimed.
Point 31.5

31 Capital allowances on qualifying hotels

Point 31.1: *Capital allowances can still be claimed in respect of capital expenditure incurred on a building which is used for trading purposes as a qualifying hotel. However, these allowances are being phased out in the period to April 2011.*

Capital allowances are available in respect of structural expenditure on hotel buildings. The rules follow closely those for industrial buildings and in many respects the points raised in Chapter 30 above apply equally to hotels. As with industrial buildings allowances, the allowances for hotels are being phased out in the period to April 2011 as mentioned in Point 31.2 below.

An hotel must satisfy the following conditions in any year to be eligible for relief:

(1)   The hotel must be open for at least four months in the 'season' (ie from April to October inclusive); and,
(2)   when open:
    (a)   the hotel must have at least ten letting bedrooms available to the public;
    (b)   the sleeping accommodation offered must consist wholly or mainly of letting bedrooms;
    (c)   services should be provided which normally would include breakfast and evening meal, the making of beds and cleaning of rooms;
    (d)   the letting bedrooms must be available to the public generally and not in the same occupation for more than one month.

(*CAA 2001, s 279*).

Point 31.2: *Writing-down allowances are available on capital expenditure on qualifying hotels although the annual allowance is diminishing from 4% in financial year 2007 to nil from April 2011.*

The rules for hotels are similar to those relating to industrial buildings and reference should be made to Point 30.2 for a discussion of the position and the transitional position during the phasing out of these allowances. As with industrial buildings, there is a restriction if more than 25% of the building is in a non-qualifying use (*CAA 2001, s 283*).

Point 31.3:   *Allowances claimed on a hotel are permanent as no clawback of allowances can now arise* if a *building ceases to be used as an hotel or sold*

As with other aspects of the transitional rules, the position in relation to hotel building allowances mirror those of industrial buildings allowances. See Point 30.3 regarding the removal of balancing adjustments following the 2007 Budget announcements.

Point 31.4:   *When a 'used' hotel is acquired the purchaser can continue claiming writing-down allowances until April 2011 by reference to the vendor's 'residue of qualifying expenditure'.*

The eligibility for allowances when a second-hand hotel is bought will depend on whether the purchase was pre or post 21 March 2007. See Point 30.4 for a similar discussion of this point in relation to industrial buildings.

Point 31.5:   *A chargeable capital gain can arise on the sale of an hotel but an allowable capital loss cannot, to the extent that capital allowances have been given.*

See Point 30.5 for a discussion of the similar rules for industrial buildings.

CHAPTER 32 – CAPITAL ALLOWANCES ON AGRICULTURAL BUILDINGS

Annual allowances are available up to April 2011 to the owner or tenant of agricultural/forestry land on capital expenditure incurred on the construction of buildings used for farming.

Point 32.1

Allowances are available on up to one-third of the cost of a farmhouse. A farm cottage can attract full allowances.
Point 32.2

Since 21 March 2007, no balancing adjustment arises on the sale or demolition of an agricultural building.
Point 32.3

32 Capital allowances on agricultural buildings

Point 32.1: *Annual allowances are available to the owner or tenant of any agricultural or forestry land in respect of capital expenditure incurred on the construction of buildings used for farming. However, these allowances are being phased out in the period to April 2011.*

Agricultural buildings allowances are available in respect of capital expenditure incurred on the construction of agricultural buildings (*CAA 2001, s 361*). However, as with industrial buildings allowances and allowances for hotels, agricultural building allowances are being phased out in the period to April 2011.

Expenditure on a qualifying agricultural building attracts an annual 4% writing-down allowance in 2007/08. After that, the allowances reduce to 3% in 2008/09, 2% in 2009/10 and finally 1% in the last year 2010/11. These are the writing-down allowances available on the expenditure on the construction or purchase of new unused buildings and also apply on the purchase of second-hand buildings in relation to the written-down cost inherited from the seller. As noted in Point 32.3 below, no balancing adjustment can now arise on the sale of an agricultural building.

The buildings that qualify for allowances currently include:

(a) farmhouses and farm cottages – see Point 32.2 below;
(b) farm buildings – these include barns and sheds for the storage and protection of stock, livestock and tools;
(c) other works – these include items such as drainage and sewerage works, water and electricity installations, walls, shelter belts of trees, silos, farm roads and the reclamation of former agricultural land.

(HMRC Capital Allowances Manual CA 40000–41420 generally; for 'other works', see CA 40100).

The expenditure must be incurred in connection with 'husbandry' activities and the building must be used for these purposes. 'Husbandry' comprises any form of agriculture and, in addition, intensive rearing of livestock or fish on a commercial basis for human consumption (*CAA 2001, s 362*).

Where the building or works is used for a purpose other than husbandry initially, the related expenditure cannot qualify for allowances and, indeed, will never qualify even if the building etc is in agricultural use in later years (*CAA 2001, s 374(1)*).

To claim an allowance, a person must have a 'relevant interest' in the land in question (*CAA 2001, s 361(3)*). A relevant interest would include a lease or freehold.

Point 32.2: *Allowances are available to April 2011 on up to one-third of the cost of a farmhouse unless the residence element is out of proportion to the size of the farm. A farm cottage, which is treated as a separate category of dwelling, attracts full allowances.*

The residence occupied by the person who runs the farm (whether as owner or tenant) is treated as a farmhouse. Allowances are available on one-third of the expenditure on the construction, re-construction, alteration or improvement of farmhouses. This could be further reduced if the accommodation and amenities of the farmhouse are out of proportion to the nature and extent of the farm (*CAA 2001, s 369(3), (4)*).

The one-third restriction gives rise to an important distinction between a farmhouse on the one hand and a farm cottage (agricultural worker's dwelling) on the other.

As mentioned, a farmhouse is a building which is occupied by the person running the farm. This need not necessarily be the owner but could be the farm manager or even the head employee (*Lindsay v IRC* (1953) 34 TC 289).

A building occupied by an employee who is not running the farm is a farm cottage. A building occupied by the owner of the farm is also a cottage if the farm is not run from that building. However, a building is not a farm cottage, whoever occupies it, if it is on such a scale as not to be a cottage in the accepted sense of the word.

No restriction applies on the expenditure incurred on farm cottages. This could be particularly useful if several members of the family are involved in the farming business. It has been held, for instance, that where a house was built for a farmer's son who was a partner in the farming business, this was a farm cottage rather than a farmhouse for ABA purposes (*IRC v John M Whiteford & Son* (1962) 40 TC 379).

One general rule applying to any farm building other than a farmhouse is that if it is also used for any other purpose or activity, expenditure is apportioned for ABA purposes (*CAA 2001, s 369(5)*).

A farm employee's cottage does not have to be situated on the farmland. It can be in a nearby town.

Point 32.3: *Since 21 March 2007, allowances claimed remain permanent. On the sale or demolition of an agricultural building no balancing capital allowances adjustment will arise.*

In the past, agricultural buildings allowances have differed from allowances on industrial buildings and hotels in the treatment of balancing adjustments. As a general rule, no balancing allowances or charges were made in respect of the disposal or demolition of an agricultural building. On sale, the purchaser continued claiming the allowances until the cost has been fully allowed.

It was, however, possible for an election to be made for a balancing adjustment. On sale, if both the purchaser and vendor elected, a balancing charge or allowance could have been made which was computed on similar lines to the balancing charges and allowances available in respect of industrial buildings. On demolition or destruction, the election could have been made by the owner of the building for a balancing allowance equivalent to unclaimed allowances at the date of demolition or destruction (*CAA 2001, ss 381, 382*).

This election has not been available where these events occur after 21 March 2007, when changes to these capital allowance regimes were announced in the 2007 Budget. Since that date, neither balancing allowance nor balancing charge can arise on the disposal or demolition of an agricultural building.

CHAPTER 33 – CAPITAL ALLOWANCES ON ENTERPRISE ZONE BUILDINGS AND RENOVATIONS/CONVERSIONS IN ASSISTED AREAS

100% initial allowances can be claimed on expenditure on qualifying enterprise zone buildings, although there are now only limited circumstances when this can arise.

Point 33.1

A balancing charge arises if the building ceases to be used commercially.
Point 33.7

Granting a subordinate interest on sale may avoid a balancing charge, but subject to anti-avoidance rules.
Point 33.8

100% allowance may continue to be available after the ten-year zone period expires on a pre-existing building contract.
Points 33.2 & 33.3

The initial allowance may still be available to buyers of unused buildings after the expiry of the zone.
Point 33.4

Initial allowance may still also be available on a purchase within two years of first use.
Point 33.5

If seller trades as a builder or developer, the buyer can claim on the price paid, less the land element.
Point 33.6

Any capital loss on sale will be restricted to the extent of any allowances claimed.
Point 33.9

The purchaser of a second-hand building can claim writing-down allowances up to April 2011.
Point 33.10

A 100% allowance is available for the conversion and renovation costs of bringing a building back into commercial use in certain designated areas.
Point 33.11

33 Capital allowances on buildings in enterprise zones and renovations/conversions in assisted areas

Point 33.1: *Expenditure on a building situated in an enterprise zone can attract a 100% capital allowance within ten years of creation of the zone. However, the last enterprise zones were created in 1996, so the only ongoing claims will be on a very few situations where expenditure is still being incurred under an old building contract.*

For a number of years, qualifying expenditure on a commercial building in an enterprise zone has been potentially eligible for a 100% initial allowance (*CAA 2001, s 271(1)(b)(iv)*). The rules relating to enterprise zones were similar to those in respect of industrial buildings allowances (covered in Chapter 30) although with some modifications.

Generally, to qualify for the initial allowance the expenditure must have been incurred within ten years of the site's designation as an enterprise zone (*CAA 2001, ss 298(1), 305(1)*). However, as will be noted from the list of enterprise zones in Appendix II, none of these ten-year periods extended beyond 2006. Accordingly, there are now no zones for which expenditure can continue to attract the initial allowance on this basis.

There are other qualifying circumstances as mentioned in Points 33.2, 33.3, 33.4 and 33.5 below. In view of these, there will still be opportunities to claim the 100% allowances for a number of years – in fact for a further ten years after the last zone expired in 2006. It is likely that there will only be a few situations where the circumstances fit the technical requirements necessary to qualify for the 100% allowance,

For those who have benefited or can still benefit from this allowance, the rules for enterprise zone allowances operate similarly to those for industrial buildings allowances generally. Therefore, matters such as what is the relevant interest and how a leaseholder can be entitled to allowances are subject to the same rules as referred to in Point 30.1 dealing with industrial buildings allowances.

An enterprise zone building qualifies if it is in any commercial use. There is a restriction of allowances if more than 25% of the building is in non-commercial use.

Where a second-hand building is acquired, the purchaser may be entitled to claim writing-down allowances on the residue of qualifying expenditure (see Point 33.10). Note that these have not been affected by the phasing out of capital allowances on other commercial buildings. There is one situation where a buyer of a used building less than two years old can claim the initial allowance, which is covered in Point 33.5 below.

Point 33.2:   *A 100% initial allowance may still be available if expenditure is incurred under a binding contract which was entered into during the ten-year designation period.*

Although the ten-year period of the zones listed in Appendix II has expired, there are circumstances in which the initial allowance can still be claimed. To qualify in this instance, the expenditure must be incurred under a contract which was entered into within the ten-year life of the zone even if the money is spent after that time (*CAA 2001, s 298(1)(b)*). The money must be actually spent within ten years of the expiry of the zone.

EXAMPLE 1

On 1 November 2005, Phillips Limited contracted with builders, Reid Limited, for the construction of a warehouse for its own use in the Bassetlaw enterprise zone in East Midlands. The contract was for £4m.

The designation period of that enterprise zone ended on 16 November 2005.

On 1 March 2007, building work commenced and was completed a year later as specified at a cost of £5m, including a further £1m extra works.

Since Phillips Limited incurred expenditure under a contract entered into before the expiry of the enterprise zone, the subsequent expenditure under the contract attracts full enterprise zone allowances up to the extent of the works under the original contract. The extra work of £1m would not, however, qualify.

The money under the contract needs to be spent before the tenth anniversary of the expiry of the zone. In the above case, that would have to be by 16 November 2015. If a proportion of the actual expenditure was incurred or contracted for after the ten-year period, then the amount eligible for allowances is restricted by the appropriate proportion. Thus, if £1m out of £5m represented expenditure after the expiry of the zone, the qualifying expenditure is 80% of the total.

Furthermore, the works need to be those contracted for. Any variation of the agreement could invalidate its qualification for allowances.

Point 33.3: *The purchaser of the building with a 'golden contract' after the expiry of the ten-year life of the zone can still claim the 100% allowance on expenditure contracted for during the life of the zone – but the seller may have to pay the contract costs prior to sale.*

As mentioned in Point 33.2 above, allowances can still be claimed for a further ten years after the expiry of an enterprise zone on expenditure incurred under a binding contract entered into during the ten-year life of the zone.

Some uncompleted buildings may have been contracted for during the ten-year period. The work may not have been completed – or indeed started – for a reason. The owner may have hit financial problems or have held back on the project for other commercial reasons. If such contracts were binding agreements entered into during the ten-year life of the zone, they can confer an entitlement to the original owner and potentially any successor to allowances.

When the buyer takes over the building and there is a contract as mentioned above, it might be possible to argue that the buyer will be incurring expenditure under a contract entered into during the ten-year life of the zone. However, it is believed that HMRC hold a different view.

HMRC regard the buyer as only taking on the obligations of the contract on the date the building is purchased. On that interpretation, entitlement to allowances on further expenditure on the contract would not be available when the building is acquired after the ten-year enterprise zone period has expired. This is because the obligation to incur the expenditure as far as the buyer is concerned would not have arisen in that ten-year period.

The solution for a buyer in this position might be to require the seller to pay the builder 'up-front' the full costs of the construction. The seller has incurred expenditure under a qualifying contractual arrangement. The buyer then takes over the contract with no further costs to pay, having paid the costs to the seller as part of the purchase price.

It seems that this arrangement works where the seller is involved in the business as a builder or developer of property. This ensures that the buyer can claim allowances on the purchase price.

EXAMPLE 2

In example 1 in Point 33.2 above, Phillips Limited does not build the warehouse; instead, Varga Limited bought the site from Phillips Limited for its use in February 2007. Varga Limited took over Phillips's role in the building contract and commenced building in March 2007. The building was completed a year later as above.

HMRC may well argue that Varga Limited did not incur expenditure under a contract entered into before the expiry of the enterprise zone, but under a contract to buy the building in February 2007. The subsequent expenditure under the contract would not attract any enterprise zone initial allowances on that basis.

If Phillips Limited were to pay the entire £4 million under the contract and then sell for £4 million, the position might then depend on whether Phillips Limited was trading as a builder or developer.

If it was not, Varga's allowance would be limited to the lower of the price paid and construction cost. Arguably, that might not include the £4 million since that was not yet actual construction cost. On the other hand, if Phillips is a builder or developer by trade, Varga could claim the initial allowance on the total amount paid – less the land element.

It will be recognised that there are legal and commercial complications in structuring arrangements involving up-front payments and safeguards will need to be built in to secure the purchaser's position.

Furthermore, where any such agreement is being relied upon for allowances, it is necessary to obtain professional advice on whether the agreement is, indeed, a qualifying contract.

Point 33.4: *The purchaser of an unused building who buys it after the expiry of the ten-year life of the zone can still claim a 100% allowance.*

Where a building is constructed during the ten-year life of the zone but remains unused, a buyer can claim the initial allowance on its purchase of the building (*CAA 2001, s 300*).

As mentioned in Point 33.1 above, in some circumstances, the amount to be claimed will be based on the purchase price if the seller is a developer. In other cases, it will be the lower of the price paid and the construction cost.

The position is complicated if the seller had incurred any of the construction cost after the tenth anniversary of the site's inclusion in the enterprise zone. Such an amount may still qualify if it was incurred under a contract entered into within the ten-year period after the expiry of the zone (see Points 33.2 and 33.3 above). Otherwise, the qualifying amount for the purchaser will be restricted.

If there have been a number of sales of the unused property, the allowances apply to the last purchaser that brings the property into use.

Point 33.5: *100% initial allowance is also available on buildings situated in enterprise zones which are purchased within two years of first use.*

Initial allowances are available where a purchaser acquires a building within two years of its first use. The allowances are available on the same basis as with any unused building (*CAA 2001, s 301*). The seller will suffer a clawback of any allowances claimed as normal.

The initial allowance is only available to the first purchaser of the used building (*CAA 2001, s 301(1)(d)*).

Point 33.6:   *Where the seller is a developer, the buyer could be entitled to allowances on the price paid for the building even if that is higher than the construction cost.*

As mentioned in Point 33.1 above, if a person carrying on a development trade incurred the actual construction expenditure, the purchaser's deemed expenditure is the purchase price. That means that the buyer gets an allowance on the developer's profit as well as on the building costs (*CAA 2001, s 296(2)*). It is generally considered that this must exclude any element attributable to the land.

If there is more than one sale before the building comes into use, the amount eligible for allowances is the smaller of the purchase price paid and the price paid on an earlier sale (*CAA 2001, s 296(3)*).

The position is less straightforward if not all of the construction expenditure was incurred during the ten-year life of the zone – or under a contract entered into during that period. In that case, that expenditure will be split between elements qualifying and not qualifying for the initial allowance.

Point 33.7:   *If a building ceases to be used, a balancing charge can arise.*

Unlike the position for industrial buildings generally, balancing charges may still arise for enterprise zone buildings up to the 25th anniversary of claiming the initial allowance. One circumstance where that can arise is if the building permanently ceases to be in commercial use. As long as the building continues to be used commercially in a trade, or any cessation of use is only temporary, no clawback of allowances will arise.

Point 33.8:   *A clawback of allowances can arise on the sale of the building. This can often be avoided by granting a subordinate interest rather than an outright sale of the relevant interest owned subject to the anti-avoidance provisions for enterprise zones.*

A method of avoiding a clawback of allowances has been used commonly in the past on the sale of industrial buildings. This involved selling a lesser interest than the one held eg a very long lease out of a freehold – or a shorter sub-lease out of a leasehold interest.

This method can be used for sales of enterprise zone properties, although anti-avoidance rules can result in a balancing charge in two situations where a capital sum is realised from the grant of a lease:

(a)   where the lease is granted within seven years of the original expenditure (*CAA 2001, s 328(5)–(7), 329, 330*); or

(b)   where there are arrangements at the time the expenditure is incurred for a subsequent sale at any time.

As mentioned above, although balancing adjustments are no longer relevant for other commercial buildings, they continue to apply to buildings where enterprise zone allowances have been claimed.

Point 33.9:   *A chargeable capital gain can arise on the sale of an enterprise zone building but an allowable capital loss cannot to the extent that capital allowances have been given.*

Any excess of sale price of a building over cost (or value at 31 March 1982 where relevant) plus indexation allowance (where appropriate) would give rise to a capital gain chargeable to tax under capital gains tax rules. A loss, on the other hand, may not necessarily constitute an allowable loss to the extent that capital allowances have been claimed of that amount (*TCGA 1992, s 41(2)*).

Where a building that has always been a qualifying enterprise zone property is sold at a loss, this loss should be relieved either by way of balancing allowance or a reduced balancing charge. A capital loss cannot also arise on this amount.

Since no allowances are available on land, a capital loss would be available for any loss sustained in relation to the land element.

Expenditure for this purpose would be reduced by capital allowances given and not withdrawn. Normally, it equates to the sale proceeds.

Indexation relief can neither create nor enhance a capital loss on any disposal and so will not figure in the calculation. See Point 12.3 for a discussion of this.

As explained in Point 12.3, it still may be possible to claim a capital loss on a disposal where it arises from indexation allowance accruing before 30 November 1993 following an earlier acquisition on a no gain/no loss basis (eg intra-group sale or transfer between spouses).

Point 33.10:   *When a used enterprise zone building is acquired, the purchaser can claim writing-down allowances up to April 2011 by reference to the vendor's 'residue of qualifying expenditure'.*

As with industrial buildings, the purchaser of a second-hand enterprise zone building can claim allowances on the vendor's residue of expenditure.

It is not clear at the time of writing whether the phasing out of writing-down allowances proposed for other commercial buildings are also to apply to enterprise zone buildings. The provisions in *Finance Act 2007* confirm that no balancing adjustment applies but are silent as yet on the writing-down allowance position going forward.

The likely scenario is that the buyer will only be able to claim allowances up to April 2011 (as with industrial buildings). However, unlike the industrial building scenario post 21 March 2007, the buyer will inherit the residue of expenditure from the purchaser which will equate to the seller's cost plus any balancing charge that the seller has suffered. A suggested illustration of the position is given in the example below, which is similar to the position given in example 2 in 30.4:

EXAMPLE 3

The freehold of a qualifying enterprise zone building cost £600,000 in April 1997, excluding any land element. It was sold in April 2007 for £1 million.

The seller is assumed to have claimed the 100% initial allowance on the £600,000. When the freehold is sold, that is clawed back. The residue of expenditure inherited by the buyer is thus £600,000.

On purchase, the buyer is immediately within the new rules. The allowance in the year to 31 December 2007 will be 4%.

The year to 31 December 2008, straddles the financial year 2008, which starts for companies within charge to income tax on 1 April. For that financial year, the IBA entitlement falls by one quarter to 3%. The hybrid rate for the year to 31 December 2008 becomes 3.25% (one quarter of 4% and three-quarters of 3%)

In the year to 31 December 2009, the allowance falls by a further quarter, reducing the hybrid rate to 2.25%.

The next year to 31 December 2010 sees the allowance fall by a further quarter to 1.25%.

In the final year the purchaser will get allowances to will be to 31 December 2011 in which it will be entitled to three months at 1% taking it up to 31 March 2011. The hybrid rate for that year becomes 0.25%.

Although this is similar to example 1 in 30.4, there is one important difference. The buyer here is getting the benefit of the allowances on £600,000 – ie the seller has suffered a clawback of allowances which has been included in the buyer's residue of expenditure. Bearing this in mind, a seller may well push to try and sell a lesser interest to avoid the balancing charge in line with Point 33.10 above.

Note that the above example, as for the examples in Point 30.4, is based on interpretation of the Government's proposals in its July 2007 consultative document and the position may be subject to revision once final legislation is published.

Point 33.11:   A 100% allowance is available for the conversion and renovation costs of bringing a building back into commercial use in certain designated areas.

A 100% allowance has been available since 11 April 2007 for the cost of converting or renovating property situated in an 'assisted area' to bring it back into business use. Although the relief was introduced in the *Finance Act 2005*, its introduction was delayed pending EU consent and the consequent need to reduce the areas in which the property could be situated.

The relevant rules are now contained in the *Business Premises Renovation Allowances Regulations SI 2007/945* and the assisted areas are those specified in the *Assisted Areas Order 2005* plus Northern Ireland. The assisted areas in the UK as listed in *SI 2007/107* can be found at www.opsi.gov.uk/si/si2007/20070107.htm.

To qualify, the property must have been vacant for a period of at least 12 months, after having last been used for the purposes of a trade, profession or vocation, or as offices, but not as a dwelling.

The allowance will only be clawed back if the building is disposed of within seven years from the date it was brought into use.

A number of business uses are excluded from the relief including fisheries; shipbuilding; coal and steel; synthetic fibres; the production of certain agricultural products; and the manufacture of substitute or imitation milk or milk products.

CHAPTER 34 – CAPITAL GAINS PLANNING: REPLACEMENT OF BUSINESS ASSETS 'ROLL-OVER') RELIEF

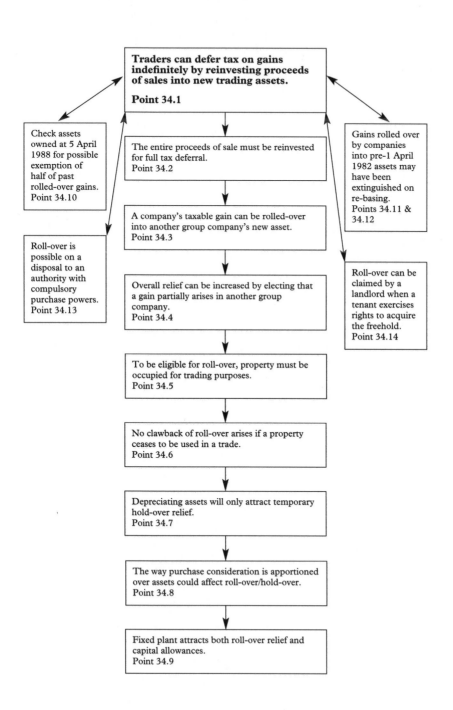

Traders can defer tax on gains indefinitely by reinvesting proceeds of sales into new trading assets.

Point 34.1

Check assets owned at 5 April 1988 for possible exemption of half of past rolled-over gains.
Point 34.10

Roll-over is possible on a disposal to an authority with compulsory purchase powers.
Point 34.13

The entire proceeds of sale must be reinvested for full tax deferral.
Point 34.2

A company's taxable gain can be rolled-over into another group company's new asset.
Point 34.3

Overall relief can be increased by electing that a gain partially arises in another group company.
Point 34.4

To be eligible for roll-over, property must be occupied for trading purposes.
Point 34.5

No clawback of roll-over arises if a property ceases to be used in a trade.
Point 34.6

Depreciating assets will only attract temporary hold-over relief.
Point 34.7

The way purchase consideration is apportioned over assets could affect roll-over/hold-over.
Point 34.8

Fixed plant attracts both roll-over relief and capital allowances.
Point 34.9

Gains rolled over by companies into pre-1 April 1982 assets may have been extinguished on re-basing.
Points 34.11 & 34.12

Roll-over can be claimed by a landlord when a tenant exercises rights to acquire the freehold.
Point 34.14

34 Capital gains planning: replacement of business assets ('roll-over') relief

Point 34.1: *A trader can defer indefinitely any tax arising on the sale of a property that has been used for the purposes of a trade by reinvesting the proceeds of disposal into appropriate assets during the requisite time period.*

A claim can be made to defer tax on capital gains where business assets are sold and replaced by new assets (*TCGA 1992, s 152*). The effect of the claim is to reduce the base cost of the 'new' assets for capital gains purposes by the gain on disposal of the old assets (*TCGA 1992, s 152(1)(b)*).

EXAMPLE 1

Freehold trading premises are sold for £1,000,000, realising a chargeable gain of £300,000. New freehold trading premises are acquired for £1,500,000. The gain on the old property can be 'rolled over' into the new asset reducing the base cost for capital gains purposes to £50,000.

A claim should be made within six years of the disposal.

On the disposal of the second asset there may be a further claim for roll-over relief. There is, therefore, the opportunity of indefinite deferral of tax on capital gains. In this way, the relief is invaluable for traders who are ploughing back capital gains on the sale of properties used to finance further expansion.

The 'old' and 'new' assets must be within the following categories:

(a)   land and buildings;
(b)   fixed plant and machinery;
(c)   goodwill (but see below);
(d)   ships, aircraft and hovercraft;
(e)   satellites, space stations and space craft;
(f)   milk and potato quotas (but see below);
(g)   ewe and suckler cow premium quotas (but see below).

(*TCGA 1992, s 155*).

Since 1 April 2002, companies have not been able to roll over capital gains against the acquisition on or after that date of the following new assets:

(a)   goodwill;
(b)   milk and potato quotas;
(c)   ewe and suckler-cow premium quotas.

This is because these assets qualify as intangible property, for which a new tax régime applies from that date. Companies disposing of intangible property are able to claim reinvestment relief (similar to rollover relief) against the acquisition of other intangible property. Special transitional rules apply to disposals of goodwill acquired before 1 April 2002 (*FA 2002, Sch 29, para 131*).

There is no change at all to the rollover rules for non-corporate taxpayers, to whom the new intellectual property régime does not apply.

The reinvestment must take place within a four-year period commencing up to 12 months before the date of sale and ending three years after (*TCGA 1992, s 152(3)*). HMRC are entitled to extend the deadlines where appropriate (proviso to *TCGA 1992, s 153(3)*). If there are particular reasons for delays in selling or acquiring assets, there may well be valid grounds for asking the Inspector for a time extension.

It is not necessary for an asset in one particular class to be replaced by an asset in the same class. An individual trader could sell some business premises and reinvest the proceeds in fixed plant for inclusion in another property.

It is also not necessary for the proceeds to be reinvested in an asset in the same trade. A sale of factory premises followed by a purchase of a retail shop would potentially attract the relief. All trades carried on by an individual or company are treated as the same trade (*TCGA 1992, s 152*).

Point 34.2:   *To obtain full deferral, the entire proceeds of sale of an asset must be reinvested. However, partial relief is available if proceeds at least equal to the base cost plus indexation allowable on the 'old' asset are used to fund the 'new' asset(s).*

Where all the proceeds of the sale of an asset are used to purchase the new asset, full roll-over is potentially available. If the extent of reinvestment in new assets over the four-year period amounts to less than the proceeds of sale, part of the gain will crystallise (*TCGA 1992, s 153*).

The part of the gain not deferred will be equivalent to the amount of uninvested proceeds.

EXAMPLE 2

A freehold property is sold for £3,000,000 realising a chargeable gain after indexation of £1,500,000. A smaller property is acquired for £2,500,000. Since £500,000 of the proceeds have not been reinvested, tax on this amount of the gain will crystallise. £1m of the gain can be rolled-over.

No deferral is available unless the reinvested amounted is more than the indexed base cost of the asset. Therefore, if, in the above example, the new property cost just £1,500,000, none of the taxable gain could be deferred.

Note that using an election (under *TCGA 1992, s 171A*) to treat a gain as partially arising in another company or companies, it is possible to increase the roll-over relief available as illustrated in Point 34.4.

Point 34.3: *Within a group of companies, it does not matter if one company makes the disposal and a completely separate company within the group makes the acquisition. The first company is entitled to roll over the gain, which is carried forward in the second company.*

HMRC treat companies within a tax group as carrying on a single trade for capital gains purposes. Therefore, the gains of one group member can be rolled over against the cost of a qualifying asset acquired by another (*TCGA 1992, s 175(2A)*).

EXAMPLE 3

Group member A Ltd, an importer of catering equipment, sells one of its warehouses for £1 million, realising a chargeable capital gain of £0.5 million. Fellow group member B Ltd, a hotel operator, acquires a freehold hotel two years later for £2 million. The gain of £0.5 million on A Ltd's disposal can be rolled over against B Ltd's hotel acquisition reducing the base cost for tax purposes to £1.5 million.

All UK-resident companies, which are under the common 75% ownership of a principal company, are within a tax group for capital gains purposes. Furthermore, since April 2000, this also includes the UK branches and permanent establishments of non-resident companies (*TCGA 1992, s 175(1A)*).

Where a non-trading group company holds properties that are used and occupied for trading purposes by other group companies within the definition of a group, HMRC treat these properties as group assets eligible for business roll-over relief.

Roll-over relief is also extended to an individual owning assets that are used and occupied by his or her personal company (*TCGA 1992, s 157*).

Point 34.4: *Overall relief can be increased by electing that a gain partially arises in another group company.*

As mentioned in Point 34.2, a gain is only partially deferred if not all the proceeds of sale are reinvested. The benefit of that partial roll-over, which is illustrated in example 2, can be increased by electing for at least part of the gain to arise in another company. Such an election is possible under *TCGA 1992, s 171A*.

Starting with the situation in example 2, we can deem that, say, £500,000 of the £3m sale arises in a second group company. That would mean that the first company's proceeds and cost are reduced to £2.5m and £1.25m respectively, giving rise to a gain of £1.25m. This gain of

£1.25m can be fully deferred because the deemed proceeds of £2.5m attributable to that company are being fully invested. We have, therefore, been able to defer an extra £250,000.

Point 34.5   *The 'old' and 'new' assets must actually be used for trading purposes to be eligible for relief.*

For business roll-over relief purposes both the old and new assets must be used for the purposes of a trade. The definition of trade includes professions and vocations. The old asset must have been used for trading purposes throughout the period of ownership. If this is not the case, only a portion of the gain may be eligible for roll-over (*TCGA 1992, s 152(7)*).

EXAMPLE 4

A freehold building was occupied as the business premises of A & Co from January 1999 to December 2007. In January 2006, new trading premises were acquired and occupied immediately. The old building is let until the end of December 2008 when it is sold.

As the old asset was used and occupied for trading purposes for nine out of the ten years of ownership, 9/10ths of the gain is eligible for roll-over.

For a property bought before 31 March 1982, only the period of ownership after 31 March 1982 can be considered in determining the proportion attributable to business use (*TCGA 1992, s 152(9)*).

An apportionment must similarly be made if part of the property has not been occupied for trading purposes. From that perspective, it may be better to try and maximise the use of the property for the purposes of a trade eg by using areas for storage.

Where the old asset has only partly been used for trading purposes, the roll-over relief is calculated on the basis that two separate assets are sold. Only the proceeds apportioned to the part used in the trade need be reinvested to obtain roll-over relief in respect of the qualifying element of the gain (*TCGA 1992, s 152(6)*).

EXAMPLE 5

A Ltd bought a freehold office building, with four equal-sized floors, in 1995 for £900,000. Three of the four floors have been occupied by A Ltd and used for trading purposes. The fourth floor has been let. In 2007, the building is sold for £1,500,000. The indexation allowance is £200,000.

	Total	Trading element 75%	Non-trading element 25%
Proceeds	£1,500,000	£1,125,000	£375,000
Cost	(900,000)	(675,000)	(225,000)
Indexation	(200,000)	(150,000)	(50,000)
Gain	£400,000	£300,000	£100,000

No business roll-over will be available on the non-trading element of the gain ie £100,000.

With regard to the remaining £300,000, rollover relief will be fully available if proceeds of £1,125,000 are reinvested in new assets. The minimum reinvestment below which roll-over would not be achieved is £825,000 (ie £1,125,000 less £300,000 – see Point 34.2 above).

The new property (or other specified asset) should be a trading asset immediately on acquisition. If the property has to be substantially refurbished before occupation, this, strictly speaking, would not satisfy the roll-over conditions. However, HMRC have published a concession under which roll-over is allowed in such circumstances providing the following conditions are met:

(a)   the owner proposes to incur capital expenditure for the purpose of enhancing the new asset's value;

(b)   any work arising from such expenditure begins as soon as possible after acquisition and is completed within a reasonable time;

(c)   on completion of the work, the asset is taken into use for the purposes of the trade and no other purpose;

(d)   the asset is not let or used for any non-trading purpose in the period between acquisition and the time it is taken into use for the purposes of a trade;

(e)   if a building is being constructed on land, the expenditure on the building will qualify if the building is to be used in the trade on completion

(HMRC Extra-Statutory Concession D24).

Land must be occupied by the taxpayer as well as used for trading purposes (*TCGA 1992, s 155*).

It should be noted that furnished holiday lettings will qualify as a trade for this purpose (see Chapter 10 in Part A).

Point 34.6   *Relief in respect of an 'old' asset will not be clawed back if a 'new' asset ceases to be used for trading purposes (unless it is a depreciating asset – see Point 34.7 below). Future roll-over relief will, however, be affected.*

The roll-over on the first asset will still be effective even if the replacement asset subsequently ceases to be used for the purposes of a trade. There will be no clawback of relief at that stage. The second property will, however, only be eligible for restricted roll-over relief on its sale (see Point 34.5 above).

There are two exceptions to this point:

(a)   if the 'new' asset is a depreciating asset, tax will crystallise on the cessation of use for trading purposes (see Point 34.6 below);

(b)   if the new asset is bought wholly or partly for the purpose of realising a gain on disposal (*TCGA 1992, s 152(5)*), no roll-over would be available.

Point 34.7:   *If the new assets are 'depreciating' assets, then only temporary 'hold-over' relief is available unless there is a subsequent further reinvestment into non-depreciating assets.*

The general rule in capital gains roll-over situations is that the cost of the new asset for tax purposes is reduced by the gain arising on the old asset. This gain will not crystallise until the new asset is sold and at that stage a further claim to roll-over may be made. On this basis, tax could be deferred indefinitely.

The rule does not apply, however, where the new assets are 'depreciating assets'. The relief then becomes a temporary 'hold-over' of the chargeable gain (*TCGA 1992, s 154*).

A 'depreciating asset' for this purpose is one that is or would become a wasting asset at any time within ten years of its acquisition (*TCGA 1992, s 154(7)*). A wasting asset by definition has an anticipated life not exceeding 50 years (*TCGA 1992, s 44*). Therefore, a lease with not more than 60 years to run would be treated as a depreciating asset as would a building built on land held under a lease of less than 60 years (HMRC Tax Bulletin 7, May 1993).

Other replacement assets including fixed plant (other than plant forming a building fixture – see Point 34.9 below), ships or aircraft would often also be 'depreciating assets'.

The held-over tax charge will crystallise ten years after the acquisition of a depreciating asset at the latest. It may crystallise earlier, however, if the asset is sold or ceases to be used for the purpose of the trade (*TCGA 1992, s 154(2)*).

On the acquisition of a depreciating asset, there is merely an opportunity to hold-over a gain for a period ending with the earliest of the events mentioned above. If there is an acquisition of a non-depreciating asset within the four-year reinvestment period mentioned in Point 34.1 above, then this asset can be substituted by making a variation of the original roll-over claim before the depreciating asset is sold or ceases to be used (*TCGA 1992, s 154(4), (5)*). The deferral of the original gain (or part of the gain) indefinitely will then be a possibility.

EXAMPLE 6

The proceeds of the sale of a building in February 2007 were reinvested, in March 2007, in a lease of new business premises with 55 years remaining. As a 55-year lease is a depreciating asset, the original gain will crystallise and tax will become payable at the earliest of the following:

(1)   the ten-year anniversary of the acquisition (ie March 2017);

(2)   disposal of the lease;

(3)   the building ceasing to be used for the purposes of the trade.

If, before February 2010 – assuming the 55-year lease is still owned and the building still occupied – a new freehold is purchased, this freehold can be substituted for the short lease, providing the cost would have been sufficient for a roll-over claim on the original disposal.

Note that the new freehold must be acquired before any of the above events. Thus, if there are plans to move out of the leasehold premises or sell them, the freehold must first be bought (ie contracts must be exchanged) to avoid any crystallisation of tax.

In view of the above, it is important to be constantly aware of roll-over claims that have been made involving acquisitions of depreciating assets. If non-depreciating trading assets are acquired subsequently within the requisite period, the claim should be amended as far as possible to include these.

It should also be remembered that the crystallisation of the tax charge on cessation of use only applies to depreciating assets. If a freehold or long leasehold property is vacated and subsequently let, the original roll-over is not affected.

Point 34.8: *In view of the position regarding depreciating assets, the allocation of consideration on the purchase of business premises may be important.*

Where new premises are acquired which are subject to a short lease, it has often been advantageous to allocate expenditure as far as possible to goodwill. However, as explained in Point 34.1 above, goodwill has ceased to be an eligible asset for corporate taxpayers from 1 April 2002. Expenditure allocated to goodwill since that date would not be eligible for roll-over relief in the hands of a UK corporation taxpayer although it is eligible for other taxpayers.

Although fixed plant is a depreciating asset, there may be a benefit in attributing a reasonable value to this item (see Point 34.9 below).

Point 34.9: *When purchasing property, the allocation of part of the consideration to fixed plant and equipment could attract eligibility for both capital allowances and capital gains roll-over relief.*

The element of expenditure attributable to fixed plant in a building should be separated in order to formulate a capital allowances claim (see Point 29.1). Such expenditure will attract roll-over relief if the plant or machinery becomes part of a building (HMRC Tax Bulletin 7, May 1993). This would apply to items such as air conditioning, sanitary fittings and lift systems.

If the plant or machinery is fixed but does not form part of a building, then the items will be depreciating assets eligible for hold-over relief. This might include certain partitioning or floor coverings.

Expenditure allocated to elements of plant in a purchased building can therefore help to defer a tax liability on a capital gain as well as being eligible for capital allowances.

Point 34.10:   *For business properties held at 6 April 1988 by companies where there may have been an earlier roll-over claim, one half of the deferred gain could be exempt from tax altogether.*

As explained in Point 11.2 there is a special relief where the following applies:

(a)   a gain arose on an 'old' asset, acquired before 31 March 1982 and sold before 6 April 1988, which was rolled over into a 'new' asset; and

(b)   the 'new' asset, which was acquired after 31 March 1982, was still held at 6 April 1988.

In this situation, 50% of the rolled-over gain on the disposal of the new asset will fall out of charge to tax (*TCGA 1992, Sch 4*).

After 5 April 2008, this relief is only available for companies within charge to corporation tax. If the 2007 Pre-Budget proposals are implemented as proposed, individuals, trustees and personal representatives will cease to benefit from that date.

EXAMPLE 7

A Ltd bought a factory in 1981 which was sold in 1987 for £1 million. The gain on sale after indexation amounted to £580,000.

In 1989, A Ltd bought a warehouse for £2 million and made a claim to roll over the gain on the factory into that acquisition.

In 2007, the warehouse is sold for £4 million.

The capital gain on the warehouse, ignoring indexation allowance, would be:

Sale proceeds		£4,000,000
Less: Cost	£2,000,000	
Less: Rolled-over gain	(580,000)	
	£1,420,000	1,420,000
		£2,580,000
Less: TCGA 1992 Sch 4 relief		(290,000)
(50% of £580,000)		
Taxable gain		£2,290,000

(Note that the indexation allowance would be based on a 'cost' of £1,710,000 ie £2,000,000 less £290,000)

A claim must be made for the relief within two years of the end of the year of assessment in which the relevant disposal is made, in the case of a company in charge to corporation tax. (For income tax payers the election had to be filed by 31 January following a year of assessment in which the relevant disposal is made.) Disposals for this purpose will also include any roll-over situations. For instance, if the property in question is sold and the proceeds are again reinvested under the roll-over rules in a further acquisition, the relief will crystallise at that time and should be claimed in respect of that roll-over situation. The effect of this will be that the relief will reduce the deferred gain that is carried over to the new asset.

Point 34.11: *Gains on assets sold before 1 April 1982 which have been rolled over into new assets may avoid tax altogether.*

As a result of the re-basing provisions in the 1988 Finance Act, an asset disposed of after 5 April 1988 which was owned on 31 March 1982 can be treated as having an uplifted base cost, for the purposes of tax on capital gains, equal to its value at 31 March 1982 (see Chapter 11).

Consider the position where a business property was sold before 31 March 1982 and the proceeds of sale re-invested in a new business asset acquired on or before 31 March 1982. Ordinarily, the original cost of the new asset would be reduced by the 'rolled-over' gain to arrive at the base cost for future capital gains purposes. However, under the re-basing provisions, if the new asset is sold after 6 April 1988 we are entitled to substitute the market value of the new asset for its base cost at 31 March 1982.

As will be seen, in this situation the rolled-over gain should drop out of charge altogether and no tax would be payable on the gain realised before 31 March 1982.

EXAMPLE 8

A property was sold in 1980 realising a gain of £200,000. The proceeds were reinvested in a further freehold property acquired in 1981 for £1 million. That property was valued at £1.5 million on 31 March 1982 and was sold in July 2007.

On claiming roll-over relief, the base cost of the second property was reduced by £200,000 to £800,000. However, since the property was sold after 6 April 1988, we are entitled to substitute the value at 31 March 1982 as the base cost. This was £1.5 million. Accordingly, the £200,000 deferred gain from 1981 will never be taxed.

Point 34.12:   *There may be cases where a gain after 31 March 1982 avoids tax altogether having been rolled over into an asset acquired before 1 April 1982.*

As mentioned in Point 34.1 above, a gain can be rolled over into an asset acquired up to 12 months before the 'old' asset was sold. There may be instances, therefore, where a property has been sold after 31 March 1982 but the proceeds deemed to have been re-invested in a property or other business asset acquired before 31 March 1982.

Following the discussion in Point 34.11 above, the base cost of an asset owned at 31 March 1982 can be its market value at that date. Accordingly, any rolled-over capital gain would fall out of charge.

EXAMPLE 9

Taking a similar situation to example 8 in Point 34.10 above, assume the property was sold in January 1983. The new property was bought one year earlier in January 1982. On the basis of the same figures quoted there, the £200,000 would similarly never be taxed in this situation. The base cost of the property acquired in January 1982 would become its market value at 31 March 1982.

Point 34.13:   *Where land is disposed of to an authority with compulsory purchase powers, a landlord can defer any tax on the gain arising by reinvesting the proceeds into new property.*

Roll-over relief is available where land is acquired by an authority with compulsory purchase powers (*TCGA 1992, s 247*). This might be, for example, a local authority or regional development agency. Note that it is sufficient for the authority to have compulsory purchase powers. It does not need to formally exercise them.

The rules for this relief operate in a similar way to those referred to above in this chapter for replacement of business assets. The reinvestment cannot be into a property used as a dwelling house nor any property which will not give rise to a chargeable gain if sold within six years (*TCGA 1992, s 248*).

The owner should not have been marketing the property or otherwise advertising the property for sale prior to the sale to the authority in question.

The relief is available to landlords as well as owners occupying their properties for trading purposes.

Point 34.14: *Roll-over relief can also be claimed by a property owner where a tenant exercises the right to acquire the freehold reversion or extension of the lease.*

The roll-over relief available to property owners whose property is compulsorily purchased (Point 34.12 above) has been extended to situations where the tenant exercises rights under the *Leasehold Reform Act 1967, the Housing Acts 1985* to *1996* or the Housing and Urban Development ACR 1993 (HMRC statement of practice SP 13/93 and RI 205, June 1999).

CHAPTER 35 – CAPITAL GAINS PLANNING – TAPER RELIEF AND BEYOND

[Note – the Government's 2007 Pre-Budget report issued in October 2007 includes proposals for the removal of taper relief. The position is summarised in the 'Stop Press' note at the beginning of this book and this is likely to impact on the points below from 6 April 2008. At the time of writing, it remains a possibility that some form of taper relief may still be retained post 5 April 2008.]

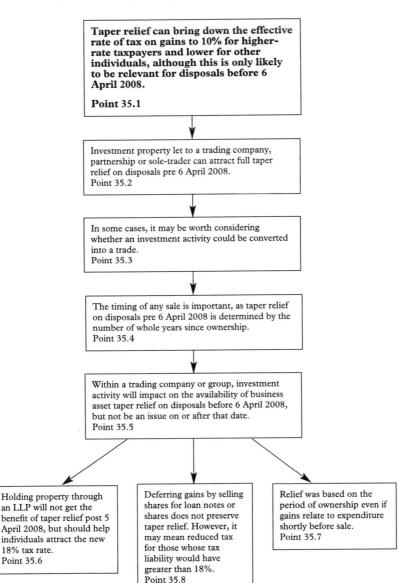

Taper relief can bring down the effective rate of tax on gains to 10% for higher-rate taxpayers and lower for other individuals, although this is only likely to be relevant for disposals before 6 April 2008.

Point 35.1

Investment property let to a trading company, partnership or sole-trader can attract full taper relief on disposals pre 6 April 2008.
Point 35.2

In some cases, it may be worth considering whether an investment activity could be converted into a trade.
Point 35.3

The timing of any sale is important, as taper relief on disposals pre 6 April 2008 is determined by the number of whole years since ownership.
Point 35.4

Within a trading company or group, investment activity will impact on the availability of business asset taper relief on disposals before 6 April 2008, but not be an issue on or after that date.
Point 35.5

Holding property through an LLP will not get the benefit of taper relief post 5 April 2008, but should help individuals attract the new 18% tax rate.
Point 35.6

Deferring gains by selling shares for loan notes or shares does not preserve taper relief. However, it may mean reduced tax for those whose tax liability would have greater than 18%.
Point 35.8

Relief was based on the period of ownership even if gains relate to expenditure shortly before sale.
Point 35.7

35   Capital gains planning – taper relief

[*Note – the Government's 2007 Pre-Budget report issued in October 2007 includes proposals for the removal of taper relief. The position is summarised in the 'Stop Press' note at the beginning of this book and this is likely to impact on the points below from 6 April 2008.*]

Point 35.1:   Up to 5 April 2008, *there have been a number of situations where the effective rate of tax paid by a higher rate taxpayer on gains from property can fall as low as 10%. For basic rate taxpayers, the rate would be even lower. However, taper relief is largely due to be removed after that date following the Government's 2007 Pre-Budget proposals.*

Taper relief for capital gains was introduced when the indexation allowance available to individuals and trustees was frozen with effect from 6 April 1998. Taper relief, which has never been available for companies, is due to be largely abolished in respect of disposals after 5 April 2008. Furthermore, individuals and trustees will not be able to claim any indexation allowance which may have accumulated up to 6 April 1998.

The removal of these reliefs arises as a consequence of the Government's Pre-Budget report. See the 'Stop Press' note in the front of the book for a summary of the relevant proposals.

The indexation allowance has, in the past, allowed individuals and trustees to increase the actual cost of investment and other capital assets by the rate of inflation to arrive at a base cost figure for capital gains tax purposes on disposal. Following the abolition of that relief for individuals and trustees, all indexation up to 6 April 1998 was 'frozen' with the frozen amount at that date continuing to be available as an addition to the tax cost of assets held.

Under 'taper relief', the percentage of the gain subject to tax fell over a period of time.

There were two levels of reduction. The higher applied to 'business assets' and could result in a 75% reduction in the chargeable gain where the assets have been held for two years or more (*TCGA 1992, s 2A*).

For 'non-business' assets, up to 40% of the gain could be exempt (*TCGA 1992, s 2A*). That was after ten years. No taper relief was available for non-business assets sold within three years of acquisition. However, where a non-business asset was held at 17 March 1998, an extra 'bonus' year was added when computing taper relief.

As far as property ownership is concerned (bearing in mind that taper relief had a more general application than merely to property), a business asset could be any of the following:

(a)   A property used by an individual in a trade that he or she carries on personally or in partnership (*TCGA 1992, Sch A1, para 5(1A)(a)*).

(b)   A property let to any unincorporated person for the purposes of a trade carried on by that person (including trustees and personal representatives)(*TCGA 1992, Sch A1, para 5(1A)*).

(c)   A property let to an unlisted trading company or the unlisted holding company of a trading group for the purposes of the trade(s); or let to a partnership of which such a company is a member for the purposes of the trade(s). The individual owning the property does not need to have an interest in that company (*TCGA 1992, Sch A1, paras 5(2), 6(1)*).

(d)   Shares or other securities in an unlisted property-owning trading company – regardless of the number of shares held (*TCGA 1992, Sch A1, paras 4(2), 6(1)(b)(i)*).

(e)   Shares or other securities in a listed property-owning trading company where the individual is a full or part-time employee or officer of the company or of a connected company (*TCGA 1992, Sch A1, paras 4(2), 6(1)(b)(ii)*).

(f)   Shares or securities representing 5% or more of the voting rights in a listed property-owning trading company held by individuals who are not employees or officers (*TCGA 1992, Sch A1, paras 4(2), 6(1)(b)(iii)*).

(g)   Shares or other securities in a property-owning investment company (ie a non-trading company or the holding company of a non-trading group, whether listed or unlisted) held by officers or employees of that company (or of a connected company) not owning directly or indirectly more than 10% of that company or of a company controlling that company (*TCGA 1992, Sch A1, paras 4(2), 6(1A)*).

Companies are connected in this context if they are both members of the same 51% group. Companies are also connected if they are associated and effectively carry on business as a single composite undertaking (*TCGA 1992, Sch A1, para 22*). Companies are associated if they are, or at any time within the previous year have been, under the control of the same person(s) or where one controls, or has at any time in the previous year controlled, the other (*TCGA 1992, Sch A1, para 22, TA 1988, s 416(1)*).

Similar rules apply to trustees.

It should be evident from the above that there have been a number of situations where individuals and trustees realising gains directly or indirectly from property were able to benefit from full business taper relief. Since the reduction is 75% of the capital gain after two whole years of ownership, a 40% taxpayer effectively only pays tax on 25% of the gain –

reducing the effective tax rate to 10%. For taxpayers paying tax at a rate of 20%, the effective rate of tax could be as low as 5%.

As for trustees, following changes introduced in the *Finance Act 2005*, they will typically be paying tax at 40%. Their effective capital gains tax rate after business asset taper relief would also be 10%. The conditions are modified in the case of trusts such that in (a) and (e) above, a beneficiary must be carrying on the trade alone or in partnership or be employed by the company.

References to listed companies would also include subsidiaries of listed companies. 'Listed' in this context means quoted on a recognised stock exchange anywhere in the world, not just in the UK. Companies listed on the Alternative Investment Market are not listed for this purpose and thus a property let to a trading AIM company or its subsidiaries can still be within business asset taper relief.

Point 35.2: *Investment property, whether let to a company, partnership or sole trader, could attract full taper relief for disposals pre 6 April 2008.*

A possibly unintentional result of rule changes made in 2002 was that it became possible to claim full business-asset taper relief for a personally held investment property let to an unlisted trading company (or the unlisted holding company of a trading group) with which the landlord needed to have no other connection. Business-asset taper relief remained unavailable, however, if the property was let to a sole trader or a partnership on the one hand and to a listed company (with one exception, mentioned below).

Because it was acknowledged that the legal personality adopted by the tenant should not influence the treatment of the asset in the landlord's hands in this way, there was a further rule change with effect from 6 April 2004. Since then, it has been possible to claim business-asset taper relief for a property let to:

(a) any individual;
(b) any partnership of which an individual is a member;
(c) trustees;
(d) a partnership of which trustees are members in their capacity as such;
(e) the personal representatives of a deceased person; or
(f) a partnership of which the personal representatives are members in their capacity as such,

provided that these persons are carrying on a trade and the property is used wholly or partly for the purposes of that trade.

This change is not retrospective, so that if the property was let to (say) a sole trader for a period beginning before 6 April 2004 and ending on or after that date, the property is a business asset only in respect of the period after 5 April 2004.

The position with letting to a company remains as it was before 6 April 2004. That is to say, the property is a business asset if and to the extent that it is let to:

(a)   an unlisted trading company or the unlisted holding company of a trading group; or

(b)   a listed trading company or the listed holding company of a trading group of which or of a company connected with which the landlord is an officer or employee; or

(c)   a listed trading company or the listed holding company of a trading group in which the landlord can exercise at least 5% of the voting rights

(TCGA 1992, Sch A1, paras 5(2), 6(1)).

As mentioned above, this relief will cease to be available after 5 April 2008 if the 2007 Pre-Budget proposals are implemented.

Point 35.3:   *In some cases, it has been worth considering whether an investment activity could be converted into a trade.*

As mentioned in the previous point, there have been circumstances where an investment property would qualify for full business-asset taper relief. In some situations, however, an investor might not have been able to take advantage of this. This would be the case with residential property or certain commercial property which is in multiple occupation.

An alternative for the investor might have been to attempt to turn the activity into a trading activity.

Generally, HMRC take the view that letting a property is investment rather than trading. Providing furnished accommodation with some services would not be sufficient in itself to persuade HMRC that a trade is being carried on. In some situations, the services may themselves constitute a trade that is separate from the letting activity.

HMRC's own manual on property income acknowledges that if regular meals are provided, it may be more likely that the whole activity is a trade. The manual states:

> It is unusual for such letting activity to amount to a trade except in the case of a hotel, guest house or similar business where services provided are substantially beyond those offered by a landlord, for example, provision of bed and breakfast, changes of linen etc.

(HMRC Property Income Manual, para 4700).

The dividing line between a guest house and a let property defines the difference between trading and investment. On that basis, a trade as compared with an investment might have the following features:

(a) the availability of food – possibly a simple breakfast (this does not need to be cooked – it can be bought in);
(b) other services eg room cleaning and laundry may be available;
(c) the property owner should have rights of entry to the rooms;
(d) lettings should typically be short-term, eg for one month, although with the possibility of renewal. The landlord should be seen to be exercising the right from time to time to terminate tenancies or at least change the rooms that the tenants occupy.

Similar criteria might also be applied to commercial lettings, which could be occupied as 'serviced offices'.

As mentioned in Point 35.5 below, it has been possible to apply to HMRC for an assurance as to whether a company or group is trading for taper relief purposes.

Point 35.4: *The timing of any sale has been important as taper relief was determined by the number of whole years since ownership. For longer-term owners, periods before 6 April 1998 are ignored.*

Taper relief reduced the chargeable gain depending on the number of complete years of ownership. Therefore, the date of acquisition and the date of sale are important.

Since the rate of taper relief on business assets after just one year is 50% and after two years 75%, the tax payable could halve by deferring for a relatively small period of time.

EXAMPLE 1

Trader, A, bought the premises used in his trade in May 2006. In March 2007, he is negotiating a sale that would give rise to a capital gain of £1 million.

If he exchanges contracts for sale before May 2007, the one complete year of ownership will mean that 50% of the £1 million will not be taxed as a result of taper relief. Assuming A is a higher rate taxpayer, the tax payable would be £500,000 at 40% ie £200,000.

On the other hand, if exchange of contracts is deferred until May, ie after the second anniversary of ownership, 75% of the gain will be taken out of charge leaving £250,000 as the taxable gain. The tax on this is £100,000 ie one half of the figure if contracts have not been delayed.

For properties or shares owned before 6 April 1998, it should be noted that the holding period is deemed to start on that date.

Point 35.5:   *Full business taper relief continued to be available as long as a company or group was substantially engaged in trading activities. To avoid losing the favourable status for shareholders, any investment activity should not broadly have exceeded 20% of the overall activity – or the activity conducted through a non-group entity.*

Having introduced a favourable capital gains tax relief for primarily trading situations, HMRC have had to distinguish situations that will not qualify because there is too great an element of investment (*TCGA 1992, Sch A1, Para 22A(1)*).

The Government has not specifically set down this distinction in legislation, so HMRC have made their own pronouncements of when they consider investment activities to have been sufficiently substantial as to affect trading status.

HMRC have stated that they consider investment activities more than incidental when they broadly exceed 20% of the overall activity of the company/group in question (see HMRC Bulletin 53, June 2001). That percentage could be applied in a number of ways eg:

- turnover;
- net or gross profit;
- asset/balance sheet value;
- management time.

HMRC clearly do not intend this to be a hard and fast rule. They recognise that the circumstances will dictate which of these criteria is more appropriate and that there should be leeway for unusual circumstances. Specifically, they have indicated that where the 20% test is breached, for instance because the company has surplus cash that is earmarked for future investment in the business, those funds will not necessarily be included in the 20% test.

With regard to property, the trading company may from time to time let surplus space, which should not be included in the test. Nor would there have been an issue where a company within a group has held property as an investment which is used for trading purposes by other companies within the group. However, there will be an issue for trading companies and groups that have held and acquired property for letting to third parties.

The problem might have arisen simply because the company chose to invest surplus funds in a property for letting. Alternatively, former trading premises may be retained long-term for investment purposes. It will also be appreciated that as long as HMRC have regard to this percentage test, a company or group could have lost its trading status by virtue of a property's investment performance improving relative to the trading activities during a particular period. The message has been that carrying out investment activities within a trading company or group can jeopardise the taper-relief status of shareholdings in that company/group. As a result, the effective capital gains tax rate on a sale could be much greater than 10%. If the investment activity was to be carried on in such a situation, it has been important to monitor its significance in percentage terms using HMRC guidelines as above. Alternatively, the activity should have been carried on outside the group, possibly by the owners personally or in a separate company.

Where a company is a 'close' company (see point 3.17 above for an explanation of close companies), any period during which the company has been inactive will not count toward the taper relief ownership period.

'Active' in this context means carrying on, preparing to carry on, or winding up a business. It does not include the sole activity of holding cash deposits, assets of insignificant securities in inactive companies or making loans to associates (*TCGA 1992, Sch A1, para 11A*).

These rules were introduced with effect from 17 April 2002 to replace previous rules that applied on certain changes of activity – for instance the commencement of an investment business.

Point 35.6:   *Property has been held through limited liability partnership (LLP) to get the benefit of taper relief as well as limited liability. Although taper relief is to be abolished after 5 April 2008, individual partners will benefit instead from the reduction of the rate of capital gains tax to 18%.*

It is common to use a limited company for business activity including property ownership as well as for trading operations. However, since April 2000, it has been possible to conduct these activities through an LLP. This is a partnership but with limited liability. Therefore, in any situation where individuals might want to limit liability but get the tax benefits of personal ownership, an LLP is worth considering as a vehicle.

The obvious benefit has been business asset taper relief where a let or occupied property qualifies. In that connection, a trading property may be held in this way and let to, say, the family company that occupies it. A commercial rent charged to the company will be a valid business expense for tax purposes and can be paid without National Insurance or PAYE being deducted. There are other forms of limited partnership vehicle that can be used. However, unlike the LLP, they rule out any direct involvement by individual partners in the partnership's activity. In all cases with limited partnerships, it is advisable to check the legal position in relation to regulatory obligations under UK financial services legislation.

With the proposed abolition of taper relief on disposals post 5 April 2008, this particular tax advantage will cease. However, partners can still benefit from the reduction in rate of capital gains tax to 18% for individuals which is expected to come in from tax year 2008/09. Companies, on the other hand, will continue to pay up to 28% corporation tax on capital gains, in addition to which there will also be further tax on extraction of the net proceeds from the company.

Point 35.7: *Taper relief on property gains was related to the total period of ownership even if the gains were attributable to enhancement expenditure shortly before sale.*

One interesting feature in applying taper relief was that the qualifying holding period of a property still commenced when an asset was first acquired even if enhancement expenditure were incurred at a later date. This means that if an asset had a relatively low value having been held for a number of years but there was an opportunity to capitalise on the renovation and significantly improve its value, the resultant gain may well be heavily tapered.

EXAMPLE 3

When A bought trading premises in May 2004, he paid £500,000. At the end of 2006, it was worth £1 million ie there is a gain of £500,000.

However, A decided to spend £300,000 completely renovating and gutting the building, increasing the usable area with the result that it is then worth £1.8 million.

Notwithstanding that this renovation might be carried out shortly before the sale in May 2007, the extra £500,000 gain generated by the exercise would still attract 75% taper relief.

This situation might also apply, for instance, where planning permission was granted which increased the value of the property shortly before a sale.

Point 35.8: *Taper relief cannot be carried forward post 5 April 2008, even where a pre 6 April 2008 gain has been deferred using loan notes or shares. However, the deferral may mean that lower capital gains tax may arise after 5 April 2008 in view of the proposed introduction of the new 18% capital gains tax rate.*

An individual or trustee selling a property or shares before 6 April 2008 may well have had their chargeable capital gain reduced by taper relief.

In the case of a share sale, there has been the possibility of deferring any tax arising by taking consideration in the form of shares or loan notes. This is subject to obtaining clearance from HMRC that they are satisfied the transaction has a bona fide commercial purpose and does not have tax avoidance as a motive.

Although the effect here would be to defer the gain from becoming taxable until the loan notes/shares are redeemed or sold, the deferred gain is calculated before taper relief. Accordingly, if the gain subsequently crystallises after 5 April 2008, tax would be chargeable on the gain without any taper relief.

Given the proposed reduction in capital gains tax to 18% after 5 April 2008, there may still be an upside here in using loan notes or shares for those individuals and trustees who might have paid a higher rate of tax on a disposal pre 6 April 2008.

CHAPTER 36 – CAPITAL GAINS PLANNING FOR COMPANIES – EXEMPTION FOR SALES OF SUBSTANTIAL SHAREHOLDINGS

Companies can enjoy complete exemption from tax in respect of gains on sales of shareholdings of 10% or more in other trading companies.

Point 36.1

Losses on the sale of substantial shareholdings are disregarded. Therefore, an asset sale might be preferable where a capital loss is likely to arise.
Point 36.2

Since sales of shares in investment companies and assets generally will not be covered by this exemption, maximisation of past and current capital losses to carry forward may still be useful.
Point 36.3

36 Capital gains planning for companies – exemption for sales of substantial shareholdings

Point 36.1: *Companies can enjoy complete exemption from tax in respect of gains on sales of shareholdings of 10% or more in other trading companies.*

From 1 April 2002, sales of certain shareholdings by UK companies are exempt from tax. These new rules (*TCGA 1992, Sch 7AC*) mean that a corporate shareholding in an associated or subsidiary company can be sold free of tax providing that the related conditions are satisfied.

The conditions can be summarised as follows:

- The disposal must be out of a 'substantial shareholding'. This means at least 10% of the ordinary shares of a company (together with an entitlement to at least 10% of the profits available for distribution to equity holders and to at least 10% of the assets available to equity holders on a winding-up), although holdings by different companies within a group can be aggregated for this purpose (*TCGA 1992, Sch 7AC, para 8(1)*).
- The company making the disposal must be a trading company or a member of a trading group before and after the sale ie the activities of the company should not include to any substantial extent non-trading activities (*TCGA 1992, Sch 7AC paras 20 and 21*). Broadly that is interpreted as meaning that non-trading activities should not exceed 20% of the total activities. The test is similar to the one discussed in relation to taper relief (see Point 35.5).
- The company being sold must be a trading company or the holding company of a trading group or subgroup before and after the transaction.
- The shareholding must have been owned by the selling company for a consecutive period of at least 12 months in the two years before the transaction. A disposal can thus still qualify up to 12 months after the holding has ceased to be substantial, as long as it had been substantial for at least 12 unbroken months in the two years leading up to the disposal (*TCGA 1992, Sch 7AC, para 7*).

Clearly, where a property disposal is contemplated out of a group but there is the prospect of selling the company along with its trading activity, this should be considered in view of the potential tax exemption on the sale of shares. In that connection, there will need to be an undertaking from the purchaser to carry on the trading activity into the foreseeable future to ensure that the transaction comes within these rules. The selling company/group also needs to carry on trading after the sale.

Where the company to be sold carries on a significant proportion of the group's trading activities, there is a danger that the group will no longer be a trading group after the sale, and hence the exemption would not apply. Consideration would need to be given to reorganising trading activities within the group before the sale in order to stay within the exemption conditions. Also, any company retaining large cash proceeds for a lengthy period after a sale without any proposals to use those funds for further trading activity may also itself fall foul of the trading activity test.

Where a trading group carries on multiple trading activities, separating the activities out individually into special purpose subsidiaries offers the opportunity to sell on those companies – together with their businesses and assets – tax free under the substantial shareholding exemption.

Point 36.2:   *Losses on the sale of substantial shareholdings are disregarded. Therefore, an asset sale might be preferable where a capital loss is likely to arise.*

The relief, mentioned in Point 36.1 above, which exempts gains on the sale of substantial shareholdings, equally disregards losses, which would not therefore be available for tax shelter elsewhere. Accordingly, where there is a property sale and a capital loss is likely to arise, alternative planning to that suggested in 36.1 should be adopted. Indeed, where a company sale is being considered where a property sale could give rise to a loss, consideration might be given to selling the property separately and then transferring the shares. An election can be made to use that loss elsewhere in the selling company's group against gains that may crystallise in other situations (*TCGA 1992, s 171A*).

Point 36.3:   *Since sales of shares in investment companies and assets generally will not be exempt from tax, maximisation of past and current capital losses to carry forward may still be useful.*

Notwithstanding the new relief for substantial shareholdings, groups will still find situations where sales are subject to tax and a gain arises. Apart from sales of assets and businesses out of companies, any sales of shares from companies which are below the 10% threshold or which are investment companies will not qualify for the exemption. Nor will sales of shares which have not been held for the requisite period.

Given these potential situations, capital losses remain relevant to many groups and opportunities to crystallise capital losses should be exploited. This might include making negligible value claims in situations where the loss would be allowable.

CHAPTER 37 – TAX-FREE STATUTORY COMPENSATION

Where a tenant is in the process of having a lease agreement terminated, any part of the consideration received which can be attributed to compensation under the Landlord and Tenant Act may escape tax.

Point 37.1

Compensation will not be regarded as tax-free if the tenant has sought to surrender the lease.
Point 37.2

37 Tax-free statutory compensation

Point 37.1: *Where a tenant is in the process of having a lease agreement terminated, any part of the consideration received which can be attributed to compensation under the Landlord and Tenant Act may escape tax.*

Where a landlord gives notice to a tenant under the *Landlord and Tenant Act 1954* that the lease is to be terminated and not renewed, there are statutory provisions for a compensation payment to be made to the tenant. This is, generally speaking, twice the rateable value of the property.

It has been established, following the 1984 tax case of *Drummond (Inspector of Taxes) v Austin Brown* [1984] STC 321, that statutory compensation payments cannot be subject to tax on capital gains since the payment arises by virtue of a right incorporated in the legislation rather than a disposal of an asset. This reinforces the principle already established in the case of statutory compensation for disturbance on surrender of an agricultural lease (*Davis (Inspector of Taxes) v Powell* (1977) 51 TC 492). In that case, it was similarly established that compensation under the *Agricultural Holdings Act 1948* was not subject to tax on capital gains. Since the payment is of a capital nature, there should not be an alternative assessment on it as income.

The exemption for such payments means that where a landlord wishes to terminate a lease, the tenant may well be in a position to minimise the tax liability on any compensation made by ensuring as much as possible is statutory compensation under the Landlord and Tenant or Agricultural Holdings Acts.

No exemption is available if the tenant receives a capital sum for surrendering the 'fag end' of his lease.

HMRC have published an 'interpretation' in this area (RI 145, see Tax Bulletin, April 1996). This followed two further unsuccessful attempts to tax compensation received by outgoing tenants (*Davis v Henderson* [1995] STC (SCD) 308 and *Pritchard v Purves* [1995] STC (SCD) 316).

HMRC now accept that where a tenant enters into an agreement to surrender a lease after receiving a genuine notice to quit from the landlord, any statutory compensation paid under the surrender agreement will not be chargeable to capital gains tax.

All other amounts under the agreement will be taxable.

Point 37.2:   *Compensation will not be regarded as tax-free if the tenant has sought to surrender the lease.*

The HMRC interpretation referred to above only covers surrenders agreed as a result of a unilateral and unsolicited notice to quit. If there is evidence that the tenant has sought to surrender the lease and a notice to quit is then issued, HMRC will seek to tax the full amount received by the tenant.

CHAPTER 38 – CONSTRUCTION INDUSTRY SCHEME

A trader that commissions construction or refurbishment work may need to satisfy the obligations of the Construction Industry Scheme.

Point 38.1

A trader that completes a building can find that it is a sub-contractor requiring to register under the scheme.
Point 38.2

38 Construction Industry Scheme

Point 38.1:   *A trader who commissions construction or refurbishment work on properties may well need to follow the procedures required under the Construction Industry Scheme.*

As already mentioned, there are certain requirements imposed on a 'contractor' within the meaning of the Construction Industry Scheme (CIS) (see Point 25.1). The term 'contractor' includes non-construction businesses where either of the following tests is satisfied:

(a)   the average annual expenditure on 'construction operations' in the three years ending with the last accounting date of the business exceeds £1 million; or

(b)   if the business has not been trading for the whole of the last three years, one-third of its total expenditure on 'construction operations' for the part of the period during which it was trading exceeds £1 million.

(TA 1988, s 560(2) (f)).

HMRC guidelines as to what constitutes 'construction operations' are set out in Appendix IV.

The important point about this aspect of the definition of 'contractor' is that the legislation is not confined merely to property developers or builders. Many commercial organisations owning property for trading as well as investment purposes spend substantial amounts annually on construction operations. A large retail or hotel organisation, for instance, may have a number of sites around the country and be continually involved in refurbishment programmes.

The obligations of a 'contractor' have already been set out under Point 25.1. It is important to recognise that failure to operate the scheme would result in the contractor remaining liable to pay to HMRC tax which should have been withheld. In this connection, the contractor must ensure that all payments to sub-contractors without a verified gross payment status are made net of tax at the prescribed rate of tax and the appropriate returns made to HMRC.

Where tax withholding is required, the prescribed rate for 2006/07 is 20% for matched (known to HMRC) and 30% for unmatched (not known to HMRC).

Point 38.2:   *Reduction in circumstances where a trader can become a sub-contractor under the legislation.*

Before 6 April 2007, the CIS could have extended to a situation where a trader owns a site and carries out a sale and lease-back arrangement under which the trader is responsible for completing the building. Often, the trader agrees to sell the site to an institution at a price equivalent to the value of the completed building less further construction costs to be incurred.

In this way, the trader could have become the sub-contractor for the institution in question and may consequently have been required to produce a sub-contractors' certificate (pre-6 April 2007) or suffer a tax withholding. However, an easement introduced on 6 April 2007 means that in many circumstances such payments are excluded from the scheme.

The trader will continue to have the responsibility of operating the scheme in respect of payments to sub-contractors that it uses itself.

CHAPTER 39 – VAT AND TRADING PREMISES

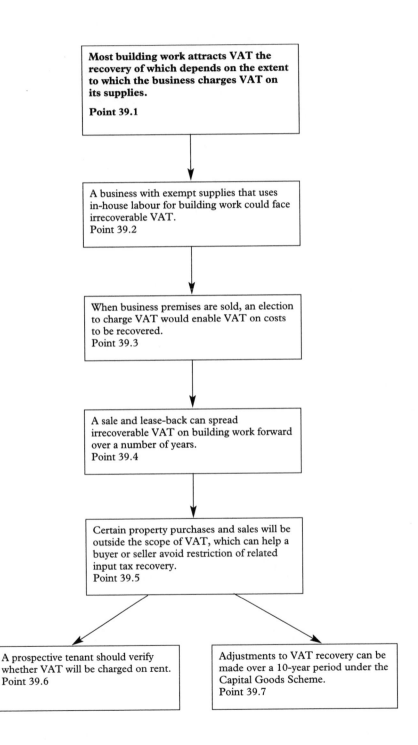

Most building work attracts VAT the recovery of which depends on the extent to which the business charges VAT on its supplies.

Point 39.1

A business with exempt supplies that uses in-house labour for building work could face irrecoverable VAT.
Point 39.2

When business premises are sold, an election to charge VAT would enable VAT on costs to be recovered.
Point 39.3

A sale and lease-back can spread irrecoverable VAT on building work forward over a number of years.
Point 39.4

Certain property purchases and sales will be outside the scope of VAT, which can help a buyer or seller avoid restriction of related input tax recovery.
Point 39.5

A prospective tenant should verify whether VAT will be charged on rent.
Point 39.6

Adjustments to VAT recovery can be made over a 10-year period under the Capital Goods Scheme.
Point 39.7

39 VAT and trading premises

Point 39.1: *Most building work is subject to VAT at the standard rate. Where a business is wholly or partially exempt, part or all of this input VAT will be irrecoverable.*

The position regarding the taxability of building work has already been discussed in relation to property investors (see Point 18.8) and for property developers/dealers (see Point 26.1).

The reader will note from the discussion under the above points that all building work on business premises will be subject to standard-rated VAT. This is regardless of whether building work is on new or existing buildings.

For the VAT-registered business with fully taxable supplies all of the input tax can be recovered from HM Customs and Excise. However, those businesses which have wholly or partly exempt supplies will be unable to recover all of their VAT. This VAT will, therefore, represent an additional cost of building work to a number of businesses such as insurance brokers, bookmakers, hospitals, banks and building societies.

Point 39.2: *A business with exempt supplies could face irrecoverable VAT on a deemed supply of construction services when it uses in-house labour to extend or alter a building.*

Where a business carries out any construction work using in-house labour, there is a deemed self-supply of construction services unless the open market value of those services is less than £100,000. Where the value of the services is £100,000 or more, VAT is chargeable on the market value of this supply.

A deemed self-supply arises with extension, enlargement or alteration work which results in an increase in the floor area by more than 10%. The VAT is charged and then recovered according to the business's input tax recovery position. For the exempt or partially exempt business, there is likely to be irrecoverable VAT unless the building itself is used wholly for taxable supplies.

The tax point for the charge would be the date on which the work is completed or if earlier the date on which the new parts of the building are occupied.

Point 39.3: *Where a business sells a property, consideration might be given to electing to charge VAT on the sale.*

The sale of business premises will generally constitute an exempt supply for VAT purposes unless the property was completed in the previous three years or the sale forms part of a transfer of the business as a going concern (see Points 39.4 and 39.5 below). This could mean that if any significant building work is carried out prior to sale, HMRC might attribute some or all of the related input tax to the sale of the property. On this basis, the input tax would be irrecoverable regardless of the status of other supplies by the business.

In every case where a business is faced with an exempt supply and the possible irrecoverability of input tax, consideration might be given to electing to waive the exemption in respect of that sale (see Points 18.1 and 26.3). This would mean that VAT at the standard rate would have to be added to the sale price. This, in turn, would mean that any input tax incurred on the property that is attributable to the sale would be recoverable.

This is also relevant to the Capital Goods Scheme, where an exempt sale within ten years will result in a clawback of VAT even if the property was used for trading purposes (see Point 39.7 below for an illustration of the Capital Goods Scheme).

There is a discussion on the option to tax in Points 18.1 and 26.3.

A separate consideration of the VAT position may be necessary if the sale of the premises is part of a sale and lease-back deal (see Point 39.4) or of the sale of the business as a going concern (see Point 39.5 below).

Point 39.4: *If a business constructs a new building for its own use and then sells it as part of a sale and lease-back transaction, VAT must be charged on the property. This can help with cash flow in respect of any irrecoverable input tax on building work.*

It will be noted from Point 26.1 that the freehold sale of a building by the developer within three years of its completion represents a standard-rated supply unless the going concern rules mentioned in Point 39.5 below apply. This will need to be borne in mind by any business that constructs its own premises and effectively re-finances the work by way of a sale and lease-back deal.

In the absence of a sale and lease-back arrangement, if the business has largely exempt supplies, any input tax incurred on building supplies would be wholly or partly irrecoverable. The mechanism of the Capital Goods Scheme would be relevant to dictate the manner in which the business can recover VAT over a ten-year period (see Point 39.7 below).

If the property is sold and leased back, VAT will have to be charged on the sale price. For this reason there should be a full recovery of any VAT incurred on the building expenditure.

The institution that purchases the building will itself be keen to recover the VAT element of the cost. It will probably achieve this by electing to tax the rentals charged to the business under the lease-back arrangement. For the exempt or partially exempt business, this results in the spreading forward over a number of years of the irrecoverable VAT that would normally arise on the construction.

It should be noted that the option to tax is sometimes disapplied under certain circumstances, including some sale and leaseback arrangements between connected parties where the tenant is partly or fully exempt. This ultimately means that the VAT that is chargeable on the sale of the building will represent a cost to the landlord, as his rental income will revert back to being exempt from VAT. This is a particularly complex area of VAT and specialist advice should always be sought in advance.

Point 39.5: *The transfer of property as part of the sale of the business may be outside the scope of VAT altogether rather than either an exempt or standard-rated supply.*

Where a business is sold as a going concern, the transaction, together with the related transfer of assets and liabilities, is outside the scope of VAT (*VAT (Special Provisions) Order 1995, SI 1995/1268, art 5*). This is also the case for the sale of part of the business. However, the following conditions must be met before this treatment applies:

(a) The business (or the part of the business which is being transferred) must be a going concern at the time of transfer.

(b) The property transferred must be for use by the new owner in carrying on the same kind of business as that carried on by the former owner. It does not matter whether this will be a new business which the transferee will be carrying on or whether he will carry it on as part of the existing business.

(c) If part only of the business is being transferred, the part must be capable of being operated separately from any other businesses the transferee carries on.

(d) The new owner must already be registered or, at the time of transfer, become liable to be registered (or accepted for voluntary registration).

(e) If the vendor has opted to tax the building, the new owner must notify HMRC before the time of supply that he too has opted to tax. This is quite strictly interpreted. Where property is bought at an auction, the election should be sent to HMRC before the auction date (*Higher Education Statistics Agency Ltd v Customs and Excise Comrs* [2000] STC 332).

(f) The new owner is now required to make a declaration to the vendor stating that new anti-avoidance legislation (see Point 18.3 above) does not apply to the transaction.

Where these conditions are satisfied, the transfer of a property as part of a sale of a business will not be deemed to be a supply for VAT purposes. Accordingly, no restriction on the recovery of input tax will arise, which might otherwise be the case if a transfer of land represented an exempt supply. For the same reason, it would not be necessary or appropriate to consider electing to tax the sale in that situation.

Point 39.6:   *When a tenancy is being entered into, the tenant should verify whether VAT is to be charged on the rents.*

As noted in Point 18.1, many investors will be considering whether to charge VAT on property lettings so that they themselves can recover any input tax on, say, construction and refurbishment.

For an exempt or partially exempt business, any VAT charged on the rents clearly constitutes an additional expense and should be resisted if possible. This may, in some cases, mean agreeing to a slightly higher rent so that the impact of the additional cost can be split between the parties. Note that where VAT is charged on the rent, this will also increase the stamp duty land tax payable on the grant of the lease (see Point 5.2 and 5.3 in Chapter 5 respectively on SDLT on lease grants and SDLT and VAT).

There may be cases where even a fully taxable business may wish to resist VAT on rents charged. As mentioned under Point 18.2, a growing business may be looking to assign or sub-let at a future date when the premises may be inadequate for its needs. If, by the nature of the location or the type of building, the premises would attract exempt or partly exempt tenants, the landlord exercising the waiver of exemption will make the rent up to 17.5% more expensive for such tenants.

Ultimately, this will be a bargaining point between landlord and tenant in future. However, in certain situations the landlord will have no option. If a landlord has already made an election for the property then any future lettings or assignments must be taxable. Furthermore, if the premises are part of a complex or precinct an election would have to cover all units within that complex or precinct.

Point 39.7:   *Where the proportion of a business's exempt outputs change, this will result in an adjustment to the VAT reclaimable on premises under the Capital Goods Scheme. A substantial clawback of VAT can arise on a sale within 10 years from purchase if the exemption is not waived on sale.*

Under the Capital Goods Scheme, there is a potential annual adjustment over a ten-year period in respect of VAT claimed on expenditure on premises (*VAT Regulations 1995 regs 112–116*).

As far as trading premises are concerned, the scheme applies to the following capital expenditure:

(a) A building (or parts of buildings or a civil engineering work) worth £250,000 or more.

(b) A building or part of a building in respect of which the owner has been subject to a self-supply charge on change of use from residential or charitable purposes, and the value of the self-supply was £250,000 or more. Such a self-supply charge is made (under *VATA 1994 Sch 10 para 1(5)*) where the owner acquired his interest in the building by means of a zero-rated supply, on the grounds that the building was to be used solely for a residential or charitable purpose, and within ten years from the date of completion of the building, it begins to be used for some other purpose.

(c) A building or part of a building in respect of which the owner was subject before 2 March 1997 to the former developer's self-supply charge, and the value of that self-supply was £250,000 or more. The developer's self-supply charge was made under *VATA 1994, Sch 10, paras 5, 6* in specified circumstances where either a developer granted an exempt interest in the building or occupied it himself at a time when he was not a fully taxable person.

(d) A building which was constructed by the owner and first brought into use by him after 31 March 1990 if the value of all taxable supplies relating to the land and taxable supplies of goods or services (other than zero-rated supplies) made to him after that date in connection with the construction are £250,000 or more.

(e) A building which the owner alters (including constructing an extension or annex) where additional floor area of 10% or more is created and the value of all taxable supplies (other than zero-rated supplies) of goods or services made to him after that date in connection with the alteration are £250,000 or more.

(f) Civil engineering work constructed by the owner and first brought into use by him after 2 July 1997 if the aggregate value of taxable supplies to the owner after that date relating to the land (other than zero-rated supplies) made to him in connection with the construction of the work is £250,000 or more.

(g) A building which the owner refurbishes or fits out where the value of capital expenditure on the taxable supplies of services and goods affixed to the building made to the owner in connection with the refurbishment after 2 July 1997 is £250,000 or more.

An illustration how this operates is given in the example below:

EXAMPLE

A building is purchased by an insurance company for £10 million plus £1,750,000 VAT.

In the first three years it is used as a branch office by the company whose recovery rate was 10%, 25% and 10% in each of those years. At the beginning of the fourth year the building is sold and the insurance company exercises the option to tax the sale. The position in each year will be:

Year	Partial exemption recovery rate	Capital goods calculation	Input tax recovered/(repaid) £
1	10%	£1,750,000 × 10%	175,000
2	25%	£1,750,000 × 15% × $\frac{1}{10}$	26,250
3	10%	£1,750,000 × 15% × $\frac{1}{10}$	(26,250)
4	100%	£1,750,000 × 90% × $\frac{7}{10}$	1,102,500
			£1,277,500

In the first year, the company recovers 10% of the VAT incurred. In subsequent years there are adjustments to that figure depending on whether the proportion of taxable supplies increases or decreases.

In year 4, because there is a taxable sale of the property, it is assumed that the property in years 4 to 10 is used in a fully taxable way. Accordingly, for those seven years, the company can recover $\frac{7}{10}$ of the total VAT on the building.

There is a potential pitfall in the Capital Goods Scheme for the trader that sells premises without waiving the VAT exemption. If, in the above example, the property were sold on an exempt basis at the beginning of year 4, there is a negative adjustment for the last seven years.

The presumption is that for those seven years, the property is used in a totally exempt way. Therefore, instead of being able to recover £1,277,500, the company must actually pay back to HMRC £122,500 (£1,750,000 × 10% × $\frac{7}{10}$). This reduces the overall VAT recovered to £52,500 (£175,000 − £122,500).

If the VAT recovery in the two situations is compared, the benefit of electing to waive the exemption on letting is evident. Taxing the sale of the property yielded a further £1,102,500 in respect of years 4–7 and a total recovery of £1,277,500.

In the second situation, virtually all of the VAT was irrecoverable.

This problem is not just confined to partially taxable businesses. If a fully taxable business were to sell premises in the same manner, it could still suffer a heavy clawback of VAT if it does not elect to waive the exemption on sale.

Part D   Private Residences

CHAPTER 40 – MOTIVE FOR ACQUISITION OF A RESIDENCE

Exemption from capital gains tax is available on the sale of a 'main residence' unless the property was acquired wholly or partly for the purpose of realising a gain. A seller may have to show that the reason for buying a property was to occupy it as a residence.

Point 40.1

40 Motive for acquisition of a residence

Point 40.1: *Exemption from capital gains tax is available to an individual disposing of his/her main residence unless the property was acquired wholly or partly for the purpose of realising a gain. Where circumstances suggest that this might have been the case, a taxpayer may have to show that the reason for buying a property was to occupy it as a residence.*

Normally, a gain realised by an individual on a dwelling house which was occupied as a main residence is exempt from capital gains tax. However, a gain on a main residence which was bought wholly or partly with the objective of realising a gain on sale is excluded from the exemption (*TCGA 1992, s 224(3)*).

This can give rise to some cause for concern. A house purchaser often expects that the property value will increase over a period of time and there is an anticipation of gain on a future sale. Many individuals and couples acquire properties which they know they will be selling in, say, two or three years time to buy larger properties.

The exclusion of the private residence exemption is clearly not aimed at normal home purchases and sales. The fact that the house has been purchased because it may have been a 'bargain' or was expected to appreciate in value does not itself prevent the exemption from applying. However, if there is a purchase and sale within a relatively short period of time, the point could be raised in a Tax Inspector's mind that the principal reason for buying was to realise a quick profit.

Where a residence is purchased and sold at a profit within a short period, it may be necessary to demonstrate the following facts to the Inspector:

(a) That the intention was to occupy the property as a main residence. This might be evidenced by reasons as to why the house and location, together with any local amenities, were particularly desirable. It may also be useful to give positive reasons for leaving the previous residence.

(b) That the property was actually occupied as a main residence. Whilst intention to occupy will help refute any contention that the property was bought with the objective of selling at a profit, no exemption will be available unless the property is actually occupied as a main residence (*Hughes v Viner* [1985] STC 235). Apart from the family's furniture being moved there, it should also be seen that the family slept in the house; cooked and entertained there; received mail there; and the address is used for local amenity purposes eg with libraries and the electoral register.

(c)   The intention to sell should have arisen after the property was acquired. It may be necessary to demonstrate special reasons for a short-term sale such as financial problems, job requirements, problems with neighbours or any other reasons why the location or house may have become unsuitable.

(d)   The timing of any advertising of the property for sale or its placement with estate agents should be consistent with the facts referred to in (a), (b and (c) above.

The main residence exemption is a valuable one. Care should be taken to ensure that the status of main residence is established beyond all reasonable doubt and, if an early sale is found to be necessary, it can be properly related to the facts above.

CHAPTER 41 – MAIN RESIDENCE ELECTION WHERE MORE THAN ONE PROPERTY IS OWNED

When more than one residence is owned, it is important to consider making an election as to which one is to be treated as the main residence for CGT purposes.

Point 41.1

Where more than one property is owned, the advantage of making a main residence election for one is that it can at any time subsequently be varied in favour of the other.
Point 41.2

A main residence election could be of crucial importance if an individual both owns and rents accommodation.
Point 41.3

During periods of overseas absence or other absence, an election in respect of the property which would otherwise have been the UK residence could be useful in establishing a continuous period of eligibility for capital gains tax exemption for that property.
Point 41.4

41 Main residence election where more than one property is owned

Point 41.1: *When more than one residence is owned, it is important to consider making an election as to which one is to be treated as the main residence for CGT purposes.*

The CGT exemption available for the main residence may require particular consideration where more than one property is owned.

If a family has more than one home, it is a question of fact which of the two is an individual's or family's main residence. Relevant factors are:

(a) where the family lives for the greater part of an average week;
(b) in which property is the main furniture kept and used;
(c) which address is used for correspondence;
(d) which address appears on the electoral list.

It is possible to pre-empt any question of fact by making a specific election that one or other of the properties shall be treated as the main residence (*TCGA 1992, s 222(5)(a)*). An election is advisable where substantial appreciation is anticipated in respect of one of the properties and there may be doubt as to whether this would ordinarily be regarded as the main residence.

An example might be where two properties are owned, one in the centre of a town and the other in the country. The town property may be used as a matter of convenience for a working couple where business commitments prevent them from returning to the country. The country home is used as the normal residence at weekends, holidays and all other times when business pressures are not too heavy. In such circumstances, HMRC may well treat the country property as the main residence as a matter of fact. However, if the town property has a higher inherent capital gain, an election to treat that as the main residence should be beneficial.

No election can be made unless the property in question is occupied as a residence (although not necessarily as a main residence). Thus it cannot be claimed in respect of a property which is let or used for other purposes. However, it may be claimed on a property which is available for use, occasionally occupied and is furnished for occupation.

Where a property has been treated at some time as a main residence, the last three years of ownership are automatically always deemed to be a period of main residence as well (*TCGA 1992, s 223(1)*). Therefore, when two residences are owned, it is generally beneficial for a property to cease to be treated as a main residence within three years of sale and another residence to be so treated. This may mean varying the election on the first property and substituting the other residence as the main residence (see 41.2 below).

As a result of this specific allowance in the legislation, it is possible in that particular three-year period effectively to enjoy the main residence exemption in respect of two properties at the same time.

An election must be made within two years of the date when it is necessary to decide the issue. Therefore, if a taxpayer wants a property to be treated as a main residence an election must be filed with the Inspector within two years of the date of acquiring (whether by buying or renting) a second residence (*TCGA 1992, s 222(5)(a)* and *Griffin v Craig-Harvey* [1994] STC 54). However, once an election has been made, it can be varied (see Point 41.2 below).

The main residence position for any taxpayer with more than one property should be kept under review in the two-year period when an election can be made in relation to changes in use of the property and movements in their market values. The making of a timely election can maximise the exemption for the property with the largest prospective gain. Also, by taking advantage of the exempt period in the last three years of ownership there is the opportunity of reducing the prospective taxable gain on another property owned at the same time.

Point 41.2:   *Where more than one property is owned, the advantage of making a main residence election for one is that it can at any time subsequently be varied in favour of the other.*

As mentioned in Point 41.1 above, a main residence election must be made within two years of an acquisition of a second property (*Griffin v Craig-Harvey* [1994] STC 54). If it is not made within that period, the taxpayer cannot choose which property should be treated as his main residence. Instead, it will depend on the facts.

Once made, an election can be varied. The election can be effective from up to two years before the date of variation (*TCGA 1992, s 222(5)(a)*).

EXAMPLE

Mr and Mrs A have lived in a cottage in the Cotswolds since 1995. On 1 June 2004, they bought a flat in North London for occasional use to spend some time near children living in London.

The Cotswold property remains the main residence as a matter of fact. If, therefore, no main residence election is made by 31 May 2006 in favour of the London property only the Cotswold property can attract exemption whilst the two properties are owned.

If the Cotswold and London properties were both sold in, say, June 2007 at a profit, the gain on the Cotswold property only would be exempt from tax. The gain on the London flat would be fully chargeable.

In the above example, if Mr and Mrs A were able to make an election for the London flat to be their main residence shortly before selling it, the entire gain on that flat could be exempt from tax as well – because the last three years of ownership of a main residence are always exempt (see Point 44.1). However, they could not make the election for the London flat because the two-year time limit had expired on 31 May 2006.

The way for Mr and Mrs A to have got the best of both worlds here would have been to make the election for the London property to be the main residence and to do this within the two-year period ie by 31 May 2006.

Electing on this basis could mean that Mr and Mrs A could then give notice to HMRC of a variation to that election enabling the London property to be treated as a main residence from two years previous to that election. That would mean the last three years that the London property is owned is exempt – which would be the whole period of ownership in this example and the Cotswold house would continue to be fully exempt for the last three years at the same time. (See Chapter 44 below for the exemption in the last three years.)

Therefore, the making of an election in the first place allows for greater flexibility – particularly enhancing the possibility of exploiting the automatic exemption for the last three years of ownership referred to in Point 41.1.

Point 41.3: *A main residence election could be of crucial importance if an individual both owns and rents accommodation.*

As stated in Point 41.1 above, in the absence of any election, it will be a matter of fact which of two (or more) properties is the main residence for CGT purposes. Whether such a property is owned by the taxpayer or occupied under lease or licence is irrelevant to this issue.

Accordingly, a person who rents a second residence could find that it is that property which is treated as the main residence. The CGT exemption in that situation would be of no benefit and on the sale of the other property, a CGT liability will arise.

An election for the owned property to be treated as the main residence would avoid this problem and is important in this situation.

HMRC recognises the potential inequity of treating rented accommodation as a main residence for CGT purposes where another property is owned and also occupied. By way of concession, HMRC are prepared to extend the two-year time limit for making such an election (HMRC Extra-Statutory Concession D21). This applies where the taxpayer's interest in one of the properties has 'no more than a negligible value in the open market'. If a taxpayer in this case has been unaware of his entitlement to make an election, HMRC will accept a late election providing it is made within a reasonable period after the person first became aware of the possibility of making the election. It will be treated as effective from the date the nominated residence was acquired.

Point 41.4:   *During periods of overseas absence or other absence, an election in respect of the property which would otherwise have been the UK residence could be useful in establishing a continuous period of eligibility for capital gains tax exemption for that property.*

As will be noted in Chapter 45, some periods of absence from a property are ignored when determining if the CGT exemption is restricted (*TCGA 1992, s 223(3)*). The potential problem is that the absences are ignored providing there is no other main residence eligible for relief (*TCGA 1992, s 223(7)*). Therefore, following from Point 41.3 above, if there is the possibility that another property may be treated as the main residence, an election should be made for the principal UK property to be so treated.

See also Point 45.2 on this point.

CHAPTER 42 – LAND AND BUILDINGS INCLUDED WITH A RESIDENCE – MAXIMISING THE EXEMPTION

The main residence exemption includes land used as grounds or for garden purposes where the total area, except in certain cases, does not exceed half a hectare. It may also extend to other properties enjoyed with the house.

Point 42.1

An area of over half a hectare may be permitted within the exemption if that larger area is required for the reasonable enjoyment of the residence.
Point 42.2

A main residence exemption may not be available on the disposal of any part of the grounds that have been retained after the sale of the house. The land should be sold at the same time as the house.
Point 42.3

42 Land and buildings included with a residence – maximising the exemption

Point 42.1: *The main residence exemption includes land used as grounds or for garden purposes where the total area, except in certain cases, does not exceed half a hectare. It may extend to other properties enjoyed with the house.*

The main residence exemption extends to land that is occupied and enjoyed with the house as garden or grounds (*TCGA 1992, s 222(1)(b)*).

The exemption provides for a permitted area not exceeding a half of a hectare (approximately one and a quarter acres or 5,000 square metres). This includes the area occupied by the house. In certain circumstances a larger area may be allowed by HMRC (see Point 42.2 below).

If the land is not enjoyed and occupied as garden or grounds, then it will not be covered by the exemption. Therefore, any area devoted to farming, grazing or stables may well not qualify whether or not the total area is less than half a hectare.

Any land that is physically separated from the house by a road, fence or other houses, can qualify for exemption. However, it is still necessary to satisfy the requirement that it is enjoyed as garden or grounds with the house.

The private residence exemption can extend to other properties within the grounds which are used in conjunction with the house. There have been a number of cases to determine whether separate buildings form part of one dwelling for the purposes of the private residence exemption. As a result of these, two principal tests have been established for the separate building to qualify with the main part of the dwelling, ie:

(a) The building must be used in conjunction with the enjoyment of the main dwelling to form part of one residence. Thus a cottage to house a caretaker and another for a gardener were held to be occupied for the benefit of the main house. This was sufficient for them to be included with the house and thus form part of the main residence (*Batey (Inspector of Taxes) v Wakefield* [1981] STC 521 and *Williams (Inspector of Taxes) v Merrylees* [1987] STC 445).

(b) The building must be adjacent or at least quite close to the main house. For this reason, a cottage on the opposite side of a large estate to the main house has been considered not to be part of the main residence (*Lewis (Inspector of Taxes) v Rook* [1992] STC 171). See also *Markey (Inspector of Taxes) v Sanders* [1987] STC 256. This test was also used to deny the exemption on additional flats in a block used by a family as additional space to the main accommodation in the block (*Honour (Inspector of Taxes) v Norris* [1992] STC 304).

Point 42.2:   *An area of over half a hectare may be permitted within the exemption if that larger area is required for the reasonable enjoyment of the residence.*

HMRC can allow the permitted area qualifying for the exemption to exceed a half hectare. However, whereas for areas of less than this it is sufficient to show that the land was part of the garden or grounds of the house, there is a stricter test for larger areas. The Inspector of Taxes (or strictly, the Commissioners of HMRC) must be satisfied that the extra area is required for the reasonable enjoyment of the property given the size and character of the house (*TCGA, s 222(3)*).

It is not sufficient for this purpose that the property owner has his or her own special requirements. For instance, an individual may use extra grounds to keep horses or vintage cars. That does not mean that area is necessary for the reasonable enjoyment of the property as other occupiers may not have this requirement (*Longson v Baker (Inspector of Taxes)* [2000] STC (SCD) 244).

Where the grounds exceed half a hectare, it may be crucial that the land is bought and sold with the house. If it is bought or sold separately this would indicate that a previous or subsequent owner did not 'require' this land for the 'reasonable enjoyment' of the residence.

Point 42.3:   *The main residence exemption may not be available on the disposal of any part of the grounds that has been retained after the sale of the house. In view of this, it is advisable to sell the land before, or at the same time as, the sale of the house.*

In Point 42.2 above, it was mentioned that land greater than half a hectare would normally have to be bought and sold with the house to satisfy the requisite test. Although this is not essential for the general exemption for land, it should be noted that a problem could arise in relation to any part of the land retained after sale of the house.

At the time when land is sold it must have been owned and used for enjoyment with the house. This condition cannot have been met where any portion of the land had been kept after the sale of the house. Accordingly, the gain on such land will not, strictly, come within the main residence exemption (*Varty v Lynes* [1976] STC 508). This is the case even if the original total area was less than half a hectare.

The above technically applies regardless of whether the gap between the sale of the house and the land was several years or one day. Furthermore, no exemption at all is available for the remaining land notwithstanding the fact that it may have been occupied with the house for most of the period of ownership. Nor is the deemed final three years of residence (see Point 41.1) applied in the case of the land only.

HMRC have stated in the past that they would not seek to assess tax on land sold in such circumstances unless it had development value. However, HMRC varied their view in August 1994 when they stated that no relief is due on the sale of a garden which takes place after a sale of the house (HMRC Capital Gains Manual, paras CG 64377–64387).

Where the land is over half a hectare, the exemption may be restricted whether it is sold before, at the same time as or after the house is sold. As stated above, once land can be shown to be separable from the main residence then it must weaken the argument that the land is required for the reasonable enjoyment of the dwelling house.

CHAPTER 43 – CONVERTING, RECONSTRUCTING OR REFURBISHING A MAIN RESIDENCE

If construction, refurbishment or improvement work is carried out on a private residence to enhance its value on sale, part or all of the gain arising may not be eligible for the capital gains tax exemption.

Point 43.1

Where an opportunity arises to commercially develop a private residence, it might be appropriate to transfer the property to a company or partnership before any work is carried out. This could help ensure that the gain to the date of transfer will be exempt from tax.
Point 43.2

The profit on the sale of a private residence following reconstruction, conversion and refurbishment could be taxable as income.
Point 43.3

43 Converting, reconstructing or refurbishing a main residence

Point 43.1: *If any construction, refurbishment or improvement work is carried out on a private residence to enhance its value on sale, part or all of the gain arising may not be eligible for the capital gains tax exemption.*

Gains attributable to expenditure incurred wholly or partly for the purpose of realising a gain on the sale of the property are excluded from the main residence CGT exemption (*TCGA 1992, s 224(3)*). Therefore, any development and building profit arising from applying for planning permission and incurring construction costs could be fully assessable to CGT. The related provision is also sufficiently wide to catch any improvements that increase the value of the property on sale. This includes the acquisition of the freehold reversion by a leaseholder. Note that simply incurring expenditure on planning permission or having a restricted covenant released will not itself result in any loss of the exemption (HMRC Capital Gains Manual CG 65243/4).

To some extent there are similar considerations here to those mentioned in Chapter 40 above. Improvements may well be carried out with the expectation that the value of the house will be increased as a result. Any such expenditure could, technically, result in a restriction of the exemption. Accordingly, it may be necessary to be able to demonstrate, where appropriate, that the whole or main objective of any work done was to improve the amenities of the property for the owner's benefit and not to realise a profit.

If the property is sold shortly after any work is carried out, this must add support to a possible argument that the expenditure was incurred with a profit motive. Where this inference is incorrect, the taxpayer may have to be prepared to present to the Inspector evidence that the intention to sell arose after the work commenced. In this connection, any special reasons for an unexpected sale might need to be put to the Inspector, eg financial problems, job requirements or problems with neighbours.

Point 43.2: *Where an opportunity arises to commercially develop a private residence, it might be appropriate to transfer the property to a company or partnership before any work is carried out. This could help ensure that the gain to the date of transfer will be exempt from tax.*

The legislation does not specify how a gain arising in the circumstances of Point 43.1 above should be computed. HMRC's approach is to apportion the total gain between original cost and subsequent enhancement expenditure to determine the taxable part (see HMRC Capital Gains Manual at CG65270/1). If the base cost is small in relation to enhancement expenditure, then the pro-rated exempt part of the gain could be unreasonably low.

To achieve some measure of certainty in this situation, the property could be transferred at full market value to a property dealing/developing company or partnership prior to carrying out any work. That would crystallise the exempt gain at that point in time. As mentioned in Point 43.1 above, HMRC do not apply any restriction if the only expenditure incurred is obtaining planning permission or removing restrictive covenants. If there is a proposed change of use of the property and it is likely that planning permission will be successfully obtained, the transfer value of the property after planning permission could reflect some development value. In that way, the exempt gain could reflect part of that development value.

The further gain on the property in the hands of a company or partnership would almost certainly be taxable as income. This would most likely be as trading income (under *ITTOIA 2005, s 5* for income tax payers or under *Schedule D Case I, TA 1988, s 18(3)* for companies within charge to corporation tax), but possibly as unearned income (*ITA 2007, s 755/TA 1988, s 766*) – see Point 43.3 below.

Point 43.3:   *The profit on the sale of a private residence following reconstruction, conversion and refurbishment could be taxable as income.*

Apart from capital gains treatment, profits from land transactions can also be taxed as income. In certain circumstances, the profit could be assessed as trading income or as unearned income (under *ITA 2007, s 755*).

An isolated transaction can constitute an adventure in the nature of a trade for tax purposes. When an Inspector considers that this is the case, some or all of the profit arising is potentially assessable as trading income.

It is rare for an individual to be treated as trading in a property which has been used as a private residence. However, this cannot be ruled out where a person has a history of property dealing or developing. In this case, HMRC would treat the property as appropriated to trading stock when it appeared that steps were taken to exploit it commercially. The capital gain up to that date should be covered by the private residence exemption. The gain after that date would be taxable as trading income.

Trading treatment can sometimes be more beneficial than taxation as a capital gain. Financing costs, for instance, can be deducted. Furthermore, if a spouse with no other income is actively involved as a partner or employee in relation to the development, any profit share or reasonable wages paid to him or her can use up personal allowances or lower tax rate bands. Note that if this is merely used as a way to divert income to a spouse to reduce tax, HMRC use anti-avoidance rules relating to settlements to counter this (*ITTOIA 2005, s 624*). The Government have also announced, in their Pre-Budget report issued in October 2007, that they intend to introduce further measures to counter 'income splitting' arrangements.

HMRC sometimes seek to tax a gain as unearned income in the following situations:

(a)   land, or any property deriving its value from land, is acquired with the object of realising gain from disposing of the land; or
(b)   land is held as trading stock; or
(c)   land is developed with the sole or main object of realising a gain from disposing of the land when developed.

(*ITA 2007, s 752*, formerly *TA 1988, s 776*).

Although these provisions are quite wide ranging, they are generally used as an anti-avoidance measure. In this connection the following should be noted:

(a)   It does not apply where the property being developed was a private residence at the time of the intention to develop (*ITA 2007, s 767*).
(b)   It cannot apply where the proper treatment of the transaction was as an adventure in the nature of trade. Unearned income treatment can only apply where the gain is otherwise of a capital nature (*ITA 2007, s 772(1)*).

CHAPTER 44 – MAIN RESIDENCE: TAKING ADVANTAGE OF THE EXEMPTION FOR THE LAST THREE YEARS OF OWNERSHIP

Since the last three years of ownership of a main residence will always qualify for exemption even if it has not been occupied as such in that period, two properties may qualify at the same time.

Point 44.1

A main residence election can help two properties to benefit from the capital gains tax exemption in the last three years of ownership where one of the properties is not occupied as a main residence.
Point 44.2

44 Main residence: taking advantage of the exemption for the last three years of ownership

Point 44.1: *Since the last three years of ownership of a main residence will always qualify for exemption even if it has not been occupied as such in that period, two properties may qualify at the same time.*

Normally, if a property has not been occupied as a main residence throughout the period of ownership, there will be a restriction on the amount of gain eligible for exemption. The gain attributable to the period of main residence will be calculated on a time apportionment basis and that element of the overall gain treated as exempt. The balance would be a chargeable capital gain.

This calculation proceeds subject to the important proviso that the last three years of ownership are always regarded as a period of main residence, regardless of whether or not the property is occupied as such in that period (*TCGA 1992, s 223(1)*).

EXAMPLE

Mr and Mrs X bought a London property in 1997 which they occupied as a residence until 2002. At that time, whilst retaining the house in London, they bought a flat in Bournemouth to be near an ageing parent. The house was subsequently let until 2007 when it was sold.

Out of the ten years' ownership, Mr and Mrs A only occupied the house as a residence for five years. However, as the last three years of ownership are treated as a period of main residence, 80% of the gain is exempt (ie eight years out of ten) rather than just 50%.

In this example, the Bournemouth flat is also a main residence for a period and will similarly benefit from this last three years of its ownership being treated as a period of main residence. The example in Point 41.2 illustrates how the main residence exemption can be used in conjunction with this three-year rule to increase the gains exempt from capital gains tax where more than one property is owned.

Point 44.2: *If a second property is used as a residence – but not a main residence at any stage – a main residence election can help both properties to benefit from the capital gains tax exemption in the last three years of ownership of one of the properties.*

As explained in Chapter 41, a main residence election can ensure that more than one property is eligible for capital gains tax exemption at the same time. This can be particularly used to exploit the advantage of the last three years as a period automatically included in the qualifying period. This would be relevant where one of the properties would not normally be treated as a main residence.

See Points 41.1 and 41.2 for further explanation of this.

CHAPTER 45 – TEMPORARY ABSENCES –
PRESERVING THE EXEMPTION

A taxpayer who spends a long period living away from his main residence can still be entitled to the full capital gains exemption if he subsequently resumes occupation of that residence. This can apply even if the property has been let during the period of absence.

Point 45.1

An election may have to be considered where another property is occupied during this same period.
Point 45.2

45 Temporary absences – preserving the exemption

Point 45.1: *A taxpayer who in certain circumstances spends a lengthy period living away from his main residence can still be entitled to the full capital gains exemption if he subsequently resumes occupation of that residence. This can apply even if the property has been let during the period of absence.*

A period of absence from a main residence would normally result in the pro-rata restriction of the main residence exemption referred to in Point 44.1. However, following the re-basing of capital gains at 31 March 1982 (see Chapter 11), periods of absence before 31 March 1982 can be ignored (*TCGA 1992, s 223(7)*).

There are also three situations where periods of absence are ignored providing the property is occupied as a main residence at some stage before and after the period in question. The three situations are:

(a) A period of absence of up to three years for whatever reason. The absence may be in the UK or abroad. In arriving at the period of three years, all shorter periods of absence are aggregated during the total period of ownership.

(b) Any period of absence, regardless of length, provided that throughout the whole period the individual was required to perform the duties of an employment outside the UK.

(c) Any period of absence up to four years during which the requirements of an individual's employment prevented him from living in the house. As with (a) above, the period of four years may be made up of shorter periods aggregated during the period of ownership.

(*TCGA 1992, s 223(3)*).

The property need not have been left vacant during the period. Even if it had been let, the house can still be treated as a main residence.

As mentioned, it is fundamental that the property in question is the individual's main residence at some time both before and after the period of absence. It can be crucial, therefore, that the individual does re-occupy the property at some time after the above periods have come to an end, at least for a short period.

EXAMPLE

A buys a house in February 1989 for £150,000. After living there for three years in February 1992, he and his family are sent abroad by his employer.

On his return in February 2004 it was valued at £400,000.

A sold the house in March 2007 without resuming occupation. Assuming an indexation allowance of £100,000, and A is paying 40% tax, the CGT position would be:

Sale proceeds	£400,000)
Cost – February 1989	(150,000)
	250,000)
Indexation allowance (to March 1998)	(100,000)
Total gain	150,000)
Exempt*	

Occupation as main residence	3 years	
Last 3 years	3 years	
	6 years	

Total ownership 18 years	
Exempt 6/18 × £150,000	(50,000)
Gain before taper relief	100,000)
Complete years of ownership after March 1998	
	= 9

Add: Bonus year	1/10	
Taper relief: 40%		(40,000)
Tapered gain		60,000)
Annual exemption – 2006/7		(8,800)
Chargeable gain		£51,200)
Tax at 40%		£20,480)

*If A had resumed ownership for a short period, the entire gain would have been exempt and tax of £20,480 avoided

For disposals after 5 April 2008, neither taper relief not indexation allowance can be claimed. Both reliefs are removed for individuals, trustees and personal representatives. In their place is a single capital gains tax rate of 18%, In the example, that would give rise to a tax liability of over £30,000 – some £10,000 more than in the pre 6 April 2008 illustration shown. See the 'Stop Press' note at the beginning of the book regarding 2007 Pre-Budget changes.

There are circumstances where HMRC concessionally do not require a taxpayer to re-occupy the property. This applies in situations (b) and (c) above where the taxpayer is unable to re-occupy the residence because the terms of his employment require him to work elsewhere (HMRC Extra-Statutory Concession D4).

Point 45.2: *Notwithstanding the permitted period of absence above, an election may have to be considered where another property is occupied during this same period.*

The provisions regarding the permitted periods of absence in Point 45.1 above only apply where there is no other residence eligible for relief (*TCGA 1992, s 223(7)*). Whilst the objective may have been to prevent two properties being eligible for relief at the same time, it also creates a pitfall where long-term absences are involved.

A family having to live away from their usual home for an extended period will need residential accommodation elsewhere. Whether this is within the UK or abroad, this accommodation must technically be the taxpayer's only or main residence during that period and is eligible for the exemption.

It would make a nonsense of the permitted period of absence provision if HMRC did not overlook at least certain types of accommodation. This might include hotel suites, company-owned property, rented houses or apartments. However, there could be a problem if another property is acquired for occupation during the period. Accordingly, where a second property is bought, it may be advisable to elect to treat the first property as a main residence (see Chapter 41). If the second property is rented, the relief mentioned in Point 41.3 may be relevant – ie the ability to make an out-of-date election in respect of the owned property.

If a second residence is acquired and the first property temporarily let, the Inspector of Taxes may not accept a main residence election in respect of the let property. In this case, the message must be that buying a second residence during a period of absence could well prejudice the availability of a full CGT exemption on the first house particularly if it is let during the period of absence.

CHAPTER 46 – TAKING ADVANTAGE OF THE EXEMPTION ON LET PROPERTY

> An owner who takes up a short period of occupation in a residential investment property can gain a substantial capital gains tax reduction when the property is sold.
>
> **Point 46.1**

46 Taking advantage of the exemption on let property

Point 46.1: *An owner who takes up a short period of occupation in a residential investment property can gain a substantial capital gains tax reduction when the property is sold.*

Let property, which was the owner's residence at some time during the period of ownership, attracts an additional capital gains exemption on disposal. The extra exemption is the lower of £40,000 and the main residence exemption in respect of this disposal (*TCGA 1992, s 223(4)(b)*).

EXAMPLE

A house is owned since 1997. In 2000 it was used as a main residence for 12 months. For the remainder of the period it was let. A total gain of £200,000 was realised on sale in 2007.

Total gain	£200,000
Main residence exemption (4/10 × £200,000)*	£80,000
Letting exemption (lower of £40,000 and main residence exemption)	£40,000
Total exemptions	£120,000

Since the property has been a main residence, the last three years of ownership are treated as a further period of main residence (see Point 44.1).

One year's occupation of the property has therefore attracted a total exemption of £120,000.

To obtain some capital gains exemption, it is not necessary to occupy the property as a main residence. Even where there is occasional occupation in a period, provided it is in fact his residence, an election can be made for a property to be treated as a main residence (see Chapter 41).

In view of the potential capital gains tax exemptions the occupation of a property to take advantage of a main residence election could well prove worthwhile if at all practical. This may be the case where the property has already been owned for some years and substantial appreciation in its value has already taken place.

Letting during a period of absence from the property may not affect the availability of the full exemption at all where the circumstances discussed in Point 45.1 apply.

As discussed in Chapter 47, periods prior to 31 March 1982 are ignored in determining the appropriate period of exemption. Thus, in the above example, if the period of occupation had been in 1981 then this would have been ignored. The last three years would still be exempt.

CHAPTER 47 – PRIVATE RESIDENCES: PERIODS BEFORE 31 MARCH 1982

Periods before 31 March 1982 are ignored for the purposes of the private residence exemption. This could be helpful where absences or letting have taken place before that date.

Point 47.1

Where the owner occupied the property as a main residence before 31 March 1982 but not since, the last three years should still be exempt.
Point 47.2

47 Private residences: periods before 31 March 1982

Point 47.1: *Periods before 31 March 1982 are ignored for the purposes of the private residence exemption. This could be helpful where absences or letting have taken place before that date.*

In Chapter 11, the effects of the re-basing provisions were discussed for assets owned at 31 March 1982. It is possible to calculate a gain by reference to the 31 March 1982 market value of a property instead of cost for capital gains purposes.

As far as main residences are concerned, it will be noted from Chapters 44, 45 and 46 that a gain on a private residence may not be totally exempt where there have been periods during which the property has not been occupied as a main residence. This may also be the case where a taxpayer owns more than one residence since he can only elect for one to be treated as a main residence at any time (see Chapter 41).

In conjunction with the introduction of the re-basing provisions, the private residence exemption was amended so that periods prior to 31 March 1982 are ignored in determining the amount of exemption. Clearly this would be beneficial where there has been a period of letting or absence from a property which only occurred before 31 March 1982.

EXAMPLE 1

Mr and Mrs A bought a holiday cottage as residential investment in 1970. It was let until March 1982. They subsequently occupied it until 2007, when the property was sold.

The entire gain on the property would be exempt. The period of letting occurred prior to 31 March 1982 and is, therefore, ignored.

Point 47.2: *Where the owner occupied the property as a main residence before 31 March 1982 but not since, the last three years should still be exempt.*

Following on from the point in Point 47.1 above, where a property had only been occupied as a main residence before 31 March 1982, none of that period can qualify for exemption. This raises the question, however, of whether a taxpayer would still be entitled to have the last 36 months of ownership treated as a period of qualifying residence.

It does appear that entitlement to the main residence exemption in the first instance arises where there has been at any stage occupation of the property as such. The restriction of the period of ownership to that period after 31 March 1982 seems to be relevant only for the purposes of determining the fraction to be applied in computing the extent of the exemption (*TCGA 1992, s 223(7)*). For the purposes of this fraction, however, the last 36 months of ownership are always assumed to be a period of occupation of a main residence (*TCGA 1992, s 223(2)*).

EXAMPLE 2

In the above example, if the property had been occupied as a residence between 1970 and 1982 but let thereafter, 3/25ths of the total gain would be exempt.

CHAPTER 48 – RENT A ROOM: INCOME TAX EXEMPTION ON PART LETTING OF A MAIN RESIDENCE

There is exemption from income tax where part of a home is let and the annual gross receipts do not exceed £4,250.

Point 48.1

HMRC do not accept that rent a room relief may be exploited for business letting although this view may be open to challenge.
Point 48.2

48 Rent a room: income tax exemption on part letting of a main residence

Point 48.1: *There is exemption from income tax where part of a home is let and the annual gross receipts do not exceed £4,250.*

The government introduced the 'rent a room' relief in 1992. This applies where an individual or individuals let furnished rooms within their main residence (*ITTOIA 2005, ss 784–802*).

The relief applies where the 'relevant sums' received from the accommodation do not exceed £4,250 per year (*ITTOIA 2005, s 789*). The receipts are fully exempt from tax.

Relevant sums include charges for items such as meals, cleaning, laundry and similar items in addition to rent (*ITTOIA 2005, s 786*). Expenses and capital allowances cannot be deducted.

Where the property is owned by more than one person, the relief is halved (*ITTOIA 2005, s 789*). This is regardless of the number of owners. Therefore, a husband and wife owning the property would each be entitled to earn £2,125. If four friends own a property which is their main residence, each would also have an exemption of £2,125. In that case, total exemptions would be £8,500.

If the receipts exceed the exemption, the individual can elect to be taxed on the excess without any deduction for expenses or capital allowances (*ITTOIA 2005, s 795*).

Rent a room relief applies in respect of furnished accommodation. Relief is only available in respect of accommodation let in the individual's main residence. If more than one property is owned it is a question of fact which is the main residence. No election is possible, unlike the position for capital gains tax.

If a taxpayer makes a loss in a year which can be offset against other income, it may not be beneficial to claim the rent a room exemption. The individual can opt out of the exemption for that year by notifying the Inspector on or before the first anniversary of the 31 January next following the year of assessment ie 22 months after the year end (*ITTOIA 2005, s 799*).

HMRC accept that the letting of accommodation which is an integral part of a main residence will not affect the capital gains exemption available on the sale of the property. However, if it is self-contained, the taxpayer may have to rely on letting relief for capital gains tax exemption (see Chapter 46).

Point 48.2:   *HMRC do not accept that rent a room relief may be exploited for business letting although this view may be open to challenge.*

Rent a room relief was undoubtedly introduced to encourage private letting of residential accommodation.

Although this is not specified in the legislation, HMRC do not consider that the exemption is available where a house is used for business purposes.

A condition of the relief is that it applies to a building or part of a building which is occupied or intended to be occupied as a separate residence (*ITTOIA 2005, s 787*). HMRC's view is that, where part of a property is used exclusively for business purposes, this condition is not satisfied. The counter argument may be that, unless the business use is permanent, the property is always intended to be occupied as a residence.

An employee using the facilities within his or her house for business purposes may seek a form of rent payment from the company or partnership he or she works for. It is open for them to treat this as tax-free if it is within the £4,250 rent a room limit. However, full disclosure of this treatment must be made and a challenge must be expected from HMRC.

CHAPTER 49 – EXPENSE DEDUCTIONS FOR BUSINESS USE OF HOME

Where some business use is made of a property, the taxpayer should ensure that expenses are claimed for tax purposes.

Point 49.1

Any claim that part of a residence is used exclusively for business will result in a restriction of the main residence capital gains tax exemption.
Point 49.2

49 Expense deductions for business use of home

Point 49.1: *Where some business use is made of a property, the taxpayer should ensure that expenses are claimed for tax purposes.*

Many individuals use their properties to a greater or lesser extent for the purposes of a trade or employment carried on by them. This could well mean that there is an entitlement to claim related household expenses for tax purposes.

A person carrying on a trade, profession or vocation can deduct any expenses that are wholly and exclusively incurred for the purposes of the trade etc (*ITTOIA 2005, s 34*). This could include heating, lighting and power costs resulting directly from his use of the property for business purposes. Often this can be estimated based on the amount of time spent on business activities in the home and the space occupied.

In addition, where an individual exclusively uses part of the premises for business purposes (eg where it is used as a doctor's surgery or as a self-contained office), it may also be possible to claim an appropriate portion of other expenses, such as rent repairs, insurance, interest charges and council tax. Strictly, such expenses are only deductible if they are exclusive to the business area being used. In practice, Inspectors of Taxes do allow pro rata expense claims provided an area is exclusively used for business. However, the possible restriction in the capital gains tax exemption should be noted (see Point 49.2 below). In practice, HMRC are prepared to accept apportioned sums in respect of heating, lighting and council tax (rates in Northern Ireland) where business use of a room or rooms is not exclusive, as will usually be the case (Business Income Manual, para BIM 47815).

An employee may similarly be entitled to deductions where an area is occupied exclusively for his work. However, the employee has the additional burden of showing that the expense was necessarily as well as wholly and exclusively incurred. Thus an employee or director who chooses to do certain work at home rather than at the office would probably not satisfy the necessarily test. On the other hand, a travelling salesman or area manager who is required to use his home as a base may well need to use a room in his home as an office. Where rooms are not used exclusively for the purpose of the employment, HMRC are prepared to accept the extra cost of heating and lighting the room(s) while in use for business. However, in contrast with the Schedule D position for the self-employed (see above), no deduction may be claimed for council tax (see Employment Income Manual, para EIM 32810).

Point 49.2:   *Any claim that part of a residence is used exclusively for business will result in a restriction of the main residence exemption.*

If part of the house is used exclusively for business purposes, then it is not covered by the main residence exemption (*TCGA 1992, s 224(1)*). Examples are doctors and dentists who have used two or three rooms within their house for the purposes of a surgery and waiting room. However, many individuals do set aside part of their house as a study or office either informally or as a formal business address. In other cases, garages or sheds within a garden area are converted into workshops for trading purposes.

If a claim is made that a particular room is being set aside wholly for business purposes, then it will be necessary to estimate the portion of the gain attributable to that room. This will be excluded from the main residence exemption. If one room in a ten-room house is being so used, then it may be reasonable to assume the figure is 10%, although it could be higher or lower depending on the size of the room in question relative to the rest of the house. In addition it may be possible to claim a portion of the interest paid on the loan to purchase the property.

A high rate taxpayer may be better off with the income tax relief than the capital gains exemption.

EXAMPLE

Between 1 April 1998 and 1 April 2008, an individual who was paying tax at the marginal rate of 40%, agreed with HMRC that part of his house was used exclusively for business purposes. His bills for utilities, insurance, repairs and maintenance plus interest charges averaged £20,000 per year and 10% of this was allowed as trading expense.

The house cost £200,000 in April 1998 and was sold for £600,000 on 1 April 2008.

Income tax saving over 10 years:

1997/98 to 2007/08

$10 \times 10\% \times £20,000 \times 40\% =$	£8,000
Capital gains position	
Sale proceeds	£600,000
Cost	200,000
	400,000
Indexation allowance – say 10%	(40,000)
	360,000

	Non business	
Business		
Exempt – 90% (non business)	(324,000)	36,000
Business asset taper relief @max 75% on 10%		(3,600)
Non-Business asset taper relief @max 40% on 90%		(12,960)
Chargeable gain		19,440
Annual exemption		(9,200)
Chargeable gain		10,220
Tax payable at 40%	£4,088	

In this example of a disposal pre 6 April 2008, indexation allowance and taper relief bring down the chargeable gain significantly.

Under the Pre Budget proposals announced in October 2007 neither indexation allowance nor taper relief will be available to reduce chargeable gains realised by individuals, trustees and personal representatives after 5 April 2008. On the other hand, there will be a lower rate of 18%. The impact of these proposals on this illustration would be to increase the tax due by over £1,000. However, there is still a net benefit to claiming the income tax relief each year.

As mentioned in Point 49.1 above, even if part of a house is exclusively used for business, the allowance of certain expenses on a pro-rata basis may be more a matter of HMRC practice specific to the circumstances of the case.

Appendices

Appendix I

Items of Expenditure on Buildings and Structures Qualifying and Non-Qualifying as Plant (CAA 2001, Part 2, Chapter 3)

[*Note* – The Government's consultative document on proposed changes to the capital allowances regime includes the creation of a new category of 'integral fixtures' in a building. Expenditure on these items attract a lower 10% rate of annual writing-down allowance. Details of the assets in this category are still to be announced at the time of writing and may include some of the items below. In addition, other items which have been regarded as structural may be included in this category and thus attract allowances for the first time. See Point 6.5 in Chapter 6 for further commentary on this]

I. *Qualifying expenditure – items which become part of a building (section 23, List C)*

(1) Machinery (including devices for motive power) not within any other item in this list.

(2) Electrical system (including lighting systems) and cold water, gas and sewerage systems provided mainly:
    (a) to meet the particular requirements of the qualifying activity; or
    (b) to serve particular machinery or plant used for the purposes of the qualifying activity.

(3) Space or water heating systems; powered systems of ventilation, air cooling or air purification; and any ceiling or floor comprised in such systems.

(4) Manufacturing or processing equipment; storage equipment (including cold rooms); display equipment; and counters, checkouts and similar equipment.

(5) Cookers, washing machines, dishwashers, refrigerators and similar equipment; washbasins, sinks, baths, showers, sanitary ware and similar equipment; and furniture and fittings.

(6) Lifts, hoists, escalators and moving walkways.

(7) Sound insulation provided mainly to meet the particular requirements of the qualifying activity.

(8) Computer, telecommunication and surveillance systems (including their wiring and other links).

(9) Refrigeration or cooling equipment.

(10) Fire alarm systems; sprinkler and other equipment for extinguishing or containing fire.
(11) Burglar alarm systems.
(12) Strong rooms in bank or building society premises; safes.
(13) Partition walls, where moveable and intended to be moved in the course of the qualifying activity.
(14) Decorative assets provided for the enjoyment of the public in the hotel, restaurant or similar trades.
(15) Advertising hoarding; signs, displays and other similar assets.
(16) Swimming pools (including diving boards, slides and structures on which such boards or slides are mounted).
(17) Any glasshouse constructed so that the required environment (namely air, heat, light, irrigation and temperature) for the growing of plants is provided automatically by means of devices forming an integral part of its structure.
(18) Cold stores.
(19) Caravans provided mainly for holiday lettings.
(20) Buildings provided for testing aircraft engines run within the buildings.
(21) Moveable buildings intended to be moved in the course of the qualifying activity.
(22) The alteration of land for the purpose only of installing plant or machinery.
(23) The provision of dry docks.
(24) The provision of any jetty or similar structure provided mainly to carry plant or machinery.
(25) The provision of pipelines or underground ducts or tunnels with a primary purpose of carrying utility conduits.
(26) The provision of towers to support floodlights.
(27) The provision of:
    (a)   any reservoir incorporated into a water-treatment works; or
    (b)   any service reservoir of treated water for supply within any housing estate or other particular locality.
(28) The provision of:
    (a)   silos provided for temporary storage; or
    (b)   storage tanks.
(29) The provision of slurry pits or silage clamps.
(30) The provision of fish tanks or fish ponds.
(31) The provision of rails, sleepers and ballast for a railway or tramway.
(32) The provision of structures and other assets for providing the setting for any ride at an amusement park or exhibition.
(33) The provision of fixed zoo cages.

Note:

Items 1 to 16 do not include any asset whose principal purpose is to insulate or enclose the interior of a building or to provide for an interior wall, floor or ceiling which (in each case) is intended to remain permanently in place.

II. *Non-qualifying expenditure – assets treated as buildings (section 21, List A)*

(1) Walls, floors, ceilings, doors, gates, shutters, windows and stairs.
(2) Mains services and systems, for water, electricity and gas.
(3) Waste disposal systems.
(4) Sewerage and drainage systems.
(5) Shafts or other structures in which lifts, hoists, escalators and moving walkways are installed.
(6) Fire safety systems.

Note:
Items in this list are subject to list C in section 23 (see I above), ie if they appear in list C, they nevertheless qualify as plant or machinery.

III. *Non-qualifying expenditure – structures and other assets (section 22, List B)*

(1) A tunnel, bridge, viaduct, aqueduct, embankment or cutting.
(2) A way, hard standing (such as a pavement), road, railway, tramway, a park for vehicles or containers, or an airstrip or runway.
(3) An inland navigation, including a canal or basin or a navigable river.
(4) A dam, reservoir or barrage, including any sluices, gates, generators and other equipment associated with the dam, reservoir or barrage.
(5) A dock, harbour, wharf, pier, marina or jetty or any other structure in or at which vessels may be kept, or merchandise or passengers may be shipped or unshipped.
(6) A dyke, sea wall, weir or drainage ditch.
(7) Any structure not within items (1) to (6) other than:
    (a) a structure (but not a building) within the definition of an industrial building for the purpose of industrial buildings allowances;
    (b) a structure in use for the purposes of an undertaking for the extraction, production, processing or distribution of gas;
    (c) a structure in use for the purposes of a trade which consists in the provision of telecommunications, television or radio services.

Note:
Items in this list are subject to list C of section 23 (see I above), ie if they appear in list C, they nevertheless qualify as plant or machinery.

Appendix II

Enterprise zones

The following areas have had designated enterprise zones. All of these designations have now expired. However, there remain limited opportunities to claim 100% allowances in respect of buildings in those zones whilst within the ten-year period after the expiry of the zone. Details of these opportunities are set out in Chapter 33.

	Number of designatory Statutory Instrument	Cessation of operation
Lower Swansea Valley	SI 1981/757	10 June 1991
Corby	SI 1981/764	21 June 1991
Dudley	SI 1981/852	9 July 1991
Langthwaite Grange (Wakefield)	SI 1981/950	30 July 1991
Clydebank	SI 1981/975	2 August 1991
Salford Docks	SI 1981/1024	11 August 1991
Trafford Park	SI 1981/1025	11 August 1991
City of Glasgow	SI 1981/1069	17 August 1991
Gateshead	SI 1981/1070	24 August 1991
Newcastle	SI 1981/1071	24 August 1991
Speke (Liverpool)	SI 1981/1072	24 August 1991
Belfast	SR 1981/309	20 October 1991
Hartlepool	SI 1981/1378	22 October 1991
Isle of Dogs	SI 1982/462	25 April 1992
Delyn	SI 1983/896	20 July 1993
Wellingborough	SI 1983/907	25 July 1993
Rotherham	SI 1983/1007	15 August 1993
Londonderry	SR 1983/226	12 September 1993
Scunthorpe (Normanby Ridge and Queensway)	SI 1983/1304	22 September 1993
Dale Lane (Wakefield) and Kinsley (Wakefield)	SI 1983/1305	22 September 1993
Workington (Allerdale)	SI 1983/1331	3 October 1993
Invergordon	SI 1983/1359	6 October 1993
North West Kent	SI 1983/1452	30 October 1993
Middlesbrough (Britannia)	SI 1983/1473	7 November 1993
North East Lancashire	SI 1983/1639	6 December 1993
Tayside (Arbroath)	SI 1983/1816	8 January 1994
Tayside (Dundee)	SI 1983/1817	8 January 1994
Telford	SI 1983/1852	12 January 1994
Glanford (Flixborough)	SI 1984/347	12 April 1994
Milford Haven Waterway (North Shore)	SI 1984/443	23 April 1994
Milford Haven Waterway (South Shore)	SI 1984/444	23 April 1994
Dudley (Round Oak)	SI 1984/1403	2 October 1994
Lower Swansea Valley (No 2)	SI 1985/137	5 March 1995
North West Kent	SI 1986/1557	9 October 1996
Inverclyde	SI 1989/145	28 February 1999

Sunderland (Castletown and Doxford Park)	*SI 1990/794*	*26 April 2000*
Sunderland (Hylton Riverside and Southwick)	*SI 1990/795*	*26 April 2000*
Lanarkshire (Hamilton)	*SI 1993/23*	*31 January 2003*
Lanarkshire (Motherwell)	*SI 1993/24*	*31 January 2003*
Lanarkshire (Monklands)	*SI 1993/25*	*31 January 2003*
Dearne Valley	*SI 1995/2624*	*2 November 2005*
East Midlands (North East Derbyshire)	*SI 1995/2625*	*2 November 2005*
East Midlands (Bassetlaw)	*SI 1995/2738*	*15 November 2005*
East Midlands (Ashfield)	*SI 1995/2758*	*20 November 2005*
East Durham (Bracken Hill)	*SI 1995/2812*	*28 November 2005*
East Durham (Peterlee North West Industrial Estate)	*SI 1995/2812*	*28 November 2005*
East Durham (Peterlee South West Industrial Estate)	*SI 1995/2812*	*28 November 2005*
East Durham (Seaham Grange)	*SI 1995/2812*	*28 November 2005*
East Durham (Fox Cover)	*SI 1995/2812*	*28 November 2005*
East Durham (Dawdon)	*SI 1995/2812*	*28 November 2005*
Tyne Riverside (North Tyneside)	*SI 1996/106*	*18 February 2006*
Tyne Riverside (North Tyneside) (No 2)	*SI 1996/1981*	*25 August 2006*
Tyne Riverside (North Tyneside and South Tyneside)	*SI 1996/2435*	*20 October 2006*

Appendix III

Definition of Industrial Building

Industrial buildings allowances continue to be available until April 2011 for qualifying expenditure incurred on the construction of a building or structure that is, or is to be, in use for the purposes of a qualifying trade (*CAA 2001, s 271*). The allowances are, however, being phased out over the period to April 2011. Commentary on the position can be found in Chapter 30.

A qualifying trade is (*CAA 2001, s 274*):

(a) a trade of a kind described in Table A below; or

(b) an undertaking of a kind described in Table B, if the undertaking is carried on by way of trade.

TABLE A
Trades that are qualifying trades

Category	Description
Manufacturing	A trade consisting of manufacturing goods or materials.
Processing	A trade consisting of subjecting goods or materials to a process. This includes maintaining or repairing goods or materials.
Storage	A trade consisting of storing goods or materials: (a) which are to be used in the manufacture of other goods or materials; (b) which are to be subjected, in the course of a trade, to a process; (c) which, having been manufactured or produced or subjected, in the course of a trade, to a process, have not yet been delivered to any purchaser; or (d) on their arrival into the UK from a place outside the UK.
Agricultural contracting	A trade consisting of: (a) ploughing or cultivating land occupied by another; (b) carrying out any other agricultural operations on land occupied by another; or (c) threshing another's crops. For this purpose, 'crops' includes vegetable produce.
Working foreign plantations	A trade consisting of working land outside the UK used for: (a) growing and harvesting crops; (b) husbandry; or (c) forestry. For this purpose, 'crops' includes vegetable produce and 'harvesting crops' includes the collection of vegetable produce (however effected).

Category	Description
Fishing	A trade consisting of catching or taking fish or shellfish.
Mineral extraction	A trade consisting of working a source of mineral deposits. 'Mineral deposits' includes any natural deposits capable of being lifted or extracted from the earth, and for this purpose geothermal energy is to be treated as a natural deposit. 'Source of mineral deposits' includes a mine, an oil well and a source of geothermal energy.

Note:

Maintaining or repairing goods or materials is not a qualifying trade if (a) the goods or materials are employed in a trade or undertaking; (b) the maintenance or repair is carried out by the person employing the goods or materials; and (c) the trade or undertaking is not itself a qualifying trade.

TABLE B

Undertakings that are qualifying trades if carried on by way of trade

Undertaking	Description
Electricity	An undertaking for the generation, transformation, conversion, transmission or distribution of electrical energy.
Water	An undertaking for the supply of water for public consumption.
Hydraulic power	An undertaking for the supply of hydraulic power.
Sewerage	An undertaking for the provision of sewerage services within the meaning of the *Water Industry Act 1991*.
Transport	A transport undertaking.
Highway undertaking	A highway undertaking, that is, so much of any undertaking relating to the design, building, financing and operation of roads as is carried on: (a) for the purposes of; or (b) in connection with; (c) the exploitation of highway concessions.
Tunnels	A tunnel undertaking.
Bridges	A bridge undertaking.
Inland navigation	An inland-navigation undertaking.
Docks	A dock undertaking. A dock includes: (a) any harbour; and (b) any wharf, pier, jetty or other works in or at which vessels can ship or unship merchandise or passengers, other than a pier or jetty primarily used for recreation.

Appendix IV

Construction operations for the purposes of the Construction Industry Scheme

The following list produced by HM Revenue and Customs gives guidance on which types of construction work are within the scheme and which are not. Where a contract relates to a number of operations some of which appear in the 'Operations excluded' column, the contract as a whole will be one relating to construction operations and the deduction scheme should be operated for all payments under the contract.

Planning

Operations included

None

Operations excluded

Professional work (including the ancillary work of engineers, draughtsmen, scientists and technicians) of architects, surveyors or consultants in building, engineering, decoration (interior or exterior) or landscaping.

Site Preparation

Operations included

Demolition of buildings, structures, tree-felling, etc.
Preparation of site and site clearance, earth-moving on the site, excavation, tunnelling, boring.

Operations excluded

Delivery of materials.

Transport of spoil from site.

Construction

Operations included

Installation of public services.
Installation of closed-circuit.

Preparation and laying of foundations and piling.

Operations excluded

Manufacture or off-site fabrication of components or equipment, materials, plant or machinery and delivery of these to the site.
For example

traditional building materials
prefabricated beams and panels
ready mixed concrete

Actual construction, alteration or
repair of a permanent or temporary
building or civil, chemical or other
industrial engineering work or
industrial plant or structure.
For example:
storage tanks
silos
pylons
cranes or derricks
pumps

Operations included	*Operations excluded*
Construction of site facilities.	Manufacture and delivery of pre-fabricated site facilities. Running of site facilities such as canteens, hostels, offices, toilets and medical centres or the supply of security guards.
Installation of power lines, pipelines, gas mains, sewers, drainage, cable television and telecommunications distribution systems.	Installation or replacement of telecommunication or computer wiring through pre-existing ducting in buildings.
Installation of closed circuit television for purposes other than security (such as traffic management).	
Installation of public services.	
Construction, repair and resurfacing or roads and bridges, including white-lining.	Delivery of road-making materials.
Provision of temporary and permanent roadways and other access works such as drives.	
Erection or dismantling of scaffolding falsework and formwork.	Hire of scaffolding equipment (without labour).
Plant hire with operator for use on site.	Delivery, repair or maintenance of construction plant or hire equipment with an operator. For example concrete mixers, pumps and skips.

Installation of fire protection systems designed specifically to protect the fabric of the building (such as sprinkler systems, fireproof cladding) rather than a fire warning (alarm) system.

Installation of fire alarms, security systems including burglar alarms, closed-circuit television as part of a security system, and public address systems.

Installation of pre-fabricated component or equipment under 'supply and fix' arrangements.

Transportation of materials on site.

Transport of materials from site to site on the public highway.

Assembly of temporary stages and exhibition stands, including lighting.

Operations included

Operations excluded

Internal cleaning of buildings and structures carried out in the course of, or on completion of, their construction, alteration, extension, repair or restoration.

External cleaning (other than painting or decorating) of buildings and structures.

Work done on installations (such as rigs, pipelines, construction platforms) maintained or intended to be established for underwater exploration for, or exploitation of, minerals where the work is on land or in UK territorial waters.

Drilling for, or extraction of, oil or natural gas.

Extraction of minerals, boring or construction of underground works for this purpose.

Installation of systems of heating, lighting, air conditioning, ventilation, power supply and distribution, drainage, sanitation, water supply and distribution, and fire protection works.

Manufacture, delivery, repair or maintenance of these items.

Installation of lifts, plant, or machinery needed by the specification of a building under construction or alteration.

Servicing, repair or maintenance of these items.

Construction and repair of industrial plant.

Site restoration and landscaping.

Tree planting and felling in the ordinary course of forestry or estate management.

Installation, structural repair and painting of lamp standards, traffic lights, parking meters and street furniture.

Manufacture and delivery of lamp standards.
Routine maintenance such as cleaning and general replacement.

Construction of concrete and marble floors.
Fitting of eye bolts, whether internal or external.

Manufacture off-site and delivery of flooring materials.

Installation and repair to:
glazing
doors and rolling grills or security shutters
kitchens and bathrooms
shop-fittings including fixed furniture (except seating).

Manufacture and delivery of:
glazing materials
computer and instrumentation systems
thermal insulation materials
heating and ventilation systems
doors and rolling grills
painting or decorating materials.

Painting and decorating the internal or external surfaces of any building or structure.

Operations included

Operations excluded

Manufacture, delivery and installation of seating, blinds and louvred shutters.

Manufacture, installation and repair of artistic works (for example, sculptures and murals) which are wholly decorative in nature (not functional items caught by the Scheme which incidentally have artistic merit).

Manufacture and installation of solar, blackout or anti-shatter film.

Signwriting and erecting, installation and repair of signboards and advertisements.

Fitting of:
floor coverings, such as vinyl, linoleum (but not carpet) and laminated wooden flooring
new locks
pigeon mesh
TV aerials and satellite receivers

Installation of refrigeration units.

*But only where these finishing
operations render complete a building
or structure that has been constructed
or altered.*

Index